D'ANNUNZIO

The Poet as Superman

D'ANNUNZIO

The Poet as Superman

ANTHONY RHODES

McDOWELL, OBOLENSKY INC.
NEW YORK

To Rosaleen

Acknowledgments

The late G. A. Borgese was kind enough to make some suggestions to me for the way in which D'Annunzio should be regarded. This study is based upon his ideas, which are set out in the Preface.

I am also most grateful to Signor Luigi Barzini, Mr. Bernard Wall and Mr. Archibald Colquhoun, who were kind enough to read the manuscript and make some valuable suggestions; and to Signorina Pallavicini of the Italian Institute, London, who checked many details.

There are few studies in English of D'Annunzio, but I gratefully acknowledge help and quotations from those by: Sir Osbert Sitwell (*Noble Essences* and *Discursions,* published by Messrs. Macmillan & Company); Nardelli and Livingstone (*D'Annunzio,* published by Messrs. Jonathan Cape); G. Griffin (*The Warrior Bard,* published by Messrs. Harrap); and Francis Winwar (*Wings of Fire,* published by Messrs. Alvin Redman).

Contents

Preface

The circumstances in which the Italian people had increased, particularly between the Alps and Tuscany, their inheritance which had survived the Dark Ages, their geographical position, and finally their climate, had made them, by the sixteenth century, the greatest imaginative and creative community known on earth since the Greece of Pericles. Two thousand years of almost continuous civilization had given Italy a special place among the nations of Europe, many of them richer and more powerful. When at last, in the mid-nineteenth century, Italy appeared as a modern state, united as she had never been since classical times, from the Alps to Sicily, many Italians believed she was destined for yet another period of greatness. Her influence in Europe, her new power as a centralized state, could only be humane and humanizing. Mazzini, the architect of that state, saw his country as the first nation in the world with a civilizing mission, with a future more glorious than that of other nations, because her past was more glorious. He saw the new power of Italy in terms of the Communes of the Middle Ages, by whose improvised armies the German emperors had been driven back into their woodlands and glaciers. When he looked back to Rome, he saw not the Rome of the Caesars, but the Rome of the civil liberties. Italy's new force was to be an instrument of defense, menacing no one. Surrounded by her Alps and seas, she would be self-sufficient, in the service of mankind.

Mazzini was, to employ an anachronism, almost a Wilsonian, believing in the League of Nations in the mid-nineteenth century. There had been plenty of Utopians before him. Poets, philosophers, dreamers had believed in the idea of a united mankind, free from hatred and bloodshed. But no one had put it into force. Even Achilles, at the dawn of civilization, had pronounced in a sudden pause between the slaughter, a prayer that strife among men might cease. Charlemagne, Henry IV, Sully, had dreamed of federation. But it was not until the nineteenth century, in Mazzini, that it seemed anything more than a dream. Ideals such as these were repeated by most of the writers of the day; and Italy's first poet, Carducci, said in 1861, when he acclaimed the new unified Italy, "No more Caesars, with their slaves and spoils!" He had watched all the phases of the *Risorgimento,* and in his poetry the nation seems to be young again. There is a sensuous joy and life which we search for in vain in the earlier nineteenth-century poets, like Foscolo and Leopardi, who, with all their magnificence, can only depict the sad conditions of the time. Moving from them to Carducci, we seem to come to something newer, as well as older. Carducci is the first poet who seems to go back not only to ancient Rome, but to be of modern Rome. The papal domination, the Renaissance, the Spanish night, have passed him by, and the Latin spirit of Horace lives in a Latin poet again. Men like Carducci, Mazzini, and Manzoni, imbued with these ideals, were the creators of the new Italy, their patriotism summed up in Mazzini's, "I love my homeland, because I love all homelands."

When the young D'Annunzio came to Rome in 1881, it was still the city of Carducci and Mazzini, as near as it had ever been, or was to be, to that Dantesque ideal capital of Europe and the planet, where shortly a great council of mankind would sit, to rule in harmonious collaboration with everyone else in the world. No nation had traveled in so short a time the road Italy had traveled since her unification. Legislation was as liberal as in any nation of the West; bureaucracy was, relatively, conscientious and honest; illiteracy was disappearing; Catholicism had taken on a sense of social responsibility. Architecture and engineering were again restoring to Italy her technical supremacy. Mazzinian Rome was beginning to resemble Victorian England.

Why, then, did all this change so rapidly? Why were these ideals so short-lived? Why, at the end of the century, could Carducci himself write instead, "Prepare the way for the *Signore* who is to come, for the spirit of Italy, grand and great, for the genius, the beatings of whose approaching wings we already hear. . . ?" Why, within fifty years, had the most idealistic state in Europe become a Caesarean dictatorship, the pseudo-Roman Italy of the nationalists?

Within fifty years of the death of Mazzini, the eldest son of Italy's ruler was writing the following article in a newspaper, ". . . I had anticipated glamorous explosions in the style of the American films; whereas the low Ethiopian huts, made of clay and brushwood, did not afford any satisfaction at all to my bombs. They simply disintegrated like chaff. . . ." Vittorio Mussolini was here referring to the Ethiopians, a few million half-naked, half-starved, half-nomad, half-savages, being treated by the Italian air force to a liberal dousing of mustard-gas and other skin-charring, lung-rending exhalations. And D'Annunzio, the greatest of Italy's living poets, was writing these words about the splendid age he thought was dawning, ". . . these men in the new torpedo boats will go forward at the great enemy vessel under an incessant hail of bullets from the guns and machine guns, capable of firing six hundred bullets a minute. They will advance to within 400 meters and launch their first torpedo! . . . their second! And no human joy can equal theirs, when they see the monstrous enemy ironclad on its side, the muzzles of its guns pointing futilely to the skies—and then suddenly sink with all its turrets and batteries, in a vast, measureless vortex."

To understand how this change could come about so quickly, it is necessary to go back in history, and see how this myth of modern Italian power was born.

The Italian-speaking nation arose, as did all the others in Europe, towards the end of the Middle Ages. Unlike them, however, Italy was not the product of kings and warriors, but of a poet, Dante. It is to Dante that we must trace back the events of the late nineteenth and early twentieth century which concern us here.

Dante had in his own lifetime been a failure. He had tried to be a Florentine, a member of the city-state in which he was born. He had failed, through no fault of his own—but as a result of the capricious political systems of the day. He could not be an active citizen of any of the smaller cities and principalities in which he was guest and refugee; his political career was ruined. But this ruin turned him into a thinker and a poet. The unwelcome political holiday gave him time to write *The Divine Comedy*. Thus, these events, which Dante looked on as a misfortune, were responsible for the greatest poem in the Italian language, as well as the creation of that language, and, in turn, of a nation.

It is well known that Dante's repressed sexual love and frustrated family affections found in this poem their sublimation in the phantom of the celestial Beatrice. In the same way, the thwarting of his political ambitions was sublimated in it into something almost as celestial and impossible in that age of growing city-states: the Roman Empire. As conscientiously as the Emperor Charlemagne five hundred years before, Dante now started to rebuild that empire, in his mind.

Thirteen centuries before, the Roman people had unified themselves under an empire, which had in turn unified practically the entire known world. Nine centuries before Dante's birth, this empire had collapsed, and all the efforts of northern emperors and conquerors who had crossed the Alps to restore it, in the form of a Christian monarchy, had failed. By the time of Dante, this medieval "Holy Roman Empire" was already a ruin, upon whose rotting framework new and spontaneous forms of life, national states and communes, were growing. But Dante preferred to ignore them. His hatred of the one commune that had spurned him colored all his political thought. Hatred for the walled city of Florence, love for a boundless empire of mankind under a revived Rome, these were his twin beliefs. Whatever came in the way to conflict with this theory, new kingdoms like France and England, nations and principalities he had not foreseen, he either cursed or ignored. In his treatise *De Monarchia* he expounded these views.

Here, he admitted that the Roman Empire was a pagan institution, but he claimed that it later merged with Christianity, thereby becoming spiritually perfect. It was true, too, that the Romans had conquered the world by war and violence; but their triumphs on the battlefield were the judgments of God that they were to rule the world. Of this intention God gave further proof, in that he caused His own Divine Son, Jesus Christ, to be born at the time of the foundation of the Roman Empire, and to die at the hands of its officials. God Himself, choosing the Roman Empire as the executioner of His Son, thus acknowledged the divine right of that empire as the only legal authority on earth. Convinced by his own sophisms, Dante continued to argue that the elect people of Rome, bathed in the blood of innumerable vanquished nations, besprinkled with the blood of the Divine Lamb, was the depository of all divine authority on earth.

At this point comes what is perhaps the most interesting and individual of his conceptions. He now said there was no need for the Emperor to be by birth or race a Roman. The ancient Romans in their later empire had never recognized this necessity themselves. Were not most of the later Emperors foreigners, Spaniards, Dalmatians, colonials? It was clear from the last five centuries that the legitimate descendants of the Caesars were now the German war lords who had been descending into Italy every half-century, trying to assume their heritage. Dante did not know these unkempt barbarians, who were clad in fur and iron, but he was prepared to like them; as one can only like things one does not know. He refused to recognize that the most redoubtable of them all, Frederic Barbarossa, had been defeated only a century before Dante's birth by a league of the Italian free communes, in one of the most significant victories of Italian history, Legnano, pointing the way to that new political entity, the city-state. Of this episode, he only remembered with glee that Barbarossa had punished and razed rebellious Milan; he forgot entirely about Milan's resurrection after, and the battle of Legnano. So when, in Dante's lifetime, a German Emperor, Henry VII, came again to Italy to claim his inheritance,

Dante welcomed him and wrote a letter to "the most wicked
Florentines," urging them to open their gates to the lawful master
of the world. The Florentines did not open their gates. Their republic lived on, and the German Caesar died mysteriously some-
where in Tuscany—to be given a fitting burial in the Ghibelline
city of Pisa, and a distinguished seat in Dante's Paradise.

Is it not significant that in the most splendid of Italian centuries,
the thirteenth, Dante, the greatest of Italians, should have only
lament for the past and malediction for the present? For it was then
that Florence dominated Europe with her bankers; that Genoa and
Venice ruled the known seas; it was then that in every Italian city
were upreared those cathedrals and bell towers that still remain
the marvel of the world; when religious belief gave Francis of
Assisi to the world, and Italian poetry surpassed Provençal, with
Guido Guinizelli and Guido Cavalcanti. But this counted for nothing to Dante. He saw only one thing; that the political unity of
Christian society was broken, because the Roman Emperor lived
beyond the Alps, and Italy had ceased to be *il giardin dell' Impero.*

More important than *De Monarchia* was *The Divine Comedy* in
which, together with some of the most beautiful poetry in the
world, Dante incorporates these political beliefs with his views on
religion, in particular on what he considered should be the proper
relations between Emperor and Pope. For the Papal See was still to
him the depository of eternal truth, the bestower of eternal happiness—occasionally, he admitted, occupied by rogues and criminals,
like Boniface XIII (to whom he assigned one of the lower rungs
of the *Inferno*). But he saw both powers, Emperor and Pope, the
lay and the sacerdotal, as parallel authorities, never coinciding with
one another, working in harness, deriving from the same source,
God. The Emperor would go about his business of ruling undisturbed by the Pope; the Pope would confine himself entirely to
spiritual matters. The Emperor, for his part, would pay homage to
the Holy Father, a kind of homage which might, in practice, never
be more than lip-service. The effect of these theories put into a
poem was startling. They created a nation.

Already in earlier times, a powerful personality or genius had been responsible for the creation of a people or a religion. Moses, Solon, Cyrus, St. Paul are examples. But they had all been legislators or warriors. Even Luther and Calvin were far more than mere theologians and preachers; the tests to which they had to put their doctrines in the administration of a city, or in the material struggle with other earthly powers, gave their State the practical quality which earthly systems must possess. But Dante was neither a legislator nor a conqueror. Real responsibility and action never interfered with his imagination. His State, like Plato's, was written on the clouds. In this way Italy was born, a phantom searching perpetually to return to the past of a thousand years before. When in the nineteenth century she seemed at last to have matured to the level of other nations in Europe, the belief in this phantom destroyed her.

This Dantesque conception of a revived Roman Empire lay dormant in the Italian mind for nearly six hundred years, until it was associated in the twentieth century with Italy under the Savoyard kings, and Dante's dream seemed to have become a reality. But in the meantime, a new and less attractive ideal had arisen, to graft itself onto the Dantesque myth. In 1514, Machiavelli wrote *The Prince*. This takes Dante's notion of Roman and Italian greatness a stage further, modernizes it, gives its nebulous quality something practical, prepares it for the age of D'Annunzio.

Machiavelli had been forgotten since the middle of the seventeenth century, until he fell into the hands of the nineteenth-century professors and idealists who, while expounding his thought, had read him lectures on morality for his most un-Victorian attitude towards Power. Ambition and bitterness were Machiavelli's chief inspiration, as they had been Dante's. Political failure was for him, too, the unwelcome opportunity for his literary genius. He too wrote about Florence and his beloved Italy, but not in terms of universal monarchy. The Empire was no more than a word; the Roman Church was torn by heresy outside, by skepticism and corruption within. The real, the tangible in Europe was, to Machiavelli, the growing nation-state which Dante had overlooked. Europe was being conquered, Machiavelli saw, with his own eyes, not by the World Emperor with his World Priest, but by Kings with their swords and horsemen.

During Machiavelli's own lifetime, not *one* King of France, but three, had entered Italy, to conquer it almost without firing a shot, "with chalk" as they said (for during that extraordinary pageantry parade of the French down the peninsula, Charles VIII's Marshals had stopped wherever they liked in Italy, merely marking with white chalk the lodgings they considered fit for their troops). After France, it was the turn of Spain to govern Italy. Spanish grandees, German *Knechte,* Swiss mercenaries, tussled with one another up and down the peninsula without consulting its inhabitants for the next four hundred years. Mercifully, Machiavelli died before the Sack of Rome by the Imperial armies, nor did he live to see the fall of Florence and the Spanish night which now descended on his land. Instead, in its dusk, he wrote *The Prince,* which, just as Dante's was the greatest piece of Italian poetry, is the greatest piece of Italian prose.

The Prince enunciates a simple, even obvious, theory: that political activity is unconnected with ethics. Machiavelli here differs from Dante who, however mistaken his political thought, does at least base it on "goodness" and "wisdom." Force and cunning, Machiavelli states blandly, rule the world. Although this idea was not new, it had never been stated in such an outspoken way before. Cruelty, treachery, violation of the given word, inclemency to the vanquished, all this had happened before. But from the start of our civilization in Greece, it had been deplored. Even in the *Iliad,* Achilles displays remorse for some of his politically justifiable deeds. Homer refers to sin and punishment, and treats his heroes according to whether they behaved honorably or not. Plato developed an ideal state full of rules and justice and good behavior, in which the sacredness of Embassies and treaties was taken for granted. With the arrival of Christianity and the importance of Faith by Works, this rough system of ethics received further endorsement.

Instead, Machiavelli substituted the law of the jungle, reinforced with all the power of human intelligence. "Disarmed prophets," he wrote, "perish. Armed prophets prosper." To arms, he entreats his Prince to add cunning, to be the fox as well as the lion. "The Prince who minds what things *ought* to be, instead of what they *are*," he says, "learns the way to his disaster and not to his preservation, since the man who wishes to be in everything good, must necessarily be ruined among those who are not so good." And, "it is a thing natural and ordinary to lust for acquisition; and those who have that lust and the force thereto will always be praised, and not blamed. Only when lust is without power are there blame and error. . . ." Or this precept for popularity, ". . . offenses should be committed at once, all together, so that, there being less time to taste them, they may offend less. On the contrary, beneficences should be done little by little, in order that there may be more time for others to savor them . . ." It would be best for a Prince to be feared *and* loved, he says; but if only one of the two is possible, "then it is safer to be feared than loved." He then examines all the examples of treasons, duplicities, cruelties, sacrileges and tortuous policies of the tyrants, with his usual frigid and exhaustive analysis.

Having described his ideal Prince, Machiavelli now set about looking for him. He had the chemical formula and, like Faust's assistant, Wagner, who knew scientifically all about the composition of man, he tried to create him in the heat of his furnace, this *homunculus politicus*. It was harder than he expected. His assumption that the only standard by which actions must be judged is whether they succeed or fail implied that his own doctrines must stand that test too. They did not. He chose Cesare Borgia, a man who seemed admirable for the role, and who has lived on in the frightened mind of posterity almost as Antichrist, the son of a Pope, half-genius, half-hero, traitor, assassin, incendiary, a sacrilegious and incestuous bastard who, after renouncing his blood-red Cardinal's hat, had conquered most of the cities and castles of Central Italy. He was at this time planning to set up a hereditary Roman Papacy on his father's death. But then, when limitless fame and power seemed within his grasp, through the death of his Holy Father, he died too, partly as a result of his own excesses. "He told me," says Machiavelli almost ingenuously, "that he had thought of everything that might happen if his father came to die, and that he had found an answer for everything, except that he had never thought of the possibility that, while his father was dying, he too might be near death!" Machiavelli relates this conversation, as if quite unaware of the Shakespearean irony of the situation: the fate of this man, who had fulfilled almost every condition laid down for a successful ruler in *The Prince*.

We find then, at Machiavelli's death some years later, Italy at the feet of foreign conquerors, about to undergo a three-hundred-year period of subordination, possessing notions not only of Dantesque Italian greatness, but of Machiavellian means of achieving them. The period of foreign domination that now set in, while it increased the backward-looking for past glories, also increased the cynical attitude of the Italians, giving them an inferiority complex. When a nation becomes aware that it cannot govern itself, that strangers must always give it law and order, a feeling of unworthiness and shame arises. Initiative disappears; courage and honor are stifled; economic competition slackens. With the extinction of social liberties, all the branches of the arts begin to wither. The written word, the art most connected with freedom of expression and thought, was the first to decline in Italy after Machiavelli's death. There was no Italian writer of European stature after the death of Tasso until the nineteenth century. The Spanishified poets of the sixteenth and seventeenth centuries wrote only verses in honor of the Catholic powers at war with the Turks, or of the rather feeble fights of the Knights of the Order of Santo Stefano against some lateen sail of a Moslem pirate; or again, poems on the Virgin and Mary Magdalene. They were patriotic songs without a *patria*.

This inferiority complex caused by foreign rule is by no means dispelled by Machiavelli himself. Indeed, he almost revels in his countrymen's baseness and lack of heroism. In his *Florentine History*, he depicts the Italians as a people of intelligence, imagination, great reasoning power and eloquence, but without character, loyalty, pride, and above all, without physical courage. Some of his pictures of the *condottieri* in the typical battles of the Renaissance are well known. Of the battle of Molinella in 1467 he says, ". . . the captains of the Florentines rushed closer to the enemy, so that they came to a regular fight which lasted half a day, without either of the parties yielding. Nevertheless, no one died; only a few horses were wounded, and one or two prisoners taken. . . ." Of another, the battle of Zagonara in 1424, he writes, ". . . in so great a rout, widely spoken of throughout Italy, only Ludovico degli Ubizi died, together with two of his men, who having fallen from their horses, drowned in the mud. . . ."

Nor has Dante done much to raise Italian self-esteem. The greatest Italian shows life in medieval Italy as morally contemptible. If Italy was sacred as an idea to him, the Italians were anathema. Siena, Lucca, Arezzo, all the Tuscan towns, not to mention his own native Florence, were so many pouches of Hell on the surface of the earth. And as for Pisa—giving his poetic imagination full play, he regretted that the Tyrrhenian Islands could not move towards the coast and close up the mouths of the Arno, so that the river might pile up and drown all the inhabitants of that immoral city.

For centuries the Italians had complained about their reputation abroad for lack of courage, a feeling of humiliation and revolt against a dishonorable reputation which explains much of the history to be examined in the time of D'Annunzio. Yet they have helped to spread the reputation themselves. Even in our own times, the battle of Caporetto is known as the most notorious defeat in the Great War, not because it was bigger or worse than other defeats—than for instance the British rout at St. Quentin in March 1918, or the French defeat on the Argonne—but because the Italians *wanted* it to be thought the biggest and worst defeat, and continually announced it as such to the world.

Such then were the political ideals of Italy when D'Annunzio came to Rome in 1881, a compound of Dantesque myth and Machiavellian method, savored with the Mazzinian idealism and a permanent inferiority complex. Italy had at last found liberty and unity; she seemed destined to be one of the first nations of Europe. But the very word Italians used for the great experience they had just passed through to achieve this unity, *Risorgimento* or Resurrection, was a dangerous word, implying that they were still looking back to the myth of Roman greatness.

D'ANNUNZIO

The Poet as Superman

Gabriele D'Annunzio

Gabriele D'Annunzio was born on March 12, 1863, in Pescara, on the Adriatic coast of Italy. About his origins and name there is some doubt, which he assiduously fostered himself. His father, whose real name was Rapagnetta, had changed it some years before to D'Annunzio, the name of his mother's brother-in-law. Not content with such a complicated change, D'Annunzio, in his auto-biographical sketches, takes the ordinary facts of his childhood and turns them into myths, interpreting with symbols and parables his adolescence, creating an allegory of himself, mixing truth and imagination. "I come from an ancient breed," he writes. "My ancestors were anchorites on the *Maiella*. They flagellated themselves till the blood came. They filled their fists with snow, and ate it; they throttled wolves; they stripped eagles of their feathers, and scratched their seals on giant rocks with the nail Helen took from the Cross. . . ." He claims, furthermore, that he was born on a bark, in a gale, on the high seas. This is certainly untrue. Of his earlier forebears not much is known, except that there is talk of a man who made his living by going from house to house restuffing mattresses, one of the humblest occupations of Italians.

The names of the parents, Don Francesco Paolo D'Annunzio and Donna Luisa de Benedictis, are full of poetry, perhaps more than they were themselves. He was the son of a merchant plying a carrying trade across the Adriatic; she, the daughter of an Ortona bourgeois. The father was a full-blooded, good-natured man, who liked the company of pretty girls. He became Mayor of Pescara and finally went bankrupt. The mother, on the other hand, was always to remain virtuous, one of those typical examples of Italian motherhood, whom we seem to see (from her son's fond accounts), always sitting in the front room knitting, wearing that bombazine black beloved by the Italian peasantry, worn, it seems, in keeping with the colorless mildness, the resignation, the drabness of existence.

In the father the worst carnal instincts soon appeared. A slave of the senses, he was, at the end of his life, sleeping with the girls born of his concubines, and he ran through his small patrimony, so that his son later had to pay the family debts. Portraits reveal Francesco D'Annunzio looking like a villain out of burlesque opera, with a great black beard, huge mouth, thick lips, bulbous nose and fleshy hands. In one of his son's early novels, *Il Trionfo della Morte,* there is a clear autobiographical description of his father, ". . . Desire was awakening in Giorgio's flesh with unheard-of violence. A small thing could start it off, a breath of warm air, a scent, a sound—enough to send a flame pulsating through his veins, sending him into a state of excitement bordering on delirium. For he carried with him, in the depths of his being, the germs he had inherited from his father. He, a person of reason, of thought and feeling, had in his flesh the fatal heredity of his coarse being. . . . Certain impulses of animalism, gusts of it, moving like storms across cultivated ground, were destroying the spiritual side of his life. They shut off every source of interior light, they opened great voids of misery. . . ."

From his parents, then, D'Annunzio inherited very different gifts; from the mother, a kind of holy benediction in keeping with her name, which was to express itself throughout his life in acts of sudden generosity; from the father, a sexual gift, bordering often on frenzy.

Of the rest of the family, there was the brother, Francesco, who became a musician and emigrated to South America; Elvira, D'Annunzio's favorite sister, who married a pharmacist; Ernesta, the "ox-eyed," who married an engineer; and Anna, who seems to have done little except accompany herself on the piano. These relations disappeared early from D'Annunzio's life, and we find few references to them in his books and diaries. He seems glad to have forgotten them when he reached Rome. Only his mother, who remained always dear to him, appears again and again in his life.

The earliest portraits of D'Annunzio reveal a dark-skinned, crinkly-haired boy with lively eyes, and something of the Abyssinian in his expression; a sharp nose, mobile lips and, as he often pointed out himself, beautifully shaped ears which, he contended, were a sure sign of breeding. He was to remain throughout his life the reverse of his coarse-looking father; he was dapper, polite, ceremonious, alert. When he became famous, he always regretted not having the face of a Foscolo, a Shelley or a Musset. Had he even been ugly, like Beethoven, or hideous like Socrates and Verlaine, he would at least have had something positive in his appearance. But this remarkable and very individual Italian had a mediocre, perfectly ordinary face such as you might see in any barber's shop. Later, Isadora Duncan was to say of it, "Perhaps the most remarkable lover of our time is Gabriele D'Annunzio. And this notwithstanding that he is small, bald, and, except when his face lights up with enthusiasm, ugly. But when he speaks to a woman he likes, his face is transfigured, so that he suddenly becomes Apollo. . . ."

The physical courage which was to distinguish his later life developed early. In *Faville,* one of his few autobiographical writings, he says, "When my father, to teach me to swim, threw me into the river and told me to swim for my life, I always swam by instinct *against* the current. In the sea, I always went where the waves were biggest, as if with a desire to dominate them." At the age of nine, he cut his finger deeply with a knife, while trying to open a seashell. He was about to go for help; but he decided first that he would open the shell, as he had intended. While he did so, he sucked the bleeding flesh and watched the handkerchief redden, thereby obtaining a strange sensation, a satisfaction almost, which caused him to see how long he could last, without fainting. With these and other self-imposed tests, such as standing on a high roof to gauge his powers over giddiness, he seems to have wanted to discover the limits of his endurance.

The father, for all his crudeness, appreciated that there was something remarkable about his son, and he decided to give him a good education, at the well-known Cicognini College in Prato. The classical education was one of the best in Italy, and here the Abruzzese would learn to speak Tuscan Italian. D'Annunzio profited from this to such an extent that he was capable of apt quotation from the Latin and Greek classics all his life. This classical education also developed his first feelings of pride in being an Italian, and of Latin stock. "I glory in being a Latin, and I look on all other races as barbarians," he said. The cult of the Italian heroes was first expressed in a poem he wrote at school at the age of thirteen, to celebrate the visit of King Umberto:

"New days are breaking for our Italy, days which once again will see the triumphant armies marching the streets of Rome, and a laurel-crowned conqueror riding in a chariot along the Sacra Via. While children strew his path with flowers, and the waving flags dip low, to brush the hispid lines of victorious soldiers. Conquer O Mighty King! And let the star of Savoy glow like a sun upon the soil of our regenerate land. . . ."

It was at the Cicognini College, too, that his interest in uniforms awoke. On one occasion, he went into Florence wearing the college full dress uniform. When some soldiers appeared, the twelve-year-old schoolboy put on such an air of authority as he strutted along, that they thought he must be an *aspirant* or Second Lieutenant, with his silver arm-loops, such as ADCs wear; and they saluted. D'Annunzio boasted of this to his school friends, and it came to the ears not only of the school authorities, but of the Minister of War, who gave instructions that, in future, the college dress must be modified, so that schoolboys should not undermine the discipline of his troops.

D'Annunzio spent seven years at this school, where the most important event took place in his last year, when he fell in love with Griselda Zucconi, the daughter of one of the language masters. Although the friendship was short, and he forgot about her almost as soon as he reached Rome a year later, she may legitimately claim to be the first woman in his life, as well as the first

inspiration of his early poems, *Primo Vere,* which he wrote at
school. One of his letters to her is remarkable, in that it describes
a scene which he turned into verse. It shows how the young poet
uses his own experience. In the letter to her, he says:

". . . I feel I can almost see you, my darling, seated on the balcony, beautiful, pensive and pale. And in those fawn-colored eyes,
I can read your far-away thoughts. Yes, you are thinking of me, as
you sit there, aren't you? You are sitting in the sun on the balcony,
dreaming. . . . Do you know what has come from these thoughts as
I write? A poem! It is full of the scent of the *zaphir,* full of desire,
of tropical heat growing here in January, like camellias in a hot-
house. O, my beloved Elda, you are my muse, my poem. My darling, the finest images, the sweetest harmonies, are all inspired by
you."

This is transformed in *Primo Vere:*

For you germinate the eclogues and the eases
    Of a summer afternoon, beside the salt sea air,
The bird songs and the orange blossoms;
    For you, the golden fruit shines on among its greenery.
While on the distant Adriatic the red sails
    Cluster on the sea-front, and the sands are quiet.
All this I see, my Elda, in your pallid cheeks,
    A sudden flower that opens there, desiring and desired.
And then the sun shines in your fawnlike eyes,
    And in your mouth that opens like a pomegranate,
I smell again the fragrance of your kiss.

Unequal though these poems were, modeled on his readings of
the Latin poets and Carducci, there is a genuine lyrical strain running through them, with an original choice of images, words and
colors. In the preface to the second edition, he acknowledges the
classical influences from his education, and he tells how he wrote
them in obedience to advice received from Venus, who appeared
to him in a dream. They were addressed in the classical manner to

a young lady. As Ovid had his Corinna, and Propertius his Cynthia, so D'Annunzio gives himself a Lilia, the name he bestows on Griselda in the poems.

They were very well received in Rome, where the critic, Chiarini, reviewed them in the *Fanfulla della Domenica* on May 2, 1880, in these patronizing terms:

". . . Stretching out into the great flood of contemporary verse that assails me unremittingly day by day, doubtless sweeping away things that are good in its vast siltage of rubbish, I am glad to extend my hand to a recent volume of verse, and make an effort to drag it to a safe landing. My new poet is a youth of sixteen. His name is Gabriele D'Annunzio. . . ." He then went on to speak of them most favorably.

There were other good reviews, and D'Annunzio became known overnight in Rome as a rising young poet. Although the poems were lyrical, the decadent note also creeps in, in imitation of the *fin de siècle* poetry of Baudelaire, then in fashion in France:

No longer do I crave the sweetness of ideal romance,
    The softness of the apple and the milk; nor songs
And gentle carols 'mid the flowers and soft west wind;
    No longer Nemean games and girls and languid notes . . .
No Satan, you I crave beneath your brazen wing,
    To stand beside me and to fill me with your ill.
I long for madness that prostrates the soul and sense,
    While hymns of evil fill the priests with fear;
I crave infernal dances and insensate sounds,
    The breasts of Grecian concubines to pass the night.
I crave long orgies and strange unknown forms of love.
    Among the kisses and the wine-cups will I madden.
Satan yes, 'tis you I crave. . . .

Of this Chiarini wrote more severely: "But a poem like *Ora Satanica* is poetically and morally ugly. A well-brought-up young man of sixteen, full of obvious talent, should not be filling his head with 'infernal dances and insensate sounds, and the breasts of Grecian concubines to pass the night.' Such images can only be the froth from a brain stewing at an unhealthy moment. We may be sure that time and study will purge him of these faults. . . ." Little did he know! Another critic said that if he had been D'Annunzio's teacher, he would have given him a gold medal and a sound whipping.

But for a schoolboy this was an achievement, and articles about the "sixteen-year-old poetic prodigy from the Abruzzi" soon appeared all over Italy. After this, D'Annunzio was naturally anxious to leave school and reach Rome as soon as possible, although this involved leaving his Lilia. She seems to have been a quiet, good-natured girl, well content with her provincial life. André Germain, in his *La Vie Amoureuse de D'Annunzio* (a sort of chrestomathy of D'Annunzio's sex life), does not give her a place among the dozen or so selected ladies. As he has gone into these matters in some detail, one must assume that this was very much a puppy-love friendship. But most amorous letters to her from D'Annunzio have been found: ". . . my divine, my beautiful, my good, my sacred love! So greatly did I long for your letter that, on arriving back, I went up the stairs three at a time—a hundred and thirty-four steps! I found your letter, I kissed it, I opened it with shaking hands. Ah, how wonderful is this fire of love, of me for you, and you for me. My only, only, sole, unique, my only one. Ever, ever, ever, ever, ever, ever, ever, ever, ever, ever, your Gabriele. . . ."

The schoolboy proposed to her, she accepted, and he promised to return and marry her when he had made enough money, by writing, in Rome. It was the first of the many promises he was to make to women, and not to keep.

2

Rome in the '80's

"What a stupendous spectacle is this city strewn with the mighty monuments of the Past, a wilderness from which nothing now springs but grass, fever germs and noble thoughts! Will a new humanity ever rise from the ruins of this city?"

So wrote the young D'Annunzio when he arrived in Rome in 1881, at the age of nineteen. Having read Carducci at school he was, like most of the youth of his time, powerfully stirred by the patriotic *Odi Barbare,* which recalled the times of classical greatness. But, unlike the earlier great poets of the century, Leopardi and Manzoni, who put into their verse not only love of Italy but of mankind, Carducci had loved only Italy. *They* united Italy with the world; Carducci isolated her. All D'Annunzio's verse is marked with Carducci's *Romanità.* The young poet was soon writing:

> Rome, Rome, in you alone,
>   In the circle of your seven hills,
> Will the thousand discords of humanity
>   Find at length the universal harmony.
> You alone can give the bread of life.

When he arrived, the epoch of materialism which we call Victorian had set in. Rome was still the *urbs et orbis* of the Popes, full of operatic flights of stone steps leading nowhere, with the façades of baroque churches, which are elegant façades onto nothing. The world of Bernini still lingered among the altarpieces, surrounded by hearts and idols and fetishes hanging from the walls. But new buildings for the army of bureaucrats who had accompanied the Savoyards from the north were now being erected. Large areas belonging to Pius IX's minister, Monsignor de Merode, had been forcibly acquired for new streets and vistas, around Santa Maria Maggiore. Twelve large buildings in the heavy northern style had been recently erected. Typical of these was the new Ministry of Finance, which was disliked by the Romans as a symbol of Savoyard tax-collecting.

The old idea of Italy, as a place of ruins, landscapes and museums, fit only for honeymooners, archaeology students and young women in search of amorous excitements, was beginning to change. People might deplore the electrical tram-wires in the Corso, and think wistfully back to *diligences,* but the heroic excitements of the *Risorgimento* were over. Rome was becoming pacific, bourgeois, Victorian. The petty bourgeois and his wife, pushing the baby carriage in the Pincio gardens, could enjoy their Sunday afternoons, in the certain knowledge that the crepitations of the new Gatling guns (used for the first time in the war of Liberation) would not add an unwelcome counterpoint to the familiar harmonies of the brass band. In the afternoons—D'Annunzio writes in his first journalistic articles—the pretty Roman girls were to be seen walking in the mild Roman air, "large-eyed, slow-paced, fattening ladies who, between the Mass and the promenade, would have a meal at an *osteria*—the long noodles, the veal spiced with aromatic herbs, the strawberries in May, the figs in October, all washed down with three or four glasses of slightly but surely intoxicating Frascati."

Roman society, too, was at last beginning to model itself on western lines. The aristocracy had, for three centuries, been arrogant and cloistered, distinguished neither by ability nor culture, living in an almost feudal manner, the servants and lackeys playing cards and eating at table with their masters. It had now begun to acquire the etiquette of England, where middle class snobbishness, money-making and refined manners went hand in hand. Some Italian nobles, so obsessed with this English model, even deigned to try their hand in the new Commerce; but they did so with small success and most suffered financial ruin. The best account of what was happening is given by Luigi Barzini in his *Italy and her Aristocracy.*

"During the last decades of the century, that varicolored hodge-podge of illustrious and ancient, less illustrious, unknown, totally new, genuine and almost genuine families which, for good or ill, went to make up the aristocracy's *Book of Gold,* began searching confusedly for a new unifying principle. The Kingdom was new, life seemed to be changed, new industries and fortunes were being built, railroads were reaching out almost everywhere—it was neces-sary to be modern. The old traditions seemed to have been left behind and appeared dangerous to the principle of Unification. Everybody was looking for foreign models to imitate. The states-men debated the national problems in the halls of Montecitorio dressed in *rédingotes* as were being worn at the Palais Bourbon. The Parliamentary Rules of Order or *Statuto* had been taken di-rectly from the Belgians. The cotton mill owners of Milan played at being Englishmen, some of them even going fox hunting in red jackets. The bankers were studying their German counterparts. In the Army, the cavalry sent for a lance from the German Uhlans at Berlin, to copy; and they hired a famous Austrian horseman as their instructor.

"In those years, servants waiting at table in the old houses sud-denly became mute, just as in England; until then, they had always been permitted to participate respectfully in the conversation. Many nobles tried to prepare their sons for their responsibilities by sending them to the universities to study. Other nobles began serving their new King with punctilious faithfulness. Still others, following the pattern of the English Lords, plunged into voyages of exploration and hazardous big-game hunts. Some nobles threw open their old *palazzi,* redecorating them in accordance with the period's taste, gave large receptions, frequented high international society, married the daughters of foreign nobles, and traveled all over Europe visiting their friends. But there were also humble country counts, belonging to the newest group of the nobility, who enlisted in the old Piedmont regiments and felt obliged to behave

like the descendants of the Crusaders, scorning all dangers, putting
on haughty airs, sometimes challenging peaceful-minded bourgeois
to duels or throwing away part of their inheritance in wild gambling. In other words, the Italian nobles for the first time set about
acting the part of 'nobles'; they ceased to be patriarchal, with a
place in the people's ancient way of life, in order to live a fic-
titious literary and choreographic existence."

The literary world, which was the only world D'Annunzio knew
when he arrived, was also acquiring this western or "bourgeois"
stamp. Until the arrival of Sommaruga some years before, there
had been no publisher in the idle and sleepy city. It took the
capital many years to rival the more "western" cities of upper Italy,
Turin and Milan, which boasted publishing houses and newspapers. Sommaruga's magazine, *Fanfulla,* to which D'Annunzio
contributed, had all the hallmarks of the modern Bohemianism, as
it was known in France. Its writers were in continuous struggle
against innumerable (and often non-existent) adversaries, classi-
cists, romanticists, traditionalists and philistines of all kinds. Min-
istries were made and unmade in these intellectual circles; the
problem of Free Will and the existence of God were questioned;
and it was agreed that it was harder to write a good line of poetry
than to win a battle. The whole thing was salted with piquant
erotic poetry. Satanism was the fashion, and D'Annunzio, we have
seen, had written one or two *fin de siècle* odes.

Most of the literary men circulated round Sommaruga, meeting
in the offices and coffee-houses, in particular at the Café Aragno
which had, from 1880 onwards, its select literary *terza saletta.*
When D'Annunzio arrived in Rome, he had introductions to these
writers, his claim to recognition being his small book of poems,
Primo Vere, telling of "mountain tops and cathedrals, the open
sea and closed-in marshes, human suffering and delirious love. . . ."

Of the world he was later to depict, and for which he is best
known—his ornate descriptions of balls, palaces, great houses, receptions, beautiful women and their jewels—there is nothing yet.
He was, in his first two years in Rome, the young Abruzzese, who

had been favorably received by the literary men. His natural habitat was the intellectual or Bohemian circle of journalists, poets, café politicians and *avant-gardistes,* all people who, unlike corresponding circles in Paris and London, remained relatively remote from the aristocracy and ruling classes. He took a small room in via Borgognona, and enrolled as a student at the University; but he soon gave up lectures in favor of his literary friends. In one of his last letters to poor Griselda Zucconi, he wrote: "Here in Rome is a seething literary life. From morning to night I am on the go, from place to place, listening to a speaker here, airing my own views there, discussing, arguing, even fighting, with my little band of friends. . . ."

To another old friend, Paolo de Cecco, at Pescara, he wrote: ". . . forgive me for not having written sooner. These last months I have lived in an absolute whirl of excitement and energy. I have thrown myself into the Roman maelstrom of pleasure and struggle, to such effect that I seem guilty of forgetting you, old friend, although you are always in my mind. I have been too idle and too tired to write, to free myself from the torpid fevers of my own sensuality [*sic*], to give up even one hour to the people like you, dear Cicollo, who really love me. . . ."

We see him in these first days, from his own letters, as a child of nature, delighted to be among the literary men, in and out of the cafés and editorial offices, with sonnets, reviews, articles. The young man who was later to become the arbiter of Italian taste behaved in those days as the most modest of provincials. The future Beau Brummel went about in a black suit and open-necked shirt. (Black is the male costume in the Abruzzi for smart occasions. On Sundays, holidays, festival days, every Abruzzese puts on black.) There is one particularly unattractive photograph of him at this period, looking like a young Calvinist pastor up in the capital for the first time. His friend, Scarfoglio, describes him as "a little fellow with curly hair and softly feminine eyes." Another friend, Ugo Fleres, said, "a little bucolic fellow with crinkly hair, and a pair of great, glaucous eyes with almond lids."

But his forceful and ambitious character soon began to make

itself felt. There are other letters in which he confesses, "My desire
for glory sometimes gives me a tormented melancholy"; so he
quickly learned to place himself determinedly at the best café
tables in the piazza di Spagna and summon the waiters peremptor-
ily, by beating hard on the ground with his newly-acquired marble-
headed cane, to let the other people in the café know he was there.
He soon felt the need to offer flowers to ladies and to possess
elegant visiting-cards. He already looked on life as a "vast garden,
full of fruit and flowers to smell, touch, eat, with a kind of diffused sensuality." He wanted to absorb, he claimed, with all his
senses, every form of beauty, from the simplest to the most sublime. Later, he was to say that he compared the first longings of
his youth in Rome with the forward movement of horses, greyhounds and hawks—to give some idea "of the ardor, impulse and
voracity with which I hurled myself towards life." He expressed
it in poems of this kind, *A Paean to Joy:*

> Sing of Joy! I love to surround you
>   With all the flowers; to celebrate
> The Joy, the Joy, the Joy,
>   This magnificent giver of life.
>
> Sing of the immense joy of living!
>   Of being strong, of being young:
> Of biting with white teeth the fruits of earth;
>   With healthy, white, voracious teeth.
>
> To place audacious longing hands
>   On all that is sweet and tangible,
> To bend the bow towards
>   Each thing the soul desires.
>
> To hear all music,
>   To regard with burning eyes,
> The divine force of the world,
>   As a lover looks into his loved one's eyes.

To adore each fleeting form,
    Each vaguest hope and vanishing desire,
Each transient grace for their
    Brief appearance in their hour.

With all the flowers I would surround you,
    Transfigured thus you should extol,
The Joy, the Joy, the Joy,
    This invincible giver of life.

His early articles on Rome, and the exciting discoveries he was making, of its beauty, architecture and history, contain the best of his prose, which had not yet become inflated and baroque. Fabrizio Sarazani, in his study of D'Annunzio's early days in Rome, points out that his writing then contained none of the elaborate similes, the endless metaphors, the continual comparisons, which deface his later work. "The writing is direct, even dry; it is all matter, concrete, with a jealous economy of expression and image," he says. D'Annunzio's later unfortunate notion that the Italian language possessed "musical elements, various and powerful enough to compare with the great Wagnerian orchestras" had not yet appeared. His early prose is full of straight descriptive passages like the following: "The commercial street is narrow, at its far end lined with industrial buildings and wine-booths, where Roman wine is sold, while men play bowls. Then, gradually, past great walls stained and reddened with overhanging moss and with the tops of cypresses visible above, the atmosphere changes—into one of convent-like stillness. We are in the area of religion."

His magnetic quality of voice and manner, meanwhile, had made him friends outside the literary world. Isadora Duncan describes later, if with some exaggeration, how he must have first made his entrée into the difficult patrician houses (where a writer was still looked upon as a kind of servant). "His effect on a woman is remarkable," she says. "The lady he is talking to suddenly feels that her very soul and being are lifted, as it were, into an ethereal region, where she walks in company with the Divine Beatrice. Above ordinary mortals, she goes about with a kind of imaginary halo. But, alas, when the caprice is over and he moves on to another lady, the halo dulls, the aureole diminishes, and she feels again of clay. She does not quite understand what has happened, but seems to be back on earth searching desperately for her transfiguration, aware that never in her whole life will she meet this kind of love again." With such a power, it was not long before he succeeded in making his personality felt outside the literary world of Rome.

The first signs of the change are given by Scarfoglio in his memoirs: ". . . Gabriele, who was modest, kind, ingenuous, is now becoming foppish, cunning and affected. The childlike grace, half-wild, half-timid, from the Abruzzi has been transformed overnight into the perfumed elegance, the capering mannerisms of the dandy. He has abandoned himself to the smart crowd, from whom his artist's instincts should have fatally divided him. When the doors of the great Roman houses open, he gives himself up entirely to female blandishments. I shall never forget the first time I saw him adorned, perfumed, decked-out for a smart evening. The year before, we had never been able to persuade him to wear anything but a dark suit and white tie (he occasionally forgot the tie). Now, for six months, he has been going from one party to another, from one ball to another, from a morning's riding in the Campagna, to a supper-party at the house of some pomaded old idiot furnished with nothing more than a set of quarterings. Gabriele never opens a book. Not one serious thought enters his head. He is a puppy dog on a silken thread. . . ."

That there was some truth in this is illustrated from D'Annunzio's own writings. After a few years in Rome, he had become a gossip columnist on the *Tribuna,* where he began to write paragraphs of this kind: ". . . the ladies go down the Corso in their carriages between four and five in the afternoon. The Countess Taverna wears leopard skin in the winter. Who does not know the divine pallor of the Countess? Her dark hair, full of undulations, the wide, veiled eyes and long lashes? There is nothing that can awaken in rainy weather, the desire, the intimacy of love, more than a leopard skin. . . ."

His articles become full of foreign words—*potelée, toilettes, five o'clock tea* (in English), *biscuits, fondants, noisettes, flirtation, parures.* Then there are hunting scenes where, after describing the ladies' *parures,* he writes, "I remember certain mornings in England chasing the deer in the park of Lady Horne, when we left *avant l'aurore qui tout dore."*

His literary colleagues quickly noticed the change, which transformed his physical, as well as his mental, appearance. They now disapproved of it, as a regrettable affectation. For literary and artistic people in Rome were expected to be neglected and down-at-heel. The great writers of the period, Carducci, Rapisardi, Panzacchi, were all disheveled men. Good clothes were considered an insult to the intelligence. But now D'Annunzio's English ties and impeccable riding coats, which he wore at the meets of the Campagna hunt, annoyed the intellectuals. His apparent success with fashionable women was also irritating.

". . . the Countess Robilant," he writes in his gossip column, "a lady who has conquered one of the first places in Rome with her wit, her simple elegance and manners, wore a gray dress, from the House no doubt of Worth or Morin Bloissier. The two Brook daughters, making their *entrée* into *le monde,* were accompanied by their mother. Among others present, we saw Madame Lindstrand, the Marchioness of Villamarina, Donna Amelia De Pretis, the Baroness Magliani. The Ambassadress, the Comtesse de Mornay, received the guests so graciously that, in truth, I believe she has with her smile conquered all Rome. And the French Ambassador, himself, who is also a poet of the widest culture and taste," etc., etc. . . .

From these society notes, he began composing his first full-length novel, *Il Piacere.* In the third chapter, there is a description of an auction sale in a Roman *palazzo,* at which the public consists entirely of Princes, Princesses, Dukes and Ambassadors, Lords and

Cavaliers of all kinds. But as Sarazani remarks, he was really describing an imaginary aristocracy, for what he admired was "an attenuated refinement which was far from the manners of the old aristocracy," who were coarser than he imagined. He can in fact be accused—as Proust's Marchioness of Villeparisis accused Balzac—of depicting a society which he did not really know, for it had not received him. At first, he saw all these people only from a distance, from the upper circle of the Apollo Theatre, or the Capannelle.

He was interested, above all, in the ladies. The Countess of Santafiora, the Duchess Sforza Cesarini, the Princess San Faustino, the Marchesa Theodoli, the Princess Odescalchi, the Princess Pallavicini—he depicts these ladies with the sartorial details of a knowledgeable tailor. In *Tribuna* he describes, for instance, the Princess Pallavicini in her box at the Apollo on the eve of the 1885 carnival, painting her with the detail of a miniaturist, from the color of her dress, "rich with waves of red velvet," to her hair style, "*poudrée* with a high coiffure puffed out from the neck." He notes that she wears on the top a red ribbon; while the Countess Taverna has "a white dress covered with diamond brooches and gold arabesques." In the novel, *Il Piacere,* the description of this woman's world is equally sustained and detailed. In Constanza Landbroke, who was for Sperelli, the hero, a "very subtle love," he describes in the hair "a comb made as of Grecian fretwork." He adores stuffs which are *"pailletés."* In *Il Piacere,* Elena Muti, at lunch with the Marchioness D'Ateleta, wears a "gown of very pale sky-blue," while Lady Ouless has a dress of "a marine seaweed and red fish" design, with which Sperelli is delighted, describing it as a "splendid aquarium of a dress." In this book, too, steps the "Marquis of Mount Edgecombe."

The people for whom he wrote these articles demanded above all novelty and enjoyment. He soon learned to provide this, writing long passages full of "witty," worldly dialogue in his articles; such as:

"At a bazaar sale in Rome, the beautiful Countess X was in

charge of a small stall called *L'Article de Paris.* The Duke of Y,
an attaché from one of the embassies, went by. Laughing, the
Countess called him over. *"Please buy* something, Duke! What can
I offer you?"

"Ah, Countess, but what bewitching goods you are yourself!"

"I'm not asking for compliments, my dear Duke. I'm asking for
money. *Please* buy something!"

"But you, my dear Countess, are not selling what I want."

"What is that?"

"Zounds! That is not so easy to say."

"But please *do,* dear Duke! It is for the poor."

"Well, I want simply a kiss."

"That I do not possess myself. But I am sure, dear Duke, that I
could obtain it for you."

"Indeed?"

"Yes. For a thousand lire."

"And when?"

"In a year."

"The Duke opened his wallet, took out a bank-note, which he
threw gently into the tray with the other money. He bowed and
left.

"Aha!" said a friend, the Marchioness of Z, to the Countess.
"Your business seems to be a little risky, my dear."

"The Countess pouted and laughed. "A year. A year is long.
Who knows where we will all be then? I, the Duke—and the
kiss?" And in fact, the Duke was dead in a year, in another country, in a duel. And a well-known circus director received that so
highly-paid-for kiss. . . ."

The ladies of Rome were taken with a romantic and morbid
fascination for this D'Annunzio who advertised himself (and
themselves) so well. Poetry had become for him a game for the
delectation of women, who asked for sonnets in their albums and
on their fans, just as on their bed tables they wanted Chinese jades.
In his next set of poems, *Intermezzo di Rime,* his style changes.
Poetic inspiration is less. He becomes more interested in style and

expression in themselves, aiming above all in the baroque manner, at making his readers wonder, at dazzling and shocking. He advised the ladies on furnishings, antiques, jewels, furs; he learned to describe with the minuteness of Firenzuola, the elegant postures of a beautiful woman. His poems are full of lascivious images; gums seen in a smile; the smell of the tears which a lover drinks; nude women; lines like, "Lucia getting down from the boat had her blouse full of the odor of southern fruits . . ." or "all my roses are plucked; no more garlands are left; my cup is empty. I have drunk and re-drunk, until finally no form of drunkenness is unknown to me. I have dared all. . . ." The set of sonnets called *Le Adultere* are full of luxury, beauty and obscenity, the last quality justified by the motto he quotes from *Ecclesiasticus:* "and from these, passion grows like a flame."

In the first days, when he attempted to enter society himself, he met only amused contempt on the part of the young women. They danced, joked, flirted, only with their friends, friends' relations, and friends' relations' friends. An unsurpassable barrier separated them from the young Abruzzese still smelling of journalist's ink, displaying an occasional boorishness and lack of tact, in remarkable contrast with the flower in the buttonhole, the tail-coat, top hat, and patter of conversation overheard at the last party. Moreover, he was not famous; and literary men, like any actor or mountaineer, are only taken seriously in *le monde* if they are.

But there was one *palazzo* which gave him a warmer and more sincere reception. Its owners, a mother and daughter, represented in their artistic tastes as much as in their unusual past, something of the strange history of the house of Gallese, which belonged to the "black," or papal, aristocracy of Rome.

3

A "Black" Family

Ten years before D'Annunzio arrived in Rome, the breach had been made in the walls at Porta Pia, and Victor Emmanuel had stepped in to claim his new title. The great obstacle to Italian unity, the Papal state, had been overcome, and Italy was united for the first time since the Caesars. But Rome itself was divided, into the "black" and "white" aristocracies. The Pope had refused to recognize the house of Savoy, and had shut himself up in the Vatican, beginning a self-imposed incarceration which was to last fifty years. He was Pius IX, the great intransigent Pope of the Syllabus, of the Infallibility and the *non possumus;* and Rome was divided about him into "blacks" and "whites," sympathizing with, respectively, Pope and sovereign.

The "blacks" had not, it is true, actually defended the Pope, arms in hand, at the time of the Porta Pia breach. Their loyalty to the Vatican was only platonic, and their protest against the Savoyards went no further than an ostentatious refusal to recognize the new sovereign in the Quirinale. Among these "blacks" were such famous names as Barberini, Chigi, Borghese, Aldobrandini, Theodoli, and Rospigliosi. The old Prince Torlonia so hated the Savoyards that he had changed the red liveries of his footmen, in order not to share that color with the royal grooms. The more important ladies of "black" society did not go out for their daily carriage *passeggiata* in the Corso, except during summer months, when the court had left the capital on vacation. At the Quirinale, the King's chaplain could not celebrate Mass in the chapel because that building, together with the rest of the palace, came under the papal interdiction. The King and Queen had to

go to public worship in Santa Maria Maggiore where, on one
occasion, Queen Margherita was given the ceremonial reserved for
foreign princes. The situation became even more ludicrous when
the Spanish ambassador (naturally a "black") would not allow
the King and Queen to pass through his anteroom, to visit a sale
in aid of the Andalusian earthquake victims. A special entry from
the road had to be cut into the room where the sale took place. In
short, the monarchy, which had come into power through a revolution, was in the invidious position of being unable to be conservative without depriving itself of its title rights. The Pope had
arrogated to himself the position of Supreme Conservative of
Rome.

Among the families belonging to this "black" aristocracy were
the Duke and Duchess of Gallese—neither of whom had a drop
of Gallese blood in their veins. Although the Duke bore the title
of one of the proudest families of the "black" aristocracy, he
was, by origin, a French non-commissioned officer of bourgeois
extraction called Hardouin. He had been stationed in Rome with
Louis Napoleon's forces defending the Pope, some twenty years
before. He was then handsome, and he had the tantalizing habit
of combing his beautiful hair every morning at the stables, opposite the bedroom of a young widow, the Duchess Gallese.[1] Whatever it was, she fell in love with him and, being as pious as she
was romantic, decided to marry him. What now happened illus-
trates perfectly the powerful position occupied by the "black"
aristocracy at the Papal Court. Having inherited the entire fortune
of her late husband, the Duke of Gallese, the Duchess obtained
permission from the Pope, not only for her marriage with the
French NCO, but also for him to assume her own style and title.
Hardouin became Duke of Gallese. The Pope was predisposed to
reward any Frenchman who had rallied to the cause in the difficult
days of '48; but he also respected the wishes of a "black" family.
The situation became even stranger three years later, when the
Duchess died childless, leaving her considerable fortune and *pa-*

[1] Roman gossip says, *"non si pettinava, urinava."*

lazzo to the lucky Frenchman—who married again! It was from this second marriage that the daughter was born, whom D'Annunzio was to marry. Thus, a D'Annunzio without D'Annunzio blood married a Gallese without Gallese blood.

One afternoon in the winter of 1882, D'Annunzio was invited to their house, the *palazzo* Altemps. He was already an accomplished conversationalist, able to make whoever he was talking to, particularly women, feel that they were the most agreeable persons he had ever met. Maria, on the other hand, had been brought up in the solitary manner customary in those times, in the formal atmosphere of a palace where gaiety was unknown (like all upstarts, the Duke was a stickler for etiquette), and she was quiet and unassuming. She had also, in self-defense, acquired a taste for the arts. She enjoyed the company of poets and writers, so unlike the "black" society she normally frequented. For the rest of the winter, D'Annunzio was a regular visitor to their house, where they took part in poetry readings.

At all periods of his life, people have spoken of the extraordinary power D'Annunzio's voice had over his listeners. Arthur Symons has written: "I never realized the full charm of the Italian language until I heard the Parable of the *Wise and Foolish Virgins* read by Gabriele D'Annunzio. He reads Italian more beautifully than anyone I ever heard. Delicately articulated, all those triple endings, *avano, arono, ovono,* ringing like bells, fatigued the ear as the blue of the Mediterranean fatigues the eye; there were no gray shades, and there was also no brief, emphatic pause in the music. . . ."

Both mother and daughter in the Gallese household were susceptible to these special charms. He, for his part, was delighted to have at last made an entrée into a Roman *palazzo,* which did not depend entirely upon his journalist's card.

The girl was slender, with long golden hair, and D'Annunzio tells us she had green irises to her eyes. In a letter written on April 6, 1883, to his friend, Enrico Nencioni, he wrote, "I am in love, my dear Enrico. I am at last in love, with a total abandon which makes me forget all else. Not even the gate of poetry has now time to open. . . ."

One of his first problems was to be alone with her; for the strict rules of society enacted that no unmarried daughter should ever be left alone with a young man. D'Annunzio was a good strategist, and he was helped by the governess Maria's parents employed to accompany their daughter on her walks. This governess would sometimes leave them alone together in the Roman parks, and the courting would begin. At first, Maria did not find D'Annunzio particularly attractive; he amused rather than fascinated her. In spite of all the scents and pomades he used on his hair, there was still something Abyssinian about the hirsute little face.

The romantic Maria, who had so often escaped from her family through poetry, saw in D'Annunzio the Muse itself. Much later, she said sadly to a friend, "When I married him, I really thought I was marrying Poetry." D'Annunzio realized that she was in love, but he was aware too that her parents, particularly the Duke, would never accept a son-in-law without name, fortune or position. Having climbed to the position he now held, the ex-French NCO was more Roman, and more ducal, than any Roman duke. He had planned a further advance for his family, in the form of a Colonna fiancé for Maria. In his daily arguments with his daughter he employed every means, from the threatening and violent to the sweet-tempered and flattering. When he saw that she would never marry the Colonna youth (who was, incidentally, a half-wit), he said he would give up the plan, provided she would at least marry someone of her own class. At all costs, she must get rid of the idea of these Abruzzese brigands.

But Maria was as stubborn as he. No other marriage, however brilliant, meant anything to her, she said. It was Gabriele she wanted, "Gabriele or the convent." These arguments continued for days, and weeks, with the Duke in a towering rage, and Maria in tears. After an unsuccessful attempt at an elopement, in which Maria and D'Annunzio reached Florence before being turned back, the Duke capitulated. She should marry her boor then. But let it be done quickly. There would be no dowry. The Abruzzese peasant would not get a penny. She would be cut off entirely. Her family would not see her. She would be outlawed.

So powerful was the Duke's position in Rome, not only in his own family, but also as the head of a "black" dynasty, that his word was law. Maria's childhood friends no longer came to see her, and she was ostracized from the *salons*. On the morning of her wedding, she received a visit from her favorite uncle, the Marquis Lezzani, her mother's brother, who brought the finest of wedding presents, a diamond necklace. As he gracefully laid it on the table, he added, "And with this, I see you for the last time."

D'Annunzio had too much of the Stendhalian hero in him not to feel flattered at this, at shaking one of the ancient houses of Rome to its foundations, at being the hero of a love affair the whole city was discussing. He was clever enough not to allow himself to be offended by the studied insults of the Duke which, he knew, could be excellent publicity. On the wedding day, the bride's parents refused to come to the church, and she was accompanied by the governess. They were married in a church which was empty, except for one or two friends of the bridegroom. Through her tears Maria could see only a few of D'Annunzio's journalists and then, to her surprise and pleasure, a veiled woman standing in a lonely corner of the church. It was her mother, the Duchess, who had disobeyed her husband's orders. But the pleasure was short, for the service was not over before Maria heard the brush of skirts as her mother left quickly, to avoid being discovered. A few minutes later, D'Annunzio knelt with Maria Gallese before a Cardinal, and was married into the "black" aristocracy of Rome.

4

The Novels of Violence

D'Annunzio's rise to power and influence was due initially to women. His marriage with Maria Gallese was the first rung of that ladder; and the novels he now wrote, the *I Romanzi della Rosa,* are all based on autobiographical experiences with women. To relate all his love affairs (there were eight large ones and hundreds of small ones) would be repetitive. His love affairs *are* important, but only in so far as they contribute to D'Annunzio as the Stendhalian hero, nourished on the myth of Roman greatness, determined to repeat it in his own life, to become the superman. The female element in his career has been understandably exaggerated by biographers. Although women certainly played a large part in his life, there were periods when he sickened of them so thoroughly that, like Faust who suddenly realized that he had read too many books, he retired for months into seclusion to avoid them. It was during these periods of withdrawal that D'Annunzio wrote his first novels.

But in the early married days, this feeling of surfeit had not begun. He describes this as the period of his "great debauch." He lived in Rome for six years working on the newspaper, for periods with his wife, or retiring to Francavilla on the Adriatic with his friend Michetti, or to Naples, generally in the company of a lady of the aristocracy. After six or seven years of this, he had such an indigestion of duchesses, of duchesses or adventuresses (he occasionally mistook the one for the other), that he took up with the Roman bourgeois, Barbara Leoni. He probably did not conquer as many authentic princesses, duchesses and marchionesses as he attributes in his first novel, *Il Piacere,* to the hero, Andrea Sperelli.

To seduce these great ladies with their varied appetites, he lacked two of the many charms he so generously attributed to Sperelli—a great name, and a great fortune. The novel about Sperelli is set entirely in Roman society, in a world of sumptuous balls, dinners, receptions, carriages and *objets d'art,* with dukes and duchesses centering round the hero who is, of course, D'Annunzio himself, wearing the borrowed plumage of a nobleman with a string of titles. Maria, who was the first aristocrat D'Annunzio knew, is depicted as the woman the hero comes to last, after sampling a bevy of licentious duchesses and princesses.

In spite of this, the first three years of married life with Maria Gallese were happy, idyllic even. Much later in her life, Maria told the French writer, André Germain, that when she and Gabriele arrived at the Adriatic fishing village of Porto San Giorgio for their honeymoon, "then began three years of intoxicating happiness." They spent several months here by the sea, in modest but comfortable surroundings. Maria, accustomed to the gardens, receptions and *salons* of Rome, full of the works of the great artists, showed no disdain for the bourgeois world of the D'Annunzio family. Her amiable disposition was revealed in a number of small acts of kindness towards her husband's parents. The local Abruzzesi still speak of her good nature and charm. There are letters to her mother-in-law with phrases such as these, where she calls her "Mama Lisa," ". . . I go to bed at eight, and to sleep at ten, and my mind and heart always turn towards you, my Mama, and I pray for you and for your health. . . ."; in another letter, "I always think of you, dear Mama. The happy hours we have passed together will be a memory in time of loneliness." Her nobility of character overcame the difference of origins, the contrast between the simple Pescarese house and the Palazzo Altemps. Repudiated by her father, coldly treated by her old friends, she never reproached her husband, nor her parents-in-law. D'Annunzio himself, whose fresh impulses for ever-changing life and love were to take him far from his wife, never forgot this goodness of charac ter. He always displayed a kind of reverence for her, that increased as he grew older.

In these first days, D'Annunzio was less a husband than a lover (the only role he could ever play with a woman), and many of his poems were inspired by Maria:

> Now I remember, my Maria,
>   How with that smile of goodness on your
> Flower-like lips, you followed all my
>   Movements as I rode away.
> Oh tell me then, Maria, who cured my
>   Wounds with sweet assuaging, whose tender
> Hands lay gently on those bitter hurts,
>   And cured my sleeplessness with love at night,
> And the thousand sufferings with the patient
>   Balm of your quiet voice. Tell me, oh tell me,
> My adored Signora, tell me once again
>   Of that great ease, those moments when my eyes
> Were filled with tearful laughter as I kissed
>   Your pallid lips. . . .

It was when they returned to Rome that financial difficulties created differences between them. Maria's father had kept his word and cut her off without an allowance, so that they had to live, with an increasing family, on D'Annunzio's small literary earnings. Maria adapted herself to a life of frugality unknown to her before, dealing with the bills and accounts, shopping, organizing the household, feeding and clothing the children as they appeared. D'Annunzio, with his refined tastes and growing belief in his genius, spent lavishly, bought *objets d'art* and took his social and literary friends to the best hotels and restaurants. Maria later told André Germain, "When we managed at last to settle the debts, off he would go lighthearted as a bird, to some auction or sale, to buy something completely useless, a Chinese jade, a bibelot costing thousands of *lire.* Then the struggle would begin again." His journalism for the *Tribuna,* so necessary for their livelihood, soon seemed beneath him, and he complained in a letter to the owner, Prince Matteo Sciarra:

". . . so I must go on then with this petty journalism! This is particularly galling for me just now, as I have many other things to do. I want to start serious work, in particular a long book which will be of importance to my future. . . ."

It has never been politic for a writer, however famous, to talk to a newspaper editor or owner about "petty journalism," nor to speak slightingly of the "ephemeral nature of newspapers in general." But D'Annunzio must have been on fairly good terms with Sciarra, for he goes on, ". . . this daily journalism distracts me, wastes my energies. . . . Rome has conquered me. I have by temperament, by instinct, *the need for the superfluous.* My aesthete's feeling draws me inevitably towards the acquisition of fine things. I could have eaten quite well in a modest house, sat on a simple wooden chair, eaten off common plates, walked about on carpets made in Italy. . . . Instead, fatally, I have wanted divans, Persian carpets, precious materials and stuffs, Japanese plates, all those beautiful and useless things which I love with a deep and ruinous love. . . . Also, I am anxious that Maria should not live in circumstances too different from those to which she is accustomed. She is possessed of a marvelous spirit of selfsacrifice. . . ."

This letter shows the strains to which the household was subjected, as well as the good nature of the wife, and D'Annunzio's growing conviction that he was a genius. As long as he was in love with her he was prepared, it seems, to continue the hack journalism. It was when his affection cooled and he felt he was capable of living alone, could indeed work better alone—and live cheaper alone—that he decided to leave Rome. Most of the Italian biographies of D'Annunzio are silent on the relations between husband and wife after 1888. They do not tell of the separation, they only indicate that it was slow and painful for Maria.

By the time the third child arrived, in 1887, D'Annunzio was not even present, to support his wife in childbirth. All he did was to telegraph instructions about the child's Christian name. There is an account in André Germain's book, in which Maria tells the French writer how she discovered her husband's first infidelities: "I used to brush my husband's clothes myself. One evening while doing so, a letter fell out of his pocket. I recognized the writing of one of my best friends, and I couldn't help reading it. It left no doubt as to what were her relations with Gabriele. . . ." Antongini, who was later D'Annunzio's secretary, also refers to infidelities in these early days. He describes a visit to Franz Liszt at Tivoli in 1886 by D'Annunzio, accompanied by a pretty woman whom he treated with intimacy, and who "was not his wife."

If domestic problems arose, D'Annunzio imitated the unheroic behavior of another selfish genius, Goethe, when he wished to avoid the repeated childbirths of his wife. He disappeared. He would go off for weeks at a time, sometimes without leaving his address. In this way, preferring the withdrawn life among the pine trees of Francavilla-al-mare, and the comforting sight of the Adriatic, to babies in the house and arguing with creditors, he began the series of holidays he was to take at the house of his painter friend, Michetti, where he wrote the first novels of *I Romanzi della Rosa*.

D'Annunzio's sensual nature is to be found not only in his poetry, but also in his first set of short stories, *Tales of the Pescara,* where it seems that there is no joy other than physical joy, just as there is no pain other than physical suffering. They contain an astonishing mixture of cruelty and sex. In one, he shows the local schoolmistress, a well-known and respectable local character, the embodiment of chastity, being raped by a drunken water carrier. In *La Veglia Funebre,* the widow and the brother of a dead man, in the presence of his decomposing body, give themselves to one another feverishly, as they roll on the ground before him. In another, he recounts minutely the story of a wounded sailor who is ferociously mutilated by his well-intentioned companions on the high seas; they cut up his wound, then burn it, until he is in such agony that he dies, and has to be thrown in the sea. In *La Madia* we see a deformed man who is hungry and who, while he is stealing a loaf of bread, has his hand crushed by his own brother who shuts the heavy iron bin on it.

Impassively, without indignation, without tears or laughter, the young D'Annunzio examines, notes and describes these cruel things precisely. The volume of some of his collected stories is called *Il Libro delle Vergini,* its jacket depicting three naked women dancing in a Bacchanalian orgy. D'Annunzio described it himself to his publisher. "I think it should please the public for its air of sanctity combined with audaciousness. Its scenes alternate between the church and the brothel, between the odor of incense and the stink of decay."

I Romanzi della Rosa, his first full length novels, carry this process a stage further. They are, as their title suggests, placed under the sign of the Queen of flowers—mistakenly, one might say, for the rose is the symbol of burning but at least of pure love, whereas these novels are concerned exclusively with cerebral love and lust. D'Annunzio seems to have set out to be the Italian representative of the *fin de siècle* writers already well known in France and England. In *I Romanzi della Rosa,* he develops his special Cult of the Beautiful in a manner reminiscent of Baudelaire or Pater, adding to it his own special Italian element, a kind of Machiavellianism of Beauty. Every act committed for the sake of Beauty, even a sin or a crime, is justifiable and excusable. Just as Machiavelli exalted Cesare Borgia into a superman in spite of his crimes, so D'Annunzio exalts his heroes who, in order to live their life of Beauty, do not hesitate to commit sins, including the special D'Annunzian one of incest.

For such men a special set of rules exist. He describes Andrea Sperelli, the hero of *Il Piacere,* in these terms, "He was completely saturated with Art, to the extent of being corrupted by it, demanding only experience and more experience of the sharpest kind to feed it. He was always prodigal of his own energy, for the

powerful force within him was ever expressing itself—but only at
the expense of another force, the moral force. Gradually, he found
that he lied to himself as much as to other people; it became absolutely natural, and necessary." Andrea Sperelli is a kind of autobiographical hero, a man of great culture, taste and verve, who
moves through innumerable intrigues and amorous adventures,
duels and balls, from fox hunts and horses to the composition of
elegant works of art printed on special paper for a restricted
number of friends.

A passage like the following from his next novel, *L'Innocente*,
seems today like a parody of Oscar Wilde: ". . . perverse and
curious, I thought how she would seem if I made love to her when
she was ill. Would not the voluptuousness have something incestuous about it? If she were to die? I thought. And certain words
of the doctors echoed in my mind. The sense of cruelty and danger
which, basically, exists in all sensual men attracted rather than
repelled me. I took pleasure in examining my feelings, with a
kind of bitter complacency combined with disgust. I analyzed all
the interior manifestations which seemed to furnish a proof of the
fundamental evilness of humans—in myself. Why does man have
as part of his nature that terrible faculty of enjoying more acutely
when he knows he is hunting a creature from whom he takes his
pleasure? Why must there be a germ of sadist perversion in everyone who loves and desires . . . ?"

Here, the hero is a man who desires certain sensual spasms
which he cannot find in his lover. Realizing that he can never obtain the unnatural delights he craves, he takes his pleasure in nos-
talgically imagining them.

In *Il Trionfo della Morte*, D'Annunzio goes further. Aurispa,
the hero, loves a woman so intensely that he feels he must destroy
her. He is a self-indulgent young man who passes from mad adora-
tion of a woman to nausea for her. D'Annunzio emphasizes this
by recounting her physical and mental defects, the manner in
which his hero views the deformity of her feet as they walk on
the warm sand of the beach, the physical disgust his mistress is

beginning to awaken in him. He feels he can neither live with her, nor without her, that she will somehow destroy him. The book reaches its climax with a long and gloomy meditation on sin as the supreme joy, the hero obsessed by the thought of death, wishing to die and cause to die. These two acts can best be combined in a sexual embrace, so, after a fearful hand-to-hand struggle with the unfortunate heroine, he assaults her and pulls her to death over a precipice. The epigraph he placed before this work is appropriate: *"Nec sine te nec tecum vivere possum."*

Il Trionfo della Morte is perhaps D'Annunzio's best novel because it possesses unity. The problem of this kind of dissatisfied lover is stated in the opening pages, and is carefully worked out to its conclusion. This can hardly be said for the other novels, in which the actions and the emotions which inspire them are often unconnected. As for the writing and the technique, they are always undisciplined. Even in *Il Trionfo della Morte*, D'Annunzio introduces a long exposition of one of Tennyson's poems, as well as a disquisition on Wagner.

The general sexual theme which runs through these novels cannot be considered particularly original today. Their importance lies in the hold they took on a late Victorian generation tired of gentility, confirming that in Italy, too, as in England, middle class morality existed, and had now run its course. Like Zola, D'Annunzio wished to study what is immoral and prurient in human nature, things hitherto forbidden, to reach the depths, and shrink from no investigation. Most Italians, when they speak of his works today, regret his obscenity—not because they are prudes (the Italians are not a prudish race), but from their artistic sense, because so much is overdone. In *Il Piacere,* for instance, he introduces libertine traits and incidents, such as the auctioning of a Havana cigar which has spent a day in the arm-pit of a pretty girl. There are a number of sinister or lascivious incidents, stolen direct (enemies claim) from *L'Initiation Sentimentale,* by the French author, Péladan. On top of this, aestheticism, which is unsuitable in a novel, keeps breaking in, in the Wildean manner, "A perfect line of verse is absolute, immutable, deathless. It encloses a thought as within a clearly marked circle which no force can break; it belongs no more to the poet, it belongs to all and yet to none, as do space, light, all things intransitory and perpetual. When the poet is about to bring forth one of these deathless lines, he is warned by a divine torrent of joy which sweeps over his soul."

The worst quality is the verbiage. The ability to convey meaning and atmosphere by a word or short phrase is entirely absent. In this, D'Annunzio was probably not very different from other writers of his time, French and English. The huge crowded canvases of contemporary writers and painters are all much the same, with their varied groups and contorted attitudes. D'Annunzio's descriptions are often mere inventories, painfully minute, like a mosaic with millions of little word cubes—a multiplicity of words which frequently conceals a poverty of ideas.

Against this, the incessant search for what is loathsome and cruel, the physical and moral leprosies, the verbiage, must be set D'Annunzio's very great powers of observation and description. Seldom can a writer have been so influenced by the early surroundings of his native land as D'Annunzio. The whole Adriatic coast, from the mouth of the Tronto to the banks of the Trigno, its innumerable gulfs and bays and the barren Maiella behind, together with the primitive traditions and barbarous customs of the race, appear in his early work. There is something pantheistic in his identification of the characters with the natural world around them, a kind of intoxication in his love of sounds and colors. In the passage quoted below from *Il Trionfo della Morte,* D'Annunzio catches something most true to Abruzzese life—the paganism bred in the blood of this people, mixed with the ferocity of Christian bigotry, depicted in a pilgrimage to the House of the Virgin at Casalbordino:

". . . the crowd of pilgrims was a marvelous and terrible spectacle, unlike any other assemblage of men and things, composed of mixtures so diverse, cruel and strange, that it eclipsed the most dreadful visions of a nightmare. All the hideousness of the eternal idiot, all the filthiness of vice and its stupidities, all the spasms and deformities of baptized flesh, all the tears of penitence, all the laughter of license; the mania, the cupidity, the craft, the lust, the fraud, the imbecility, the silent desperation, the sacred choruses, the howls of the possessed, the shouts of the ambulatory vendors, the clanging of the bells, the squeal of the trumpets, the lowing, the neighing, the bleating; the fires crackling under the cauldrons, the heaps of fruit and sweetmeats, the display of utensils, of stuffs, of jewels, of rosaries; the obscene capers of the dancers, the convulsion of the epileptics, the blows of the quarrelsome, the rush of thieves through the crowd; the supreme froth of corruption poured forth from the filthy lanes of remote cities and showered out onto an ignorant and astonished multitude, like horseflies on the flanks of beasts, shoals of parasites descending on a compact mass incapable of defending itself, all the base temptations of brutal appetites, all the treacheries playing on simplicity and stupidity, all the charlatanism and effronteries bared in full daylight. All these opposing contrasts were there, boiling and effervescing around the House of the Virgin. . . ."

In D'Annunzio's prose, as in his verse, he indulges a kind of lust of the eye, which feeds on every kind of beauty—and ugliness. He had defined it before in one of his poems:

> La festa ho celebrato
> De' sonni, de' colori e de le forme.

Anyone who has seen an Italian religious festival will recognize the description from *Il Trionfo della Morte*. But if there is, as has been claimed, the graphic ability of a Hogarth or a Callot in it, is there not also logorrhea? He describes his mania for adjectives in a letter he wrote to his editor in Paris. "I have such a sensitive ear, that the repetition of a word irritates me three pages away." In another letter to his translator, Hérelle, he wrote: "I am and I wish to be above all a stylist. Compare any page of mine with that of any contemporary Italian writer and you will see the difference.

... I never take account of usage when I wish to obtain an artistic effect. I give back to the word its original meaning. Between two expressions, one the normal, the other unusual, I choose always the unusual one. ..."

Such was his feeling for euphonious sounds, that he once chose two young men to be his companions on a sailing cruise in the Adriatic, simply on account of their beautiful names, Ippolito Santilozzo and Valente Valori (unsuitable qualifications for seamanship, they proved to be, for Santilozzo was unable to handle a sail, and Valori was a martyr to seasickness).

D'Annunzio came from an imaginative people, and his early work is full of these peasant images, many of them felicitous, if elaborate. For phrases of singular beauty are still to be heard among the Abruzzese peasantry. The writer has heard them himself. A middle-aged peasant woman from the Maiella said, "So long as one's mother lives, one's youth is never gone, for there is always someone for whom one is young." An unlettered peasant who could not write a word, said of a tree that was hard to fell, "He is sorry to come away, it has been his field for so long." I have read that a young Abruzzese soldier was sent to Africa on service; whereupon his brother who loved him, killed himself in despair; and their father, having lost two sons, killed himself as well. It is this inflammable imagination which makes these people so easily led away by promises and dreams of glory.

Generosity and hospitality are natural in the Abruzzi; violence is sudden, sin remorseless; crime, especially passional and political, is widespread; and the Abruzzi has produced more than its fair share of brigands. Taverns abound, teeming with smokers, cardplayers, drunkards and chatterboxes. Bargellini, one of D'Annunzio's biographers, says that the poet came from an essentially superstitious land, from "a people whose interests are undisturbed by the arts of learning." Here, he says, life is simple, death is death, earth is earth, and *il cielo incombe* (the sky looms over). One must remember, too, in connection with D'Annunzio's novels about lust and murder, that in the more primitive parts of

Italy, a criminal is always admired by most of the people. To protect him against the law, his comrades will make the greatest sacrifices; while a man who commits a passion crime is a positive hero. (The recent case of Giuliano in Sicily is an example.)

D'Annunzio was always to remain, in spite of all his acquired elegance and urbanity, fundamentally true to this background, the son of a semi-primitive people. In terms of his early environment he is easily explained, by the harsh mountains of the Abruzzi, calcined and burned by the southern sun; and by that other great inspirer of poets, the sea. If the mountains of the Abruzzi stand for all that is cruel and harsh in his work, the Adriatic, whose waves beat far away on the Dalmatian shore, once colonized by the Italians, murmurs something too of his imperialistic dreams.[1]

[1] Readers who do not know Italian can obtain his novels in the excellent French translation by Georges Hérelle. It has been compared to Gerard de Nerval's translation of Goethe, or Baudelaire's of Poe. It is certainly an improvement on the Italian version, whose excessive detail, analyses and frequent obscenities are wearisome. Whole passages are cut and chapters sacrificed, producing a milder, less unbridled, more tempered if also less impassioned result.

Hérelle, a University professor from Cherbourg, had in 1891 discovered *L'Innocente,* which, chiefly for his own pleasure, he had translated. When this was taken by a French publisher and was successful in Paris, he translated several more of D'Annunzio's works, and entered into a long and stormy relationship with the Italian writer.

5

The Mediterranean Superman

Among D'Annunzio's novels of the first period was *Le Vergini delle Rocce* which, if not the best, is certainly the most important, because it announces the Superman, the theme which he introduced into Italy from his reading of Nietzsche. If *I Romanzi della Rosa* all show the same kind of aesthete-hero, subject to a special set of laws, they also foreshadow the Superman. Most of the heroes live in a rarefied, sub-lunar atmosphere, and rarely come down on earth, to act. But Claudio Cantelmo of *Le Vergini delle Rocce* is an Italian Zarathustra. He speaks like a Teutonic man of action: "I am grateful to my ancestors, an ancient and noble race of warriors, for having given me their rich and fiery blood, for the beautiful wounds and beautiful burnings they inflicted in the past, for the beautiful women they raped, for all their victories, their drunkennesses, their magnificence. . . ." Cantelmo says he has three aims in life, "to bring his own being to a perfect integration of the Latin type; to gather the essence of his spirit and reproduce in one sole and supreme work of art, the most profound vision of his personal universe; to preserve the ideal richness of his race and his personal conquests [*sic*] in a son and hero who, under the parental training, will co-ordinate these achievements, and go beyond them. . . ."

It may seem strange to class D'Annunzio with Nietzsche, for they were as dissimilar in their lives as in their persons; one, a Teutonic Don, a recluse, a misogynist, known to the world only after his death; the other, a declamatory, self-advertising sort of Don Giovanni, with the lurid habit of writing novels about the women he had just slept with. The conception of the Superman as a southerner, too, would have shocked the Germans. To them, the Superman was a big, blond fellow, rough, arrogant, beer-swilling, meat-eating; whereas the Italians (those at least who resemble D'Annunzio) are little, dark-skinned men, wine-drinkers, lettuce-eaters, with pleasant manners, gesticulating and excitable.

Zarathustra says that there is one law of nature for all animals, including the human animal—that the strong shall have everything because he is strong, and the weak have nothing, because he is weak. But we humans, Nietzsche says, have perverted this law, because our weaker members, realizing that the law is unfavorable to them, have come together and formed a law of their own, which they call Civil Law or Justice. It enacts that the strong shall respect the weak and help him. This Civil Law takes children from the cradle and educates them with learned words and ingenious lies about Justice, teaching them that it is a crime to use strength against those who do not possess it. Thus, just as lion cubs have their claws clipped and their teeth filed when they are young, so human beings have their natural energy drained before they are grown.

This is all monstrous, says Nietzsche (and, slightly perverted, this was to be D'Annunzio's philosophy). "The noble," the "superior" type of man, whether in Greek myth or Teutonic legend, has always been the warrior intent on pillage, murder, arson, and rape, executing the vanquished amid the tears and lamentations of women and children. Like Achilles or Siegfried, he goes forward, from battle to battle, victory to victory, destruction to destruction, protected only by his armor, his sword and his strong right arm. "In all noble and aristocratic races," says Nietzsche, "it is impossible not to recognize this superb blond beast, ever in search of prey."

Nietzsche then examines what the philosophers of the past have had to say on the subject of Power. He has strong and critical words for them all; from Socrates, who claims in the *Gorgias* that it is better to submit to injustice than to commit it, down to the English utilitarians, whom he considers spineless and com-

THE MEDITERRANEAN SUPERMAN 41

mon. He condemns the Grecian, Epicurus, who applauds the pleasure instinct, as well as the Stoics, who remain impassive before
Nature. Kant, the philosopher of Pure Reason, he calls "a legless
cripple responsible for the most stunted ideas ever conceived by
man." "Kant was," says Nietzsche, "only a bourgeois from a
Northern city who regulated every daily action according to an
immutable timetable." How can Zarathustra, who permits himself
as his sole companion an eagle, and chooses as his hermitage the
top of a high mountain—how can he consider as a serious champion of Human Thought, "a professor who walks about in a tur-
ban, going four times a day on the same identical walk, at exactly
the same time, so that the good burghers of Königsberg can
regulate their watches as he passes?" (Much later this was to be
precisely the attitude of D'Annunzio towards the Italian Prime
Minister, Nitti, at the time of the Fiume crisis in 1919.)

But it is not the philosophers whom Nietzsche execrates most.
He reserves his fiercest condemnation for Christianity. The *New
Testament* is a book aimed at "general effeminization of the spe-
cies," undermining all our most natural and necessary instincts, "a
castration of the spirit," persuading wretched man that the earth
is a sort of exam-room presided over by God who keeps a mark
book, in which those who get more bad marks than good will be
punished for eternity. The Christian Church is a criminal institution aimed at the domestication of man, a hypocritical subterfuge
to assure the triumph of the weak over the strong. We must get
rid of it. Better still, we must get rid of God.

All this had been foreseen in Italy twenty years before, but in a
much less violent form, by Carducci in one of the *Odi Barbari,*
". . . I look for a man who can forget that the world has more
than eighteen centuries of Christianity behind it. I look for the
man who sees in nature the happy Gods who advised men, by
their own example, to take pleasure and forget cares. I want to
see the triumphal arches of Rome again, and beneath them a
Quadriga, drawing the victor surrounded by cries of triumph. I
want to substitute for the bourgeois dining-room the Triclinium,

the diners crowned with white rose wreaths and Assyrian scents. I
want to see man enjoying life, his lips wet with Falernian wine,
his head resting on the snowy breast of Lydia. . . ."

Such ideas appealed to D'Annunzio, and he started reading
Nietzsche, as well as Carducci. It was when he visited Greece for
the first time, in 1895, that this feeling of the Superman (and the
possibilities of a *Mediterranean* Superman) was born in the
Abruzzese peasant poet. D'Annunzio no longer wanted to write
poems and novels about decadents, but to create an epic in which
he could express Italian ideals, like Virgil's and Dante's, only
brought up to date, in a vast vision of the opening century, and
Italy's imperial role in it. "I want to write a volume of poetic
prose which will be a war cry for the Latin peoples," he wrote to
his French translator, Hérelle. "We are totally unaware that a
barbarian invasion is on us, that we are indeed already undergoing
it [1] . . . I glory in the fact that I am a Latin, and I recognize a
barbarian in every man of non-Latin blood. . . . This is no longer
the time to dream aside, in the shade of the myrtle and the laurel.
Italians of spirit and energy must now come together and increase
their efforts, and as soldiers support the cause of Intelligence
against the barbarians. They must fight against the destruction,
contagion and violation of Beauty which the barbarians bring with
them. Our Beauty must be strong—at once the Venus adored by
Plato, and the one which Caesar gave to his Legionaries on the
field of Pharsala, under the name of Venus Victrix. . . . Who
knows if the next Universal Exhibition in Paris will not be the
last manifestation of the Latin genius before the final downfall?
If the Latin races are to preserve themselves, it is time they returned to the healthy prejudice which created the grandeur of
Greece and Rome—to believe that all others are barbarians. The
work I shall write about Greece will consist of two parts; one will
be a lyrical paean to the part played by the Mediterranean races
in the world's history; the other will be a diatribe loaded with

[1] He is referring, doubtless, to Anglo-Saxon and Teutonic commercial and
imperial superiority.

imprecations and curses, against the fatal influence of the northern
barbarians. . . ." "I am grateful to those authors," he says some-
where else, "who, when Italy was the last of nations, wrote poetry
and prose which I learned by heart, and which made me weep
with shame and hope. May our children and their children remember this, and thus know what Literature can do. . . ."

The poem *Maia* which he wrote about his trip to Greece, inspired by the idea of Ulysses in these waters, is often considered
his finest, and it is certainly his most patriotic, work. "From the
furnace of my mind," he wrote, "has appeared the only poem
dealing with life completely which has been written since *The
Divine Comedy*." Like *The Divine Comedy*, it is also a comment
on the Italy of the day, for he later added sections about Rome
and Italy—in a vast vision of the opening twentieth century,
when a new sort of satanism was brewing and the world was
changing with such rapidity. The poem expresses the anomalies of
the time; a thirst for world domination in every European country
—and yet visions of Arcadian peace; a mad armaments race—and
yet congresses and prizes for that peace. It was the age of the
Futurists, who sang only of the punch and the slap; of the Pope
excommunicating the Modernists, and the Modernists excommunicating the Pope; of aristocrats becoming democrats—and democrats badly concealing their desire to become aristocrats. D'Annunzio's *Laus Vitae* is a poem about this modern Chaos, in an age of
chaotic men, without religion or belief. This is the twentieth
century.

True to the Nietzschean ideal, the poem shows no respect for
Christianity. The quiet doctrines of Jesus seem futile; the only
Gospel is that of Pan, or, as D'Annunzio calls it, "Desire, Voluptuousness, Pride and Instinct, the Imperial Quadriga." "With
what ardor," he cried, "we passed the limits of all the wisdoms
and ran along the edges of the precipices of the world!"

The first part, *Maia*, is an idealized version of Greece as D'Annunzio saw it, written in 8,400 lines of blank verse, in the form
of an itinerary, from the moment when he and his friends set out

from Calabria in a yacht, until he left them in Athens two months
later. It is a comprehensive portrait of Greece, its men, heroes,
mountains, museums, statues, air, sea and sky; and Ulysses is its
hero. Its argument is that only after having known the classical
world, having "drunk at its sacred fountains," having been inspired by its past, can man obtain the necessary "grace" to become
a superman:

> We lived, divinely we lived
>   And at the antique breast still full
> We drank—and killed the beast within.
>   (v. 5015, *Maia*)

In the second part of the poem, D'Annunzio shows how, after
returning from Greece serene and purified, he is assailed in Rome
by the stench of modern corruption and politics. In modern Rome
no man can live heroically. He asks himself how he can escape
this contagion and finds the answer by again turning to the Past,
this time to the Sistine Chapel and its Michelangelo frescoes.
Here, not only the Sibyls and Prophets of the Greeks and Latins,
but the very Winds of Heaven depicted on the ceiling, encourage
the hero to overcome adversity and go on to final victory. The
lesson of the poem, like that of Ulysses, is one of Self-reliance.

> You must know you are the lone one of your species,
>   For in your march through life you are alone,
> Alone at the last supreme moment,
>   Alone, you are the strongest friend you have.

Ulysses had long been important to Latin literature, from Dante,
and back again to the Latins before him, through Plutarch, Ovid
and Virgil into the mists of Homeric legend, where he possesses
wisdom, cunning, and, above all, curiosity, or the desire to learn.
D'Annunzio's vision of Ulysses is this classical one, but overlaid
with Nietzsche's Superman. More than the desire for Knowledge,

it is the desire for Power which drives him on; *virtute* has submerged *conoscenza,* and D'Annunzio's Ulysses tends towards the Superman. There is something of this in all D'Annunzio's heroes, from Claudio Cantelmo in *Le Vergini delle Rocce* to Corrado Brando in *Più che l'amore.* Anyone who has lived a life more violent and powerful than that of others is to D'Annunzio a potential Ulysses, the Mediterranean Superman.

6

Greece

The trip to Greece started on a July evening in 1895 on the yacht *Fantasia,* which belonged to Scarfoglio, D'Annunzio's journalist friend. There is a revealing letter which D'Annunzio wrote before they left, to Hérelle,[1] his French translator. With its repetition of the first person singular, it shows his growing self-confidence. "To comply with the wishes of my friend, Scarfoglio, I have at last decided on a cruise in the eastern Mediterranean. It occurs to me that you might like to come. If you join us in one of the ports, I would take you with us and put you off when you want to leave . . . On the 18th or 19th, I shall go to the Gulf of Corinth where I shall anchor and make a land excursion to Delphi; after that the Corinth canal, the gulfs of Aegina and Nauplia, then excursions to Mycenae and Tiryns, Salonica, and so to Troy. Afterwards Constantinople, Scio, Smyrna, Samos and Rhodes to finish. If we have time, I shall return past Egypt and Tripoli, Malta, and so home to Naples. The yacht is a good high-seas vessel, well stocked and equipped for two months. . . . Don't bring any good clothes. We may invite a guest or two on board—but one doesn't have to dress for dinner on deck by moonlight. I shall

---

[1] Hérelle describes D'Annunzio when he first met him: "a short figure, slim and dapper, with naturally curly hair, and a small mustache; almost hairless cheeks, expressive eyes, with a charming, almost wheedling voice. He was then aged 31, but he appeared to be about 24 . . ." Hérelle says D'Annunzio spoke French with "a bad pronunciation and uncertain syntax"; but, "he knows our authors well, in particular Flaubert, for whom he has boundless admiration. He would criticize a word I had used in translation and suggest another. When I objected to his word, he would say, 'But Flaubert used it in similar circumstances. . . .'"

try to avoid accepting invitations from ambassadors, consuls, etc. . . ."

Hérelle was a University professor, and he undertook the journey with some apprehension. He was already aware of a side of D'Annunzio's character which he, an academic man, found distasteful, the fashionable side of a man who liked the company of pretty women. "And as I am just the opposite," he wrote in the diary he kept of the trip, "I foresee we may have contrasting spirits, and the result may be embarrassment, disagreement, even hostility. . . ."

They proposed to visit most of the places by boat, anchoring in various ports and traveling inland to examine archaeological remains. The discoveries of Schliemann were attracting more and more visitors. The German archaeologist had just uncovered the three-thousand-year-old tombs of the house of Atreus, and he claimed to have identified among the fifteen skeletons those of Agamemnon and Cassandra—because, being royal, they had masks of gold leaves over their faces. D'Annunzio was well versed in Greek literature, and he intended also, as he said in the letter, to visit Troy. In fact, he got no further than Athens himself, owing to sea-sickness. "The poet of the sea," of the Adriatic and the Aegean, was a bad sailor. Moreover (Hérelle relates in his diary), D'Annunzio was a complete novice in maritime matters. "He appeared to know nothing about a ship," says Hérelle. "He occasionally asked the name of a bit of tackle, a pulley or a sheave. He showed great astonishment at the least movement of the vessel, its inclination towards one side or the other under the breeze—as if it should remain always upright!"

They had agreed to continue a translation in French of one of D'Annunzio's novels; but apart from the first days of the trip, when D'Annunzio kept a diary, he seems to have lost all interest in writing. Nor, in spite of a well-stocked classical library, did they read anything. Later D'Annunzio announced grandly, "We re-read the *Iliad* and the *Odyssey,* we plunged anew into the revivifying bath of Greek lyrical poetry. We re-enacted on the sites themselves the actions of history—in our minds . . ." But Hérelle, the professor, who must be considered more reliable, says that they talked more than they read. Moreover, the tone of their conversation was not very elevated. "They hardly ever spoke of anything but modern Rome and women," he says. "When we had the marvelous landscape of Greece ever before us, this irritated me." He also found D'Annunzio too much of a dandy at sea. "At least a score of times," he says, "D'Annunzio would grumble about not having his shirts properly ironed, or not receiving the ones he had ordered from his shirt-maker in time. He was appalled when he realized that he hadn't a top hat for his official visits in Athens and Constantinople. . . ."

D'Annunzio had expressly told Hérelle in the letter *not* to bring too many clothes, but here was D'Annunzio himself—with a dinner jacket, six suits, thirty or forty silk shirts, eight pairs of shoes, ties, socks and handkerchiefs! "I could not imagine," says Hérelle, "how a poet who was to show such emotion before the beauty that surrounded him in Greece could, at the same time, attach importance to these trivialities. . . . Some people," he adds, referring to D'Annunzio, "take a kind of ridiculous pride in that, wherever they go, in whatever foreign countries they may be, they must feel as if they were at home. They evidently want to find on board ship their own hearth, their own furniture and food. They expect to watch the foreign scenery unfold like a panorama before them. The objection to this is that they have absolutely no connection with the inhabitants of the places, no means of escaping from their own personalities, nor of knowing that delightful feeling of being another man in the midst of other men. For *me,* that is the only pleasure of travel—freeing oneself from one's own land. . . ."

The other excess which he complained of in D'Annunzio was sunbathing. The poet apparently enjoyed lying naked in the sun and roasting himself, a most un-Victorian habit in 1895. "When cooked on one side," says Hérelle, "he would turn over on to the other."

D'Annunzio's attitude throughout the trip which was to produce such reams of poetry (the *Laus Vitae* is as long as *The Divine Comedy*), seems indeed strange. Even when they were on their way to beautiful places like Delphi or Mycenae, he was always complaining that he was tired and looking forward to reaching a proper city. "How nice it will be," Hérelle reports him saying, "to get to the Café Français in Athens and sit out in the restaurant in our dinner jackets!" The dust of the road, the primitive trains, the squalor and odor of sweat in the restaurants, the repulsive resinated wine, made D'Annunzio say on more than one occasion, "I'm not made for traveling. I've had enough of Greece. When I get back to Italy, I shan't budge for ten years." In the celebrated river, Alph, he even had the impertinence to bathe!

Another of his companions, Boggiani, endorses Hérelle's complaints, less because of D'Annunzio's hedonism, than because D'Annunzio made them all travel so quickly to get to the towns, and they were thus unable to enjoy the view. The view meant a great deal to Boggiani, who was an explorer by profession. Boggiani says that D'Annunzio liked only main streets where he could travel quickly in carriages, and hotels where he could have a bath. "He showed no curiosity about the country-side, no feeling for its beauty,' says Boggiani. "He seemed unaware that when one travels, it is the fatigue, the heat, the little irritations and privations, which bring the country-side alive. . . ." He was annoyed when D'Annunzio said of a certain village, "Now that the charm of the first impression is over, the idea of remaining in this wretched Greek hole for an entire day fills me with disgust."

These different conceptions of travel conflicted throughout the journey. They all wanted something new. Hérelle and Boggiani looked for it outside themselves, in the contact with new things and people; D'Annunzio regarded travel rather as a kind of theater, which he could watch without leaving the stalls. He also adopted the attitude that the present Greeks were an unfortunate accident, carelessly thrown in among the ruins, to spoil the spectacle. It was in the most celebrated places, Olympus and on the road to Eleusis, that Hérelle found him most lacking in proper

respect, where his conversation was, frankly, "pornographic."
"D'Annunzio and Scarfoglio," Hérelle says, "asked the guides for
brothels—as if they were in Italy! When the guides replied that
there were no public women, D'Annunzio kept on pointing at
passing girls, and asking if they could be had for money!" At
Patras, they looked for whores in the slums, and at Piraeus, after
several failures, D'Annunzio brought on board a woman they had
found on the docks.

D'Annunzio also appears to have said nothing about the statues
he was to write of so enthusiastically in his poem, the Praxitelean
Hermes, the Korai in the Acropolis museum. The only words he
ever uttered in front of these works of art was, according to
Hérelle, the solitary phrase, "Ah! if one could only say something
new!"

"Something new!" cried Hérelle disdainfully. "Does not that
betray artificiality and insincerity too in a writer? When D'Annunzio speaks in his poems of this extraordinary emotion he
experienced, of the great intellectual ferment which possessed
him in the museum at Athens, the truth was simply that he was
taking literary notes for his future works. . . ." On one occasion,
however, when Hérelle reproached him with inattention, D'Annunzio spoke up forcibly, showing how his mind was working.
"I'm thinking," he said irritably. "Stop grumbling! It's all going
on inside my head. I'm trying to understand the *real* truth of all
the things we're looking at. I'm interested in the soul of these
things. . . ."

This then was the real meaning of the journey, which brought
out the main side of D'Annunzio's character. Hérelle was a professor; D'Annunzio was an artist. The professor requires a vast
panorama of objects which he can learn about; the artist takes a
narrower view, avoiding this multiple, disinterested curiosity
which, for the professor, is an end in itself. Consciously or not
the artist, just as he is always looking for something which will
prove useful to him later, has a quick awareness of what is of no
value to his work. D'Annunzio was well aware that to interpret a
countryside as full of beauty and history as the Greek, something

more than mere impressionism was required. Always in search of, "to be able to say something new," the essential outlines of a place were sufficient to set him thinking. His imagination did the rest. Much later, in the *Libro Segreto,* he wrote, "Travels are really unnecessary. I knew the real Greece before I went to Patras, or knelt before the Hermes at Olympia, before I touched the columns of the Parthenon and the gold of the Mycenean masks." He here endorses Mérimée's famous statement, "Let us write a book about Spain and, with the money it brings us, let us go to Spain to see if what we wrote is true." [1]

The poem itself reveals this distortion. D'Annunzio has consciously distorted happenings and personal experiences, to give his own vision of the classical world. It is indeed the vision of a poet, and parts of it may well lay claim to immortality. How different was reality we can see by comparing the poem with the accounts of Hérelle and Boggiani. According to them, the *Fantasia* left Gallipoli, a small Puglian port, at 4:30 on a hot July afternoon, with almost no breeze. But D'Annunzio prefers the idea of leaving, in his poem, from Brindisi, the classical point of departure for Greece, from which Virgil, Horace and other distinguished travelers set out. In the opening lines of *Maia,* the first part of the poem, D'Annunzio speaks of seeing the classical column which still stands on the shore at Brindisi. He also makes the departure, which was extremely calm, extremely rough—in keeping with the Ulyssean spirit of the sea:

[1] It was the critic Croce who condemned most harshly D'Annunzio's "desire to say something new." In a letter to his friend, Capuana, he said, ". . . people will not understand that art has been invented once and for all, and that great new works of art may well appear (when geniuses appear) but there is no 'new method' of saying things. To claim to do so is the pretension of the charlatan and the impotent. In D'Annunzio there is something of both the charlatan and the impotent—in spite of his poetical qualities and technical ability. D'Annunzio presents the spectacle of a man continually in search of his own personality. All great artists have experienced life and have had something to say. D'Annunzio has experienced foreign books *à la mode,* and he has absolutely nothing to say. It is indeed interesting to observe the degeneration of our literature from Carducci to D'Annunzio. The first had a real sense of, and enthusiasm for, Italian history and culture—by which he was able to evoke the echoes of our past. In D'Annunzio, the same cult of things Italian and Latin is no more than a puerile fixation. . . ."

And so with my faithful companions [1]
We unfurled sails one gusty summer day,
And saw upon the Apulian shore
Still standing up against the sky,
As if on guard, the Roman column. . . .

Hérelle says that because of the lack of breeze, the *Fantasia* was forced to spend an entire day and night in sight of Italy. D'Annunzio ignores this and goes immediately into classical waters at Leucadia, the famous promontory from which despairing lovers, imitating the example of Sappho, threw themselves into the sea. In fact, they did not pass this place.

They reached Greece on the third day, and landed at Patras on the gulf of Corinth. Here we have the first long extract from the poem, which can be compared with what actually happened when they landed, and which is an interesting comment on how the poet's mind worked. Hérelle describes the events in his diary.

"After dinner," he writes, "Scarfoglio and D'Annunzio insisted that they must celebrate their arrival in Greece with a night of love. They instructed the dragoman, Bertucci, to find a woman. He did his best, but warned them that it would not be as easy as in Italy, and that if they did find one, it would be *a very low class of woman.* . . . We went into the worst slums, into cafés frequented by soldiers and sailors, whom we quickly left. Finally, he took us into a small house, where we went up a wooden staircase and found, at the top, a woman dressed entirely in white, neither young nor pretty, and who so disgusted the Italians that they quickly turned their backs on her. At this moment, from a neighboring room, a very old woman appeared, clad in white, with gray hair, who asked for money. We gave her a few drachma and left. On the way down, one of the wooden stairs broke under Boggiani's foot and he nearly fell over. After that, we wandered about the streets. Many of the people, overcome by

[1] "Faithful companions" is the term used by Homer for the Odyssean shipmates. D'Annunzio makes this significant point about Ulysses early in the poem.

the heat, had dragged their beds out into the open and were sleeping on the pavements. In spite of it all, we were gay, and on the way home they laughed and joked about how love was made in classical Greece. . . ."

This short, prosaic description of a visit to a brothel is magnified in D'Annunzio's poem into a long and magnificent commentary on the degeneration of modern Greece, which D'Annunzio compares with its Past. Modern Patras he finds repulsive, and he associates it with the prostitutes and *lupanars* he and his friends attempted to patronize. In the translation I have made from verse 1156 onwards, the imagery is coarse and brutal, in deliberate contrast, it seems, with the tender sentiments the poet professes at the end of the visit, for the wretched lot of such degraded human beings. Hérelle accuses D'Annunzio throughout of lack of observation. In fact, as this shows, D'Annunzio retained far more details in his mind than his companions did in their diaries. His extensive, classical learning is also in evidence:

   . . . and so appeared to me [1]
      the ancient city of the Acheans [i.e. Patras]
  creator of past diadems
     and soft-flowing robes.
In the whitened streets today,
     beneath the clouds of dust, I saw a coffin
with its priests and croaking orisons,
    a bloodless corpse within,
uncovered, with its saffron-yellow face.
    The skinny priest stood on his dusty dais,
to croak the mysteries of his weak-kneed God,
    to ruffians and café denizens;
while in their dirty robes and greasy vestments
    his veined and mottled curates
grimaced beside him, combing through their tangled beards
    their crooked fingers.

[1] Verse 1156 *et seq. I Laudi.*

O Diana of Laphria,[1] gone is all your splendor,
    temple with its reflects in the waters
of the gulf; gone the glorious effigy,
    the statue in its shining gold,
with guadrigas of triumph.
    O Goddess armed with lance, invincible proof
of Power on land and sea.
    O beauty springing from the shrines
of great unconquered Greece;
    not Apollonian sailors on their
painted triremes; nor Tyrian traders
    underneath the sign of Heracles,
nor men of Cos, nor Rhodians, nor Athenians themselves
    with all their splendid words are here.
Here only fraud and hunger wait the modern man.

In the moonless night
    beneath the street lamps,
When the breeze from Africa had dropped,
    and only up upon the mountains the star-fire shone,
when we heard afar the sighing of the sea
    beyond the rocky moles of Patras;
then laughing, singing, but sad within
    through all the fetid side-streets
the pandar led us,
    in search of prostitutes.
And one of the dear companions [2] said,
    while husky seamen vomited their resinated wine
upon the threshold of the dusty *lupanar,*
    "Resina is distilled among the pines of Ida,[3]
where Paris pastured cattle
    as he dreamt of Spartan Helen."

[1] Laphria was the surname of Diana in classical Patras, where she had a temple with a statue of gold and ivory representing her as a huntress.

[2] Another Odyssean term for shipmates.

[3] A celebrated mountain near Troy, where Paris adjudged the prize of beauty to Aphrodite.

Within, were naked shouldered sailors,
  Footpads, boatmen with their bronzen arms
And curved backs; and ribald women with limp cheeks,
  cheap-roughed: and pansies soft as women,
experts all at haunch delights;
  the filth of many ports, and mud of all the crossroads
came together with the natives and the dagoes,
  and new-come foreigners with wealth,
all sat around the smoky lamps,
  all swilled the putrid, resinated wine,
while eyes like jets of saliva glanced their fornications,
  bought and sold for half a drachma.

Here, our pandar said,
  a Phrygian lady lived,
of hot repute, in flower-like beauty,
  who would not deign to gratify the drunken sots.
Rather, in a room apart, upon her bed of white,
  rich foreigners she stroked,
or affluent business-men from Patras.
  Up the staircase of rotting wood we went
and crossed the secret sill;
  before us now the Phrygian lady lay,
In the shadow small and tenuous,
  a she-goat with breasts that hung,
And smells that told of recent happenings.

Not one of us would near this Hellenic lady;
  but one of the dear companions with Attic accent
said, "O woman come from Greece,
  have you in the Minyeois of Homer,
or in the healthless Anigros,
  which flows between the Minthe and soft Lapithas,
have you bathed your flower-like limbs?"
  We were all very merry then; but she who could

not know the Attic salt of this
    threw at us with an oath
her insults and her sandals.
    And so, with noses held, we left her
staircase and its rotten wood. And then,
    while groping in the bitter shades beneath
a hand came forth to ask for alms.
    What antique voice came to us then, to call
from modern hunger? In doubt, we stopped . . .

By the failing light our mortal eyes
    perceived the eternal face
of Tartar's Atropos, who cuts the thread of life.
    In a moment gone was the illusion of the present,
of the narrow place we stood in,
    and the bestial laughter of the drunkards;
all the silent centuries stood, which
    demeaned this face and blanched this hair,
loosened this capacious mouth
    and dried those addled breasts,
which bent this curved back
    and crabbed this skinny hand,
and buried in the hollow cavern of her sockets
    the half-lightless eyes.
And then the Past which has filled
    such human beings with madness
and with bloody tears, surged up within me,
    to oppress my living heart.

And in my soul there trembled
    an infinite sadness, as at the sight
of someone known before,
    who comes without warning,
in Time's funereal mirror. . . .
    But my companions laughed,

and in the extended grasp
of the half-starved procuress,
I, laughing, placed a drachma.
She muttered words obscure between
her grimy gums; and then the whitened hand withdrew.
We clambered down the rotted stairs,
while on the way a step collapsed beneath
my good companion's feet, and creaking broke . .
How sweet it was again outside
to see the glittering stars!

Years later, when Hérelle read the *Laudi,* he realized how
much his apparently detached friend had seen. Small incidents,
which the others ignored, such as the shepherd at Altis or the
cigale, were given a long development by D'Annunzio. He also
describes how he and the "faithful companions" saw athletes dis-
porting for palms in the arena (this, entirely imaginary); white
processions of Orphic priests crowned with roses; Parnassus surg-
ing up in "an opaline atmosphere"; and the fountains of Castalia
which make the travelers "drunk with liquid songs." The heroes
and heroines of history appear either nude or in snow-white
robes, Telemachus, Alcibiades, Alexander, Pindar, Penelope,
Aphrodite. That pan-unity with things which the Greeks felt, a
fraternity between men and trees, stars, fountains and animals
lives on in D'Annunzio's verse.[1]
One of the principal critics of D'Annunzio's poem, Gargiulo,
later said, "The lack of clarity of the poem derives primarily from
a grave fault in its poetic inspiration—this mixture of reality,
and what I will call dream, out of which 'the journey of the soul'
is woven. Sometimes, D'Annunzio is talking of ports of call, and

---

[1] It was the ancient Greeks who first interpreted natural beauty in terms of
the human form. A river was to them a beautiful young man; a fountain, the
goddess Arethusa; a source, the nymph, Daphne. They saw a nereid in every
pool, a dryad under every oak; they heard the pipes of Pan in their caves and
spoke with the Olympians on their mountain tops. All this D'Annunzio at-
tempts to catch again in his poem.

departure from ports, in the most factual manner. At others, he moves airily from one place to another, as it were on the wings of his imagination. Sometimes we are unaware whether we are on a real voyage, or whether we have entered a dream and lost all contact with reality."

The poem was written some years later, when D'Annunzio was living at Settignano. He describes the composition in his own elliptical language. "From the furnace of my mind has appeared the only poem dealing with life completely which has been written in Italy since *The Divine Comedy*. It is composed with demoniacal art, as of someone who fashions a mirror; and it operates by continual metamorphoses on the images of the visible world, while translating them into luminous signs of interior mystery. It is the dithyramb of origins and profundity. The soul is agitated in the song like a Maenad who has ravished the secret of Orpheus before destroying it. But always the shade of Eleusis follows it. . . ." As far as his reference to *The Divine Comedy* is concerned, the poem can at least be compared in length; it is 2,000 verses longer than Dante's epic.

In a note to a friend, Ugo Ojetti, he was a little more concise. "All my ideas in this poem come from ancient Greece and Rome. They represented in their art the ideal towards which I strive today—to exalt and glorify *above all things* Beauty, and the power of the pugnacious, dominating male. Our new Latin Renaissance, which will now come, will re-establish therefore the cult of Man. And the new artists, in common with the Ancients, will demand from the new science a new faculty of creation, namely to continue Nature's role, but add to it a new form. In the age of Leonardo da Vinci and Michelangelo, Science did not conflict with Art—it co-operated with it. Behind the lines with which da Vinci drew his anatomical studies, he was glorifying the beauty of the human form. Michelangelo placed a lighted candle in the navel of a corpse, to study the human form by night. Both knew what a prodigy is Man. The new artists will therefore be direct descendants of the ancient spirit. As a fervid admirer of the Word, convinced of its superiority over all other means of expression, I know that the New Light will first be born from a book. *Ex Libro Lux!"*

This book was the *Laudi.* The very titles of the individual parts, particularly *Elettra,* where the gods of Rome replace those of Greece, describe D'Annunzio's feelings about the myth of Rome, its past and future greatness: *To Dante, To the Memory of Narcissus and Pilade, To Rome, To One of the Thousand, To the Night of Caprera.* In the last he refers to Garibaldi continually as the "Dictator" and, significantly, the "Duce"; ". . . Each combatant in his terrible drunkenness under the sun and sky, feels on him the leonine stare of the Duce, the omnipresent leader. O, harvest of youth, stronger than wine, purple of autumn, purple of death among the sweet grapes of Campania. . . ."

He also gives a catalogue of the names of the men who went with Garibaldi on the Thousand expedition, just as there is a catalogue of Aeneas' men in *The Iliad:* "Bronzetti, the Tuscan Musi, the Apuan Giorgiere, the Roman Spada, the Count from Ravenna, Boreta. . . ." Then come all the Italian cities, each with a poem describing it; Rimini, Urbino, Padua, Pisa, Lucca, and a long poem on Prato, where he was at school. Then he writes of the Liberation that will come to the Italian cities under Austrian rule. "Do not cry, O Soul of Trent, for your crown trampled underfoot. Drink up again your bitter tears. Forget your pains. Cry not! Prepare in silence. . . !"

D'Annunzio's technical achievement in this poem was that he developed the blank verse method which Leopardi had begun to use so effectively in short pieces, into a vast epic poem. "Greek poetry," said D'Annunzio, "surpasses all others. The verse of Dante is a mechanical thing by comparison. . . ." By this he meant that rhyme, for which Italian poetry has always been famous, must cease. He broke the unity of rhythm by increasing the caesuras, constructing verses of sixteen or seventeen feet. Often the thought is obscure, the words precipitate and feverish, and the verbal abundance tires the reader. Some verses seem redundant, a mere enumeration of sonorities:

"Against the storms, against the destinies, against the eternal

Gods, against all the forces which have and have not searching eyes, which have and have not words—against these will I ever fight, with my head, my fist, with the lance, the oar, with the rudder and the dart. To increase, to open my huge mortal soul against that of other men, so that they are burned up with ardor in the work of time. . . ."

Arthur Symons writes of the poem, "In all this there is a great deal of fervid and eloquent writing but, except in some of the descriptions, little that seems sincere, with more than the orator's sincerity of the moment, little that does not become tedious with the tedium of unfelt emotion. Page follows page, and soon we are wearied of this orator in verse, who expects to be listened to because he has a beautiful voice. . . ."

D'Annunzio *could* write beautiful poetry, as we have seen. What could be more lovely than:

> *Voi nella gloria, voi nel riso d'amore salendo,*
> *giungere udrete il canto "Ella, ella sola è gioia."*
> *Entro le man sue reca piu luce che non l'Ora prima.*

It has the simplicity of those immortal lines which Dante alone could write, such as *"La notte che le cose ci nasconde."* But such lines are rare in this poem, which is more didactic than lyrical. Only in the part called *Alcione* is he at his lyrical best. He even introduces passages in the poem on the technique of versification: ". . . Oh words, mystical strength of our race, fertile in works of art, and ever ready for battle among the fortunes of the ages, you have been fixed in eternal syllables! Oh words, corrupted and senile, I come to re-establish you in your virgin glory. With a chaste and robust hand, I draw you from the coffer where you were born, fresh again as the contracting corollas of the sea, colored ineffably by the new light. Shine on and sing, oh words, in this hymn which is the vast prelude to my song. I have converted you anew into human substance, into living pulp, into flesh of my flesh, into fountains of blood and tears. . . ."

The poem is a vast piece of romanticism, with its changing meters, myths, subjects, its vocabulary ancient and modern, its aestheticism, paganism, panism, hedonism, stoicism. It is very far from the simplicity and unity of the classical ideal which D'Annunzio claimed to be pursuing. It is, in fact, the work one would expect from a poet about to sing the glories of a new Roman Empire, in the twentieth century.

7

The Lost Keys of the Mediterranean

D'Annunzio's decision to become a Mediterranean superman was closely connected with the new spirit abroad, not only in Italy but throughout Europe at the opening of the century. He began therefore to associate with the new mood of national expansion, expressed variously, through Crispi and the *Africanisti;* Marinetti and the *Futuristi;* and finally, years ahead, through Mussolini and the *Fascisti.*

Although this last phase was still some way off, D'Annunzio, like a prophet, was ahead of his time. That the time was not yet ripe for Italian expansion was revealed when England suggested in 1879 that Italy should share in an international occupation of Egypt; and Italy refused. Public opinion had not yet entirely lost its Mazzinian idealism, which held that other countries should be left to look after their own affairs. The same refusal was repeated when there was an opportunity for Italy to occupy Tunis, anticipating the French. But after the Congress of Berlin and the German decision to take part in the carve-up of Africa, coinciding with British expansion in Rhodesia, Italy began to feel she was being left out of Africa, and must come into line with the rest of Europe. She had not forgotten her first defeats as a unified monarchy, Custozza and Lissa, at the hands of Austria, and she felt she must express herself like a Great Power. At the Congress of Berlin, Italy, alone of all the powers, emerged without increased territory. Austria occupied Bosnia-Herzegovina, and England's position in Africa was strengthened; but Italy failed to get even the Trentino. Diplomats were laughing. "Why on earth

should Italy demand land?" said Bismarck to a Russian diplomat. "Has she lost another battle?"

The English were already in Gibraltar and Suez, and watching
the narrow doorway between Tunis and Malta which controls the
eastern Mediterranean. Most of Africa was now divided into
"spheres of interest." In Eritrea and Abyssinia, Italy saw her last,
and only, opportunity. Certain Italian patriots, thinking back to
Latin days, said that by occupying these countries, Italy "would
be fishing in the waters of the Red Sea for the lost keys of the
Mediterranean."

These and other expansionist ideas now gained ground rapidly,
revealing that the ideal system of the *Risorgimento* was crumbling at last. The moral principles which had kept Italy for decades from a war of aggression were being discarded, in the
general lowering of European standards. When in 1871 the Germans, by a mixture of force and cunning, crushed France, the
Italian Bonghi wrote, "Europe views with dismay this new and
exaggerated use of Force. The idea of Might which, for the last
fifty years, we have struggled to subdue by the idea of Right, has
risen before us with a gibe on its lips." Visconti-Venosta, an
Italian of the old school, wrote, "Europe is gradually becoming
an armed camp again. The days of Cobden and Henri Richard
are over. With them, too, has gone the new hope that men are
fundamentally peace-loving and reasonable. . . ."

The whole of Europe was now lost in admiration for Germany;
for German universities and learning, German science, German
efficiency, German industry, even the German army. Many Italians thought that German unity was simply another kind of *Risorgimento*, with Bismarck as another kind of Cavour. Here they
were wrong. Bismarck had much more of Machiavelli in him
than of Cavour. Bismarck admired everything pragmatic: Fichte's
deification of the state, Hegel's belief in Prussia, the *Sturm und
Drang* writers in the German past. Bismarck was indeed the ideal
"Prince," whom Machiavelli would have applauded. He employed
cunning and force by turns, whenever he thought fit.

German influence was also having an effect on the finances of
Italy, on her manufactures and transport, her commerce and
press. The Germans had, for example, developed a system for
supplying agricultural districts with seeds of every kind, for which
they did not ask immediate payment. "Pay whenever it is con-
venient; I am your friend," was the German attitude to Italy.
Italians who remember these times tell how much more popular
Germany was in Italy than England before the First World War.
After years of acquaintance with an Englishman, they say, his
chief subject of conversation is still the weather. As the weather
in Italy is more or less stable and not, as in England, subject to
hourly variations, they cannot keep up that continuous interest in
it which characterizes the English. And then in speech, they say,
English utterances are for the most part confined to ejaculations of
simple civilities, or deliberate, disparaging comment. English reserve, too, is distasteful to the expansive, emotional nature of the
Italian. Nor are the scathing remarks and general air of superiority which the English adopt (among themselves as much as
with foreigners) conducive to much intimacy.

But how different are—and were then—the Germans, in Italian eyes! The Germans admired, praised and immersed themselves in Italian culture. They associated freely with Italians, and
discussed learnedly all their artistic achievements. Expansive, free
from aloofness, they took pleasure in doing those little things
which are dear to the Italian heart, such as sitting out at a café
table, ostensibly to drink a cup of coffee. When a German married an Italian woman, he took up residence in Italy and the
family became Italian. When an Englishman married an Italian,
she had to go off and live in some remote part of Northumber-
land, and try to be a squire's wife.

It was a German, too, who had taught the Italians the idea
about the state as a work of art. Burckhardt had revealed how
common this idea had been during their own Italian Renaissance
in a book which was now widely read by the intellectual youth of
Italy. The Italians who had had no real heroes for fifty years,

since Garibaldi and Mazzini, related Bismarck to their own *Risorgimento,* and admired him almost as if he were an Italian hero. With him too went Wagner, the most Teutonic of all the Germans, because he was a Jew, with his conquering and fearless Siegfried. Even William II, when he landed melodramatically on the pier at Palermo, and drove to the Royal Palace surrounded by a gaping and admiring crowd, seemed to remind Italians that the greatest period of Sicilian history had been under a German dynasty, the Hohenstaufens. The Germanic emperors and Austrian marshals had been driven out of the country only forty years before, with great bloodshed and at much expense but—such is the irony of history or the perversity of peoples—the Italians now found they could admire them from across the Alps. Some remembered, too, that Dante's Holy Roman emperor had been a German.

This military and political outlook was reflected in the literary and philosophic movements of the day, in a curious mixture of restlessness, spirit of adventure, craving for power and lust for enjoyment. Literary reviews such as *Il Regno, Leonardo,* and other papers all demanded action, and extolled Italy's past and future greatness. Indeed, modern Italian nationalism, in its vocal form, may be said to have started in 1905, when *Il Regno* was founded. Here all problems, economic, demographic, financial and political, were solved with the aid of the Roman eagles, which had not been flying for centuries. With this nationalism [1] went a reaction against the utilitarian, bourgeois approach of the last half-century. Carducci had already attacked the spiritual poverty that accompanied material "Victorian" civilization; but he had at least tried to resurrect the old classical spirit in its place. He would have been a solitary prophet in the twentieth century.

The new intellectuals, calling themselves *veristi,* believed not in the past, but in the future. In their extreme form they did, in fact, call themselves "Futurists." They believed in "reality," in

[1] Croce, the philosopher, seeing this, made one of his few humorous remarks: "Nationalism is an unnational phenomenon in Italy; it is an importation!"

describing with the most minute precision, man as he appeared to the naked eye, in broad daylight, above all in his social and unregenerate forms. They were supported by the *scapigliati*, or "dishevelled men," a group of poets and artists in the north of Italy who shared this distaste for bourgeois materialism. They expressed it in a more personal way, proclaiming that the "I" is sovereign in literature, acclaiming all the "unhealthy" poets of France, Baudelaire, Verlaine, and admiring above all the realist, Zola. Almost every year, that French writer produced a new novel, in which he laid before the public a fresh "slice of life," based on his acute observation of drunkenness, prostitution, commerce, strikes, railways and human brutishness in general. Great moral, political and religious problems which had filled the minds of Alfieri, Foscolo, Leopardi and Manzoni, were being replaced by problems of sociology, hygiene and economics.

Futurism was the goal towards which these movements were all striving, with their common contempt for museums, history, and anything that might remotely be called "Culture." In the place of these things, the Futurists installed "the cult of the Futurist future," whose highest ideals were "the fist-fight, the sprint and the kick." They pasted the bristles of shaving-brushes on to canvas if they wanted to paint a man with a mustache, and they wrote "puff-puff" if they wanted to depict a train. Their leader, Marinetti, had such a detestation of "culture," that he described traditional beauties like Venice as "a city of dead fish and decaying houses, inhabited by a race of waiters and touts." He claimed that the new Futurist Italy would be a great and insolent world power, full of cement houses, huge music-halls and trains that ran on time. In his words, "a racing-car, its frame adorned with great pipes, like snakes with explosive breath, a roaring motor-car that seems to be running on shrapnel, is more beautiful than the Victory of Samothrace."

Under Marinetti, the Futurists went from city to city and appeared, Barnum-like, on the stages of local theatres, to expound these views. Courage rather than talent was their chief quality, for they stood up bravely to the potato-peel, rotten eggs and other garbage that was thrown at them by the audience. The thicker the hail, the bigger, they considered, the triumph of Futurism.

All these groups were opposed to liberal ideas. They despised the unadventurous, security-seeking, property-worshipping bourgeois. They approved of war and dictatorship, only asking that what the socialists taught about the class war should be applied to war between nations. Blanqui's "Who has steel has bread" was their motto. Like French nationalists of *L'Action Française*, they also mocked the ideas of the French Revolution and the Declaration of the Rights of Man. G. A. Borgese has described them well in his grim and powerful novel *Rubè*. He shows what D'Annunzio's nationalism in verse meant to these young men, who saw in it, "splendid tyrannies, famous courtesans, measureless voyages, lightning conquests and the ravished daughters of barbarian kings." The glitter of D'Annunzio's style, like that of Venetian glass, redundant and stuffed with reminiscences of Greek and Roman splendor, pseudo-Biblical, pseudo-mystical, often spiced with interesting sexual detail, was intoxicating to the Marinetti group. In D'Annunzio's words:

Would you fight? Kill? See rivers of blood?
  Great mountains of gold? Flocks of captive women?
Slaves? Or other prey? Would you wish to live in marble?
  Erect a temple? And compose an immortal hymn?
Would you (Oh list to me, young man, Oh list to me!)
  Would you divinely love . . . ?

The phrase *mare nostrum* appears for the first time in D'Annunzio's poetry. D'Annunzio now wrote *La Nave,* a violent celebration of the Venetian past and a call to present action, with the celebrated slogan, "Arm the prow and sail towards the world." Such was the feeling of chauvinism infused into this play, that during the rehearsals the actors themselves became penetrated with its factious spirit, of struggle, hate and vendetta. They were in such a state of nervous excitement that, at every moment on the stage, there were outbreaks of quarrels, shrieks, and people coming to blows.

At its first night, the general exultation extended throughout the entire city of Rome and its streets. The strangest shouts and shrieks, incomprehensible to the police, who were trying to keep order, were heard: *"Arremba! Arremba!"; "Il pallio a Marco Gratico!"; "Arma la prora e salpa verso il mondo!"*—("Board the vessel! Board the vessel! The papal robe to Marco Gratico! Arm the prow and sail towards the world!"). Even the King congratulated D'Annunzio on the success of this patriotic play. But D'Annunzio was even more pleased that Austria protested officially against it to the Italian Foreign Office. It was said that the Austrian Navy Minister thereafter kept a copy of the play on his desk, to remind him of Italy's real views about the Adriatic.

In the days that followed, innumerable friends, acquaintances and unknown persons came to D'Annunzio's hotel to ask him to inscribe their copy of the play. It was typical of his attitude to them that he handed over the signing to his son, Gabriellino, who could forge his signature. He also received a number of letters from enthusiastic ladies suggesting appointments. He again suggested to Gabriellino that he might replace his father, in the case of those who were pretty, but not to his taste.

La Nave now made a triumphal tour of the principal theatres of Italy. In Venice, a banquet in honor was offered to the poet by the Naval League, at which a man from Trieste, Attilo Hortis, brought D'Annunzio a mass of wild flowers picked among the cracks of the Roman amphitheatre of Pola (then under Austria). The play particularly pleased the city of the *Bucintoro,* because a real boat was constructed on the stage, placed on a movable staircase, so that when the blocks were removed, it came down onto the stage as if it had been really launched. The prow, the masts, the armaments, were a real prow, real masts, real armaments.

At the same time, D'Annunzio was most scornful of the present state of the Italian Navy. In his *L'Armata d'Italia,* he had already said, "Italy will be a great naval power or nothing," and he had made a joke about the Italian high command. "When Julius Caesar left for Spain against Afranius and Petreius, his words were, *vado ad exercitum sine duce*. When he went to Thessaly against Pompey, he said *vado ad ducem sine exercitu*. Today, a Nelson, a Farragut, a Tegethoff coming against the Italian fleet could use both mottoes." To recall the spirit of the great commanders of the past, he read his poem about Garibaldi, *La Notte di Caprera,* to a large gathering in Milan. It shows the great Liberator returning to his rock carrying with him only a sack of seed after having conquered a kingdom. All the great feats are recalled, one by one, the Seven Victories, the suffering and the glory, even the neighing of the Hero's war horses.

D'Annunzio's attitude towards expansion in Africa is expressed in a speech he later made to some aviators:

"The Italian people were always the wisest of emigrants. In medieval times, in the Renaissance as in Latin days, the Italian was king of all the seas, ruler of all the domains, to the distant horizons and limits of empire. That Africa and Asia, which we see today as the battleground for the perfidious avarice of others, was always at the mercy of our *arditi*. *Teneo te Africa* was our motto. Who will now represent for us that wish? That attitude? That tradition?

"When the three Polos, the 'three Latins,' left Acre for their marvelous voyage, they took with them a pouch of oil from the Sacred Sepulchre, as a guard against the dangers and a cure for evil. In this way we, today, will carry a pouch of oil of our martyrs, which will warm us in the cold, will lighten us in dark and doubt, will purify us of every impure thought, will renew our courage every hour and inspire a new sacrifice in every dawn, where there glimmers a new hope. . . ."

To show that he intended to practice what he preached, he had taken up dueling. Considering himself insulted in an article by one Carlo Magnifico, he instructed his friends, Michetti and Scarfoglio, as seconds, to challenge Magnifico to a duel. Magnifico, in spite of his name, knew nothing about dueling, but he accepted and suggested pistols. The seconds in conference considered this too dangerous, and decided on sabers. D'Annunzio was short-sighted, and at one point Magnifico lunged at him clumsily, hitting not, as one should, the anatomy, but the head, in which he opened up a large wound, almost down to the nape of the neck. As with all head wounds, it bled profusely: and D'Annunzio's second took Magnifico aside and rated him, thinking his friend was dying. The surgeon who was present was also unaccustomed to duels. He was so terrified that he emptied on the head an entire bottle of ferrous perchlorate, to staunch the flow of blood.

The wound was fortunately superficial, and it did not take long to heal, forming a long vertical scar down the back of the head. But on both sides of the scar, the hair began to fall out. It continued daily, because the ferrous perchlorate had entirely destroyed the capillary bulbs on the top of the head. Never again were the beautiful chestnut locks to be seen. A fine, round, but completely bald, cranium was revealed.

After this, D'Annunzio improved as a dueler, proving it a year later when he challenged his old friend, Scarfoglio, to a duel, imagining himself insulted in some way. On this occasion thirty-five thrusts were made, before Scarfoglio suffered an arm wound, and the duelers were instructed by their seconds to stop.

The ideas which young people in Italy were absorbing from D'Annunzio, both in his behavior and in his writings, are represented by a journalist, Picciola, who wrote in the *Rivista d'Italia* (1902) about another propaganda journey which D'Annunzio had made in Istria, then under Austrian rule: "Art and Poetry! What power they have when they are directed, not at titivating vitiated intellects, but at brightening and adding high ideals to the land of their origin!" This meant, in plain English, that D'Annunzio had told them "Istria should be Italian." It is not surprising that Marinetti, the founder of Futurism, should have admired D'Annunzio as "the prodigious seducer, the ineffable descendant of Casanova and Cagliostro . . . the Monte Carlo of all literature . . ."

Everyone said that "Italy must do something in Europe," but no one could say what to do. Italy had already joined the Triple Alliance, spurred on by an odd combination of monarchists on the one hand, and men of the extreme left, belonging to the old Garibaldean *partito di azione,* on the other. The military obligations of this alliance, which were quite beyond the power of the country, were not fully understood by anyone, except one or two "bourgeois" politicians like Giolitti.

Lastly came the philosopher Croce, who did a great service to all this violent youth by publishing an Italian translation of Sorel's *Réflections sur la Violence,* with a flattering preface. This book is about universal subversion and destruction, which the author calls Religious Upheaval, or Renovation, or Syndicalism, or the Creative Myth of the General Strike. Croce approved of Sorel's scorn for optimism, humanitarianism, pacifism and "the other trashy ideals of the eighteenth century." Thanks largely to Croce,[1] Sorel was widely read by the new groups who had been nourished on D'Annunzio's verse, providing them thereby with a philosophical justification for their daydreams.

The first Italian statesman to express all these ideas in action was Francesco Crispi, a Sicilian deputy who had fought with Garibaldi, but who admired Germany and was the architect of the Triple Alliance. He had been invited by Bismarck to Berlin, where he made a fine speech in the Reichstag. He was the first flamboyant Italian with popular appeal since Garibaldi. As Prime Minister, he treated every act of ordinary administration as if it were a national event, and filled his speech with the pronoun "I." He had the Royal room at the station opened for himself whenever he met a foreigner; he brandished his fist when speaking; he generally imitated Bismarck. He organized the Italian oc-

[1] The prolix Croce, in his *Philosophy of the Practical* (1909), was to uphold Machiavelli's theory of Power and State, even inserting an apology for the Holy Inquisition, which he considered as an example of the unavoidable and legitimate use of violence.

cupation of Eritrea, and obtained an almost childish delight at seeing the new coins with the King's head, and the Latin words on them, *Colonia Eritrea.* The new nationalist newspaper, *Il Regno,* later wrote: "Crispi is the last great statesman Italy has known. We understand 'statesman' not in the sense in which many understand it today, that of a diplomat, cautious, temporizing, patient, timid—but rather a statesman in the heroic and national meaning of the word . . . with a strong national consciousness, beyond and above the cries of the *piazza,* and the petty politics of the back-stairs, having regard both to the past and future of the nation. . . ."

Crispi was mesmerized by the romantic Abyssinian names of Asmara, Keren, Archico, Adua, and he persuaded his generals to extend the occupation of Eritrea inland to Abyssinia—with fatal consequences. At a time when the other nations of Europe, England in particular, were founding empires in Africa, this was perhaps understandable—but inexcusable in the case of Italy, who had something better to offer the world than mere Imperial glitter. To attempt to emulate the practical English, the born empire-builders, was unwise. It quickly brought retribution. The expeditionary force of 15,000 men which was sent against Ethiopia in the early spring of 1896 was almost immediately annihilated.

The other typical figure of these times was Cavallotti, a popular orator. Like Crispi, he personified the vague and confused aspirations towards greatness of the younger men. But while Crispi, to make Italy great, chose the road of authority, of heavy armaments and alliances with the Central Powers, Cavallotti demanded radical democracy to bring about the "new Italy."

The Abyssinian débâcle was atoned for some years later with the conquest of Tripolitania, when it seemed that Italy at last emerged as a full-scale European power. There is a popular cartoon of the time by Matania, showing an Italian sailor on the shores of Tripoli, finding in an ancient arena the remains of a Roman legionary's armor. He is brandishing with pride a Roman sword and shouting, "Tripoli shall be Italian at the roar of the cannon!"

The dispatches from the desert about this campaign by the famous journalist, Corradini, were widely read for their "literary imperialism," their quotations and descriptions of classical ruins, together with arcane and awful presages of returning Greatness. Corradini saw every unopposed landing on the African coast before a few unarmed Arabs, who scarcely bothered to brush the flies away from their eyes while staring at the invaders, as a Roman victory. Every occupation of a small island in the Aegean, together with the arrest of a pair of bewildered Turkish *gendarmes* proclaimed, for him, the new *mare nostrum*. He saw the Tripolitanian war as a kind of redemption of some mysterious sin which the Italians, servile and unadventurous, had been committing for centuries.[1]

D'Annunzio was not yet prepared to go to war. But with Corradini to Tripoli went the futurist Marinetti, "sharing after so many years of flanneled ease, the emotions of the cork helmet and the military boot." Until now, futurism had been no more than a "movement," hardly out of the cafés and literary reviews. Its manifesto, published in Paris, seemed no more than another variant of the usual carnival of left-bank fashionable *avant-garde* fevers. Here, Italian futurism came of age.

Marinetti's *Futurist Account of the Battle of Tripoli, 26th October,* describes everything he had for years been demanding. While the journalist Corradini went about searching for old mosaics and stumps of Roman columns as signs of Italy's returning greatness, Marinetti saw the New Italy in terms of tanks, shells and motorized machine guns hurtling about in clouds of dust. His futurist prose was enriched with a host of images drawn from these instruments of speed and explosion; "projectiles whose whine is confounded in my mind with the twittering of the sparrows on the olive branches." He speaks of "a fat futurist hen roosting on the branches of a tree which quietly dropped its egg

[1] See Ansaldo's *Il Ministro della Buona Vita.*

into a box full of shrapnel shells . . ." The sound of the batteries and machine guns at Bumeliana filled him with pride; and the first aerial bombs dropped by the pilot Moizo on a group of squatting Arabs seemed to him the revelation of some sublime moral, political and artistic truth.

D'Annunzio naturally saw it in much the same light. He had already written, "my first mission is to teach my people to love their own country; the second is to hate unto death Italy's enemies, and always to fight them." The poems he wrote, *Canzoni delle Geste d'Oltremare*, dedicated to the enterprise, are full of imperial presages, heroic exaltations and visions of national grandeur. They appeared regularly in the *Corriere della Sera,* each published in big type over an entire page of four columns. They were successful, not only among a public enthusiastic about the war, but also among the troops themselves, bewitched and gratified by the flow of D'Annunzio's words (a number of which were incomprehensible to them without recourse to a dictionary). Count Sforza writes of the influence this had on the army. He says that during the war he received letters from Italian generals; "short, sober and caustic," he says, "they were mirrors of honest, simple and modest men. But if they had to draw up an order-of-the-day after a battle, they suddenly felt they must produce an ornate, swelling prose, imagining it an appropriate style for the occasion. They were the unlettered victims of D'Annunzio."

D'Annunzio's general literary fame in Italy came from this period. Until the Libyan war, the Italian middle classes suspected him, for his claim to be satanic and a superman, and also on account of his immoral novels which were bad for their young ladies. But the *Canzoni d'Oltremare* crowned him as a patriotic poet.

8

Politics

It is some credit to the King and Queen of Italy that, by the end of the century, the position of the monarchy had greatly improved. To millions of Italians, the only link with the throne was personal devotion to the individual, not to the Monarchy itself, as in England. The house of Savoy had, it was true, brought order and unity to Italy, and on the whole people felt that this control from above was good. But Italy had been disorganized for so long, that they felt they had lost something, the little pleasures and joys of disorganization, the impunity of cliques, the local passions and patriotisms, the little parochial things one enjoys when one is Italian. In 1883 at Forlí, when the agricultural-industrial exhibition closed, the Savoyard coat of arms was torn down by the mob. It was the same in higher circles. Not only was the Vatican still violently anti-Savoyard but, as we have seen, the "black" aristocracy, the most powerful families in Rome, often looked upon themselves as better than the King's family. If they did not actually try to take precedence at large functions, they considered they had every right to do so.

Umberto, moreover, was a stupid man. With his exclusively masculine and military character, went a lack of interest in the social graces. He is said to have told his son, the heir apparent, that a king needed to be able to do three things: sign his name; read the newspaper; and ride a horse. But fortunately his queen, Margherita, was a remarkable woman, and most of the credit for the revived prestige of the monarchy is due to her. Her court was famous throughout Europe, not only for its splendor, but for her democratic habit of inviting clever men to it. No nineteenth-century monarch was surrounded by, it was said, "so many clever men, and so few cavalry officers." She had a "circle" in Rome, modelled on the lines of Mathilde Bonaparte's which during the '80's and '90's met weekly, the "Thursdays of the Queen." Margherita learned Latin from Minghetti, and instead of military music, quartets were played at the palace.

Within five years of their accession, Queen Margherita, with her daily landau drives in the Pincio gardens, her visits to schools, hospitals and public institutions, her intelligent patronage of the workers' growing organizations, had become personally popular. Peasants, it was claimed, kept dried margherita flowers in their prayer books as lucky charms. Some, it was said, would not pronounce her name without making the sign of the Cross. On April 24, 1893, in Trieste (then under Austria), an Italian student called Piccolo was expelled from the University for wearing a margherita in his buttonhole. Her name was even becoming a symbol for *Italia irredenta.*

The violent events of the *Risorgimento,* the hatreds and bitterness of the "blacks" and "whites," had left their scars; but under the constitutional reign of Umberto and Margherita, public life in Italy was gradually becoming pacific, liberal, parliamentary and middle class. The philosopher Croce describes the situation in these words: "Politics, hitherto an affair of the monarch, a hidden thing, secret, coming from above, is now openly in the hands of the ministers and members of Parliament, men who alternately take the reins of government, and are forced to yield them to others. . . ."

Foreigners, too, were impressed. Gladstone said, "The keen intellect and quick mind of this ancient people has at last made it possible for them to adopt methods elaborated by others, and to use them naturally, without effort. The system of government by police has disappeared, and with it the political informers and espionage. The aroma of incense and the sacristy has been dissipated, and with it the inquisitorial methods of priests and Jesuits, who had insinuated themselves vexatiously into every department of public, as well as of private, life, and had given to the secular arm the mischievous support of the ecclesiastical mind. . . ."

D'Annunzio entered politics in 1899. It was inevitable that the career of such a man should include a period in Parliament, just as it was clear that he must later fly an airplane. In a letter to his publisher, he had written, "I have just returned from an electoral journey, my nostrils full of the most acrid human smell. This may seem to you a strange undertaking, at odds with my art and principles. . . . But, my friend, the world must see that *I am capable of everything.*" This desire, to show omnipotence, was repeated in his pamphlet, *L'Armata d'Italia.* "I am not, and never intended to be, only a poet. It may have pleased that perfect versifier, Théodor de Banville, to confess in one of his ballads, *'je n'entends que la métrique.'* But this is not for me. *All* manifestations of life interest me." His parliamentary career was short, consisting essentially of two speeches and a duel. But a good deal can be said about him as a politician.

D'Annunzio's forceful character was very far from the subtle, compromising kind required in the modern multi-party, two-chamber Parliament. He had little of that skill with which your democratic politician takes part in electoral campaigns, in which a number of promises are made, that will or will not be carried out. In May 1898 he decided, however, to stand as conservative candidate for Ortona on the Adriatic, against the socialist, Carlo Altobelli. Ortona is the next town to Pescara; it was his mother's birthplace, and he knew most of the electors.

He had hitherto spoken only with scorn of parliamentary methods, describing the members as "the elected herd." In his novel, *Le Vergine delle Rocce,* there is this passage about modern democracy, ". . . A State erected on the basis of popular suffrage and equality in voting is not only ignoble, it is precarious. The State should always be no more than an institution for favoring the gradual elevation of a privileged class towards its ideal form of existence." The Italy of the *Risorgimento* and the liberal past meant little to him for, although of bourgeois origins himself, all his leanings were towards autocratic aristocracy. He was always sarcastic about the badly dressed parliamentarians. He was to sum up his political experiences later in life, after Fiume, when some old legionaries asked him if he would stand again for Parliament (it was just before Mussolini took power). "In Rome, I see only the *cloaca maxima*. I refuse to defile myself in it."

This scorn for parliamentary government in Italy was not peculiar to D'Annunzio. It has always been common. Queen Margherita herself shared it (although her husband's reign was founded upon the democratic skill of such men as Rattazzi and Giolitti). "How out of date is parliamentary government!" she complained in a letter to a friend in 1895. "It is impossible to believe that the country can go on being governed by this flock of ill-educated and wicked men who, as soon as they get into Parliament, seem struck with a kind of madness, poisoning and lowering the life of the nation. How wonderful that we are going away from Rome to the country, for our annual holiday—to those beautiful mountains which speak a language so different from that of Montecitorio!"

The *camera dei deputati* or House of Commons at Montecitorio in the center of Rome, is always the target for general abuse— even today. Whenever two or three Italians are gathered together, it is a favorite topic of conversation, and it is always disparaged and deplored. Certain papers, in those days, like *Don Chisciotte* or *Fanfulla,* seemed dedicated to its denigration; and in 1900, a Milanese liberal, Francesco Ambrosoli, wrote a satirical book, *"Why I find members of Parliament horrid."* The great *Banca Romana* crash, a sort of Italian Stravinsky affair, gave every café frequenter the pleasure of proclaiming that all Members of Parliament were bandits, and it was rumored that worse things went on in Montecitorio even than the French Syveton affair.[1] Crispi, the most forceful of ministers, had to resign for commit-

---

[1] The President of the French Committee for Moral Regeneration, Syveton, committed suicide in 1905, because, it was asserted, he was discovered educating his younger daughter in the most voluptuous games of love.

ting bigamy. Depretis, who took over, was known as "the cynic," and he managed to keep in power by devious methods. Everyone spoke of the "Consortium," a mysterious group which no one could accurately describe. "The Consortium," said Guerrazzi. "To define it is like trying to define the *cloaca maxima*. I would describe it as a society formed of politicians united in one thing— to procure private advantage at public expense." These and other stories about Montecitorio gave Italians the pleasure of criticizing their politicians, as well as the agreeable illusion of thinking themselves more corrupt and "western" than they were, contributing thereby to the general conviction that Italy was becoming a great power.

In Italy, each electoral district sent a deputy to Parliament at that time. He was chosen from the various names which local groups or factions nominated. The faction or group of persons professed more or less common aims or views, desiring to further what may be called a Socialist policy, a Liberal policy, a Radical policy or a Clerical policy. Sometimes, however, an individual, frequently a newspaper man whose name was known to the public, would offer himself to the electors, relying on his own popularity, rather than his political views. To this latter class belonged D'Annunzio. It would not be strictly true to describe him as belonging to any particular party. For if you asked a well-informed Italian how many political parties there were at Montecitorio, he would answer that he did not know. There might be five today, eight or ten tomorrow. The truth is, that there have never been Italian political parties in the sense that we know them (except, of course, the Communists today). There are only factions—factions or splinter-groups which are constantly coalescing and splitting like amoebae. Party development and party formation are the result of individual effort, which may or may not become collective.

D'Annunzio stood in an agricultural constituency where socialism was at last beginning to make a little headway. Reform was in the air, and 5,000 peasants had just marched to Reggio Emilia, demanding a redistribution of land. Socialism, suppressed after 1848, had now left the romantic period of persecution and come out into the open. The burning problem was that of the peasant smallholder, and the justice, long withheld, which all parties promised him. D'Annunzio's opponent belonged to a socialist group and based his campaign on this question. But D'Annunzio, from among the various electoral approaches open to him, had selected none; he simply went round saying, "I must show them new ideas which will demonstrate that no one shall take the Italian people lightly, as long as I represent them." To an elector who demanded a more concrete political program, and asked him where he would sit in the chamber, he replied, "I shall not sit anywhere—because I should have to go beyond the extreme Left, where there are no seats, or beyond the extreme Right, where there are no seats." It was clear that although he was standing against a socialist and, in a sense, a revolutionary, he had something much more revolutionary to offer.

Before election day in Italy, the streets and walls of a city like Ortona are plastered with posters of all sizes and colors, bearing the names and pictures of the candidates, statements of their aims and potentialities, and an enumeration of the benefits that will come to the people from their election—and often depreciation and defamation of the opposing candidate. It is often difficult for the voter to decide which of the alluring programs he shall support (having been made aware of the defects of the opposing candidates). Unless he is sure of his politics and very steady in his opinions, he generally falls into a troubled state of conscience, and ends by voting for the candidate recommended by a friend. If the "friend" has money to spend, a motor-car to take him to the poll, it is remarkable how easily he makes up his mind.

In D'Annunzio's day, it was quite customary for the government police to help bring about the election of the candidates the government desired, by intimidating peace-loving voters.[1] The

---

[1] There were two types of police in Italy—municipal and governmental (*cara-binieri*). The latter are under the Prefect, who is a state official.

M.P.s themselves were well aware of this influence, and many understandably tried to maintain friendly relations with the men in power. These men in power were known to reward the faithful and loyal among the deputies with grants of public works, or titles such as *cavaliere* or *commandatore,* which were highly sought after. It is to D'Annunzio's credit that he seems to have given little thought to this throughout his parliamentary career. In his election addresses he spoke as a poet, above such sordid realities.

It was during the electoral campaign that his considerable oratorical powers were first revealed. His political speeches were full of references to Virgil and Hesiod, to the Parthenon, the Muses, the Furies, and there was much talk of Beauty. Instead of proposing himself as "the man who will carry out the people's will," he referred to himself as "the poet in the act of recognizing the sacred ties which bind me to my native soil." "I cannot express my art," he said to the rural electors, "without associating myself with the sweet stalks of corn, the blushing apples, the pacific regard on the face of the cattle, the oil of the pressed olive. . . ." In this way, he created a suitable agrarian atmosphere around his personality. "Although I have recently submerged myself in Rome in a flood of new ideas, aspirations, divinations and transfigurations which belong to the end of this century," he said, "I can never display my art if I dissociate myself and my passions for long from my homeland. The glow of a piece of straw in the dust helps me to new truths. By watching the baker as he takes the swollen loaf from the oven, new and luminous thoughts glow in my mind. The depths of my being are stirred when I contemplate the ewe-lamb sucking. . . ."

In another speech, he said, "I have never forgotten those streets in the Adriatic towns, as broad as rivers, green with lichen and scattered with flint paving-stones; with here and there gigantic oaks which run down from the mountains, leading the flocks to pasture on the plains. Lending my ear to unknown happiness and sadness heard in hidden paths, I shall always remember the simple and grave melopees of song, ancient and immemorial, which echo round our cradle, and at last—around our grave. . . ." Of his opponent, the Onorevole Altobelli, and the socialists, he said, "Which of these men, if they were elected to lead Italy, could show that he understands the idea towards which our race has been striving with its own genius throughout the centuries? Not one of these men is representative of our national genius! Not one has considered with a clear gaze the heights of life as lived by our race—and thus understood an ancient truth, to help them make our laws today!"

It was not until late in the campaign that he revealed his true political colors. "A human society can never reach its climax," he said, "until a man can say, 'These goods are mine. I have earned them. I enjoy them. I will protect them against everyone.'" He was, in fact, a capitalist—such a convinced one that he could condemn socialism in these words, "The more a man associates with other men in communal work, the less he retains of human dignity—for he no longer struggles."

This speech came to be known as "The Hedge Speech," because in it D'Annunzio glorified the hedge which guards a man's field. "Few things in the world," he said, "seem so full of meaning, so eternal, so inviolable, as the hedge. And by that, I do not mean the rural one, with flowers and berries in it, and nests built into it, pearly with dew—but the circular thing which surrounds a man's property, which protects all that he has justly earned. . . ."

The Onorevole Altobelli also spoke of hedges, but in a different sense—preaching collectivity within limits, of communities working in the same field. His methods must have been less effective because, when the votes were taken, D'Annunzio had 1,405, and Altobelli 1,255.

Before 1882, there had not been more than a dozen voters behind each deputy in Montecitorio, their franchise depending on property ownership. But in 1882, Depretis broadened the suffrage, to include all who had "passed the fourth elementary school stage," or taken certain courses during military conscription. By the time D'Annunzio came to Parliament, each deputy represented at least five or six thousand voters. The electoral body was now largely bourgeois, in all its various forms and graduations, from the rising industrial magnate of upper Italy, who was beginning to build railways, motor-cars and telegraph lines, to the small shopkeeper, the tenant farmer and the land agent in the country. The big urban populations of modern times were not yet completely formed. *Miseria,* as it was called in the cities, was not yet apparent. The prestige of the priests was still predominant in the rural areas; and the Pope's *non possumus,* instructing good Catholics not to vote for the King's Parliament, was still in accord with the general illiteracy and lack of interest in all but local affairs.

When D'Annunzio took his seat, what we would generically term as the Right was in power. Under General Pelloux, it was busy putting down demands for reform and concessions to the working classes. Because Pelloux had just suppressed a socialist movement in Milan, he had gained the reputation of being a bloodthirsty reactionary; but he was really a good-natured old man, given to sudden fits of conservative heartiness. Having suppressed this socialist movement, he was now about to introduce legislation to restrict the power of the growing Trades Unions.

The atmosphere in the Chamber at Montecitorio was one of continuous, truceless battle between the government and the opposition. The socialist and Garibaldean groups had joined forces, but they knew that the legislation against the Trades Unions must come into force as the vote was taken, for the government had a clear majority. They therefore did all they could to postpone it, with interminable speeches, the introduction of fresh clauses, the alteration of the agenda, every device known to parliamentary democracy for prolonging a debate. Leather-lunged orators, these socialists could go on for hours without stopping. So famous did this debate become, that it has since been known in parliamentary history as "the Obstructionist Debate." D'Annunzio's first months were passed in this stultifying atmosphere—

the government sitting in impotent silence, wanting to vote, the opposition in continuous forensic action, *not* wanting to vote. The most famous socialist orators were Bissolati, Prampolini, and above all Enrico Ferri, who once talked for an entire sitting (twelve hours).

D'Annunzio has described the atmosphere in Montecitorio. "Every time I entered the hall," he said, "I would see fifteen of my colleagues drowsing on the benches. Occasionally, one of them would bestir himself and deliver a funereal monody which lost itself in vacuity. The Marquis Visconti-Venosta, coming momentarily out of his 20-year-old sleep, spoke of a certain country called Italy, in the tones of a dying man commemorating someone long dead. . . ."

This lethargy was, however, most unusual in Montecitorio. In normal circumstances, the atmosphere is, on the contrary, one of extreme animation, providing for the curious foreigner a fascinating spectacle. The Italians who are normally the most ceremonious and courteous people in the world, here throw off all restraint, and occasionally behave as if they were in an arena. On one occasion, the writer was present during a debate when a well-known socialist orator, the Honorable X, was holding forth volubly, supported by the extreme Left with frequent bursts of applause (the center and right displayed annoyance, boredom, lack of interest, alternating with cries of derision and howls of contempt). Suddenly a deputy on the right got up, looking as if he had been tortured, so red and strained was his face. He shrieked at the Honorable X, "You are trying to hide under the dirty Y affair" (the Y affair was one of the scandals of the day). No sooner were these words out of his system (one could not say out of his mouth, because they seemed to emanate from every tissue of his body), than he leaped from his place and ran smartly across the chamber, up the steps to where the Honorable X was talking, apparently about to kill him. But before he could reach him, a nearby supporter of the Honorable X had floored him with an uppercut. Whereupon another conservative, the Honorable Z, ran around and joined in the fray. It was several minutes before they could all be separated by the pages. When calm was restored, the Chamber became aware that, through all this turmoil, the Honorable X was still talking. He had not been touched during the fight, and was now finishing his speech, not one word of which had been heard.

D'Annunzio was not an assiduous debater, nor even often present at the debates. He seems to have found that his oratorical powers were useless among these professionals. On one occasion, when he was reading a book in the parliamentary library, a page came up and said that the Prime Minister wished him to come into the lobby for the vote, as the government numbers were deficient. "Tell the Prime Minister," he said, "that I am not a number." And he continued reading.

It was during 1900 that an outside event occurred which was to alter the constitution of the government and D'Annunzio's position. General discontent after the Milan suppression of the rising caused an anarchist, Bresci, to murder King Umberto II, at Monza on July 29, 1900. In the years immediately before 1900, Italian anarchists had made quite a reputation for themselves in Europe. Caserio had murdered President Carnot in France, and had been guillotined. Angiolillo had assassinated the President of the Council, Canovas, in Spain, and had been garroted. Lucheni had stuck a hat-pin into the heart of the Empress Elizabeth of Austria in Switzerland, and had been shut up for life, in the asylum at Lucerne. Italy seemed to have made a specialty of political assassination—to such an extent that, in foreign countries, to say "anarchist" meant roughly to say "Italian." When a regicide in Paris fired a shot at the Shah of Persia on a state visit, and it was learned that he was a Frenchman, a sigh almost of relief was heard all over Italy.

But the habit returned in the park at Monza, in the summer of 1900. Bresci was not strictly an Italian, for he had emigrated to

America some years before; but at an Italian gathering one evening in a town called Paterson, he appears to have been stirred on patriotic grounds to undertake the long journey back, with the express purpose of murdering a man he had never known. Pacifists and others, who like to see the hand of fate or Nemesis in this, point out that he assassinated Umberto after the King had inspected an Italian contingent about to leave for China, to suppress the Boxer rebellion; and that, among the groups the King also addressed that day were two teams of athletes from Trent, Trieste, and the "irridentist lands" then under Austria.

The general explanation of this event was that discontent with General Pelloux's policy in suppressing the Milanese uprising rendered something of the kind inevitable. D'Annunzio's objection to Pelloux's policy was in keeping with this. One day while strolling through the outer lobbies, he heard a sound of raised voices in a side room, of men in heated discussion. He dropped in, and found the socialists and republicans holding a caucus, elaborating violent plans against General Pelloux. Fascinated (D'Annunzio relates), he sat down to listen, and the left-wing men, thinking he was a new recruit, gathered enthusiastically round him. News of this reached the press, and there were rumors that the poet was contemplating political apostasy. And some days later in the Chamber, when the usual one-sided oratory was in progress, D'Annunzio, suddenly rising from his supine position on the extreme Right, walked ostentatiously round the entire Chamber, until he reached the extreme Left. In the deadly silence that fell, he announced, "As a man of intellect, I go from death to life. From Right to Left."

This was the famous *salto di quinta,* or "leap behind the scenes," for which he has always been remembered as a politician. The socialists were delighted, particularly as, two weeks later, the government decided to withdraw their restrictive decree about Trades Unions, dissolve Parliament, and "go to the country." D'Annunzio's gesture had nothing to do with this. It had become

POLITICS   87

clear to everyone that the socialists would continue obstructing indefinitely, and that some surer indication of public opinion must be obtained. But he was no doubt sincere in his condemnation of the policy that had led to the Milan uprising and the regicide.

In the general election that followed, D'Annunzio could clearly not stand again at his mother's town, Ortona, representing a policy which was exactly the opposite of the one he had been elected to support. He therefore accepted the socialist invitation to stand in another constituency, the San Giovanni district of Florence, a city he knew well, and where he also had connections.

We have spoken of the difficulty of defining parties exactly in Italy, of factions and splinter groups. The situation of the socialists which he now joined exemplified this. They had just excluded the anarchists, and were preaching regeneration of mankind to be brought about either by evolution or by social upheaval. There were two sects, the "Syndicalists" and the "Reformists," the former being extremists, the latter being a more law-abiding body, hoping to achieve reform by constitutional means. A third group had also appeared, the "Integralists," pledged to hold the party together. But this was not easy. The Syndicalists were forever trying to promote strikes, the Reformists ever denouncing them. The Reformists finally overcame the Integralists and ejected the Syndicalists.

D'Annunzio ignored these groups, and immediately embarked on a violent campaign, consisting primarily of speeches and articles against the outgoing Pelloux government. In *Il Giorno* he wrote, "that effeminate old corporal [Pelloux], who kneels to that Levantine from San Casciano [he was referring to the Honorable Sonnino, the Member for San Casciano], can incite his political assassins to every form of knavery. He can deposit in our beautiful San Giovanni of Florence all the filth of his electoral corruption. But he cannot cause the dead thing he represents not to stink."

These and similar remarks did not impress the good bourgeois

of Florence. The electors of the Via Tornabuoni and the Via
Strozzi were suspicious of a man who went from the ultra-
conservatism of the Right, to the ultra-radicalism of the Left,
particularly as he had large outstanding accounts in their shops.
His new adversary, Cambray-Digny, was quick to sense this, and
an attack was made on his private life. D'Annunzio had been
accused of adultery, polygamy, theft, incest, sodomy, simony,
murder and cannibalism. His alliance with the socialists also
closed the doors of the theaters and public meeting-rooms, and he
had to make his speeches in the open air, often in the rain, addressing only the humbler members of the community. He complained of this in a letter to the Mayor, ". . . that same orator
who in Or San Michele, in the Loggia, initiated the Dante lectures in your presence, and was acclaimed by you on the new plat-
form with noble words, in full view of the people of Florence—
that same orator can now find no covered hall to address the people. . . ." The Mayor did not answer this letter, observing privately that literature and politics are different things.

With the Florentines, D'Annunzio employed much the same
technique as he had with the people of Ortona, speaking of their
past rather than their present—the glorious memories of Dante
and the Medici, the magnificence of Florentine art and genius,
the proud communal struggles. "This battle," he said, "is to be
fought against the violators and corrupters of the civic conscience,
in the city which has long cemented all its famous stones with
untiring popular acclaim, in the same city where humanism itself
—which once was owned only by Princes—now belongs to every
citizen. . . ." He reviled the late government, ". . . the great
national flame of the *Risorgimento* has gone out, the flame which
brought all minds together in a common striving. The Italians
today, after four decades of political unity, are intent on one thing
only, nourishing hate and hostility towards one another. The
national conscience, forged in the fire of the revolution, in which
all metals seem to fuse in one sole smithy, has gradually—as a re-

sult of misgovernment—weakened, and is today extinguished. . . .

"It is a fine and grave hour of my life—the hour when I communicate my words to you, citizens of Florence—it seems that I really fuse myself with you, placing not only my thoughts but my actions in the service of my ideal homeland, where my infancy and my adolescence received the first imprint of the village fathers, where I was 'nourished to the very brim with life,' and where I have today my silent, tranquil house, sacred to my work. . . ."

Then, alluding to his *salto di quinta,* he said, "If I have accomplished in the Assembly a decisive act, without thought of the hostility and vileness which has since arisen against me; if I have openly attacked the same men who provoked me with their servility, in that place where the struggle is most violent, where the adversary employs his most perfidious and fraudulent weapons—I have done it because I felt that I, as an Italian and worker in the Italian tongue, must by moral necessity oppose my own force—whatever may be the outcome—to the bestial tyranny which oppresses and dishonors Parliament today. . . ."

His references to Dante were more sibylline: "In Or San Michele, with the sacred book of Dante before me, I said, 'Life produces life.' The virtue of Dante is the virtue of fecundation. All his words are seeds, and it is indeed a piece of good fortune for me that where we honor him is the place that was the citizens' granary, a room destined to the custody of the crops, where we evoke the fertility of the furrow, the gesture of the sower and the miracle of the sun. Like bread, Dante serves to perpetuate the energy of the race. . . ."

He also addressed himself to the peasant, "strong, tenacious, sober and healthy." To these Tuscan workers he said, "When in the rest of Europe, the serfs were sweating like beasts in harness, you Tuscans were the first to bring the scythe and the pitch-fork into the dignity of communal life." He claimed that he had already celebrated socialism in his verse. This is true. There is a part of the *Laudi* where the workers are shown knocking down the doors that have for so long barred them from advance, breaking open the ovens and taking out the bread:

> . . . then all the teeth are pure,
> in the famished mouths that masticate
>   earth's gift, born from the furrows.
> I say again—before the grain of wheat,
>   reaped in silence or in song,
> all men are equal. This then, the first equality,
>   Earth's Right written in the sod.

But all these oratorical and literary gifts were in vain. At the general election, D'Annunzio was resoundingly defeated by the Onorevole Cambray-Digny, and the Florentines confirmed their faith in broad conservatism. (It was while fighting this seat that he had a duel with the journalist, Ettore Bernabei, whom he considered had insulted him. He wounded Bernabei in the left temple, seriously endangering his eye.)

This electoral defeat really ended D'Annunzio's political career. He continued making left-wing speeches in favor of his more successful colleagues and their intended reforms. But he never entered politics again; and in the years that followed, he even abandoned his new socialist doctrines. When, many years later, he was asked by the French paper, *Le Temps,* if he was still a socialist, he replied, "Between those gentlemen and myself there is, and always will be, a barrier. I am, and always will remain, an individualist, fervidly and absolutely. It amused me to join the socialist party for a time, it is true. I did it out of disgust —for the other party. But socialism in Italy is an absurdity. It must all be started from scratch again. One day, perhaps, I shall return to the hustings. . . ."

To sum up D'Annunzio's political career, it seems that he never had any real understanding of the electors. One of his fixed ideas, held all his life, was that he "understood the common people," that the qualities he most admired were frankness, naturalness and roughness in the workers. It is true that for the lower classes he had sympathy, but it was not of the Tolstoyan brand, the desire to be with them, rather than with other people. He was more like the great Italian nobleman who is always prepared to give large sums to the poor, provided he does not have to shake hands with them. He appreciated in the peasant, the poetic gesture by which he nobly strews the seeds in the furrow, and he saw the working man in terms of medieval guilds and craftsmanship, bending the filigree of silver, studding a brocade with foliage, or blowing a piece of Murano glass. About percentages, Trades Unions, the cost of corn, he knew nothing.

There is an apocryphal story which D'Annunzio tells of how he once saw a peasant working in a field. D'Annunzio approached him, and the peasant said that his only son had been killed in the war. D'Annunzio sympathized, but the peasant said, "No, no, you can't understand the poor. You are a gentleman."

Whereupon (says D'Annunzio) he took up the peasant's scythe, and began to work himself. After half an hour the peasant, who had originally been cynical, said, "Yes, you are right. Now, I know you can understand me."

At the end of his life, in the *Libro Segreto,* D'Annunzio speaks of the working classes in passages of this kind, ". . . the wretched peasantry are no more alive to me than those railway sidings where you see old rails, rusty and displaced. . . ." On more than one occasion, he used the uncomplimentary phrase, *plebs misera contribuens.*

An even better way to understand D'Annunzio's attitude towards the poor is to quote one of his own short stories, "The Treasure of the Poor—a Christmas Tale," published some time before in the *Tribuna:*

"Once upon a time there were two poor people, a man and his wife. They were so poor, they possessed nothing—really nothing at all.

"They had no bread to put in the bread bin, nor a bread bin
in which to put the bread.

"They hadn't a house in which to put the bread bin, nor any
field in which to build a house.

"If they had had a field, no bigger than a handkerchief, they
would at least have been able to earn enough to build a house.

"If they had had a house, they would at least have had space
to put a bread bin. If they had had a bread bin, they would certainly have managed to find, in some corner or hole in the wall, a
piece of bread, or at least a crumb.

"But having neither field nor house, nor bread bin, nor bread,
they were indeed in a very wretched state. . . .

"As they were weeping and trembling on the high road one
black winter night, they came upon a cat which was meowing. It
was really the most miserable cat you ever have seen, for it had
hardly any flesh on its bones, and hardly any fur on its flesh.

"If it had had fur on its flesh, its flesh would certainly have
been in a better condition. If its flesh had been in a better condition, it would certainly not have been clinging so closely to its
bones.

"If this had not happened, it would certainly have been a
stronger cat—strong enough at least to catch a mouse. But having
no fur, and having instead its flesh so close to its bones, it was
indeed a very wretched cat. . . ."

The story continues in this vein for some time, showing the
wretchedness of the poor, who are in fact likened to animals—
until the poor couple reach a ruined and abandoned cottage,
where they take refuge. Shuddering with cold, they see in the
dark what they take to be two glowing coals, before which they
hastily begin to warm their frozen hands. They remain like this
all night, congratulating one another on having at last found a
source of warmth, and on how comfortable they now are. Then
with morning light, they see what they thought were glowing
coals are really the cat's eyes—the eyes of the wretched cat they

met on the high road. Then the cat, before it flies away, suddenly says, "The Treasure of the Poor is Illusion."

He seems to have looked upon his presence as a poet in Parliament simply as a disinfectant; and he is heavily responsible for the later Fascist habit of deriding, and finally overthrowing, democratic institutions. "We are happy," he once said, "to record that there is more strength and wisdom in our most crumbling stones than in all the muddied brains of our statesmen." Like so many intellectuals, the French *avant-garde* men, the Bernard Shaws or Bertrand Russells of our own times, he could permit himself the luxury when confronted with public affairs, of continuously destructive criticism—for such men know they will never be put to the test. That his "socialism" was not really genuine was revealed at the end of his life, when a sympathizer, finding him melancholy and depressed because he thought he was getting old, said sympathetically, "But all of us get old." D'Annunzio replied irritably, "I am not *all*." Whatever his pronounced views of politics and social conditions, he remained essentially in politics a Claudio Cantelmo, and in social life an incurable Andrea Sperelli.

His political speeches now become notable for the Greco-Roman-Rinascimento ironmongery with which he decorated them. A fellow writer, Papini, claims that there is no political speech by D'Annunzio which does not contain the words Dante, Rome and Michelangelo; and few in which there is no reference to Greek history. Marathon, Ithaca, Argus, clever Ulysses with his sirens, powerful Theseus and the spellbinder, Orpheus, together with the Spartan twins—all are here. One should note, too, that Christ appears from time to time in D'Annunzio's work, together with Veronica who wiped the sweat off his face.

His failure at Montecitorio is described by his son, Mario, perhaps understandably, in these prophetic words (Mario later became a deputy under Mussolini): "He had little to do with the debates at Montecitorio, because of the petty rivalries of men whose mediocre interests came before every noble design—together with the low moral level which debased every virtue and sign of culture or genius. These men caused him only to frequent more elevated intellectual circles connected with music, letters and the Arts."

It is at this point that D'Annunzio's great adversary, Giovanni Giolitti, the incarnation of parliamentary government, must be introduced. As black shows up against white, so these two men were to throw one another into relief for the next twenty years, winning and losing alternately, until finally, at Fiume, Giolitti won the last and greatest battle of all. Yet there was nothing of the fighter, the worthy rival to the Superman, in Golitti. He was a Piedmontese civil servant by profession, a man who, when asked why he had not fought in the *Risorgimento,* replied, "My mother had just become a widow. I could not leave her."

A confirmed liberal, a believer in compromise, his tall, gaunt figure and lugubrious bourgeois face were to dominate Montecitorio for the first quarter of the century. An expert in elucidating the most intricate problems of finance, always ready to undertake the most laborious administrative tasks, he was Prime Minister from 1902 to 1913, and from 1919 to 1921. In foreign policy, too, he was cautious. He called a halt to African expansion, and told the Central Powers that although Italy was now allied to them (by Crispi's policy), they must not expect much military help from her. His aim was to avoid the big problems of international politics while Italy was still a young state, to concentrate on industry and commerce where, he believed, lay the real strength of the nation. Such a man was naturally anathema to the nationalists and the Dannunzians. He lacked the gestures and solemn words, the half-dramatic, half-operatic qualities, the uncontrollable logorrhea, which appeals to Italians. In his domestic life, too, he was impeccable, having made one of those permanent marriages with a fat woman, which give force to and multiply the energy of a certain type of steady man. Once when, as Prime Minister, he was accused of not speaking long enough in a debate, he made the most unDannunzian reply, "Sir, I am brief by nature. It is impossible for me, when I have finished saying what I have to say, to go on talking."

Around him had collected a number of administrators whom we now call Giolittians. How unlike the "Dannunzians" they were! The typical "Giolittian" was a provincial lawyer with a well-organized office, a University past (sympathizing with, but not being of, the Socialists), advocating "ordered progress" in the domain of industry and local government, the enlargement of a port, the construction of an aqueduct, the erection of a funicular. At Rome, if he was a Deputy, he would live modestly, seldom frequenting society, receptions or the embassies. As often as not he was, even if a lawyer, a silent man. Entire sessions would pass in Parliament without his voice being heard. Giolotti and the "Giolittians," for their part, looked on D'Annunzio as a dangerous firebrand and rhetorician, who could string meaningless words and images together. Giolitti disapproved of D'Annunzio's frivolous behavior in Parliament, the "hedge" speech, his rudeness to their old chief, Pelloux, his theatrical jump from Right to Left.

The first open clash between the two men took place later, over the set of poems which D'Annunzio wrote celebrating the Libyan war (some of which we have already quoted). Not only were they chauvinistic, but they contained personal insults to Giolitti, who was then Prime Minister. ". . . And peace was a female rabbit, who had as pandar a certain Bonturo, and a Zanche as procuress for her illegal traffic. . . ." Here Bonturo and Zanche were Dantesque references to Giolotti. The chauvinism was expressed in the prophetic tone of the poems, announcing, "a new age of ploughshares being turned into the prows of ships"; "of imperial laurel wreaths and rosa"; and "perspectives of Italian arcades opening across the ocean"—images calculated to diminish in the Italians that quality which Giolitti valued most, and which he considered most necessary for the nation in its adolescent state, common sense. D'Annunzio went further and insulted Italy's ally, Austria. If Giolitti was against military commitments with the Central Empires, equally he did not wish to offend them unnecessarily and cause international incidents. D'Annunzio called Austria ". . . the loathsome, two-headed eagle which, like a vulture, vomits up the flesh of undigested corpses. . . ." Her Emperor Franz-Joseph was ". . . the Archangel with the sempieternal gallows, the squawking hangman." Of Kaiser William II, he wrote, "A *parvenu* with a mean and tiny soul. Whenever William II wishes to cause an effect, all he can find to say or do, is to pronounce one or two words borrowed from Plutarch, and to strut about in theatrical fashion, wearing some shreds of the imperial purple of Rome." It was clear that Tripoli was not going to be enough for D'Annunzio, who hoped for war with Italy's new allies as well.

Fearing government action after Giolitti's objection, the paper refused to publish these poems and D'Annunzio, after an acrimonious correspondence, consoled himself with the knowledge that his publisher, Treves, would bring the poems out in a volume. "If there is any challenge of sequestration," he wrote to Treves, "we must take it up. How splendid this would be if . . . the filthy police were to profane the poetry I have dedicated to my country. This is a magnificent opportunity. Let us exult over it. . . ." But Treves exulted less at the certain loss of his money, and he took his time over the printing, so that the threatened sequestration order arrived before any copies were in circulation. This sequestration order, presented at his office by three policemen, is memorable in its phrasing:

"Sequestration Order. Year 1912—day 24—time—2:15 P.M.—place Milan, at the Limited Liability Company of Treves Brothers, via Palermo 12. We, the signatories, members of the Internal Police, announce that, in pursuance of our instructions, we this day and hour went to the Treves establishment, where we pro-

ceeded to the sequestration of the edition of *Canzoni d'Oltremare*, by G. D'Annunzio, published by the said house in a volume under the title *Merope IV Libro dei Dardanelli*—to wit, verses 67 to 81.

Signatories: Balestruzzi Ugo, delegate
                Viscardi Raffaele, police agent
                Basile Salvatore, police agent."

This caused much excitement in literary circles, and D'Annunzio appeared for the first time as the official adversary of Giolitti and his policy. Everyone learned the forbidden verses by heart and Treves later published two editions, in which the fourteen lines were replaced by rows of dots and this footnote by D'Annunzio: "This song of our poor deluded land was mutilated by the hand of the police, at the orders of Cavaliere Giovanni Giolitti, head of the Italian Government. . . ."

This was a declaration of war between the two men.

9

Eleonora Duse

After his failure in politics, D'Annunzio moved back to literature, but this time in search of a more immediately remunerative
muse. Until now, he had written mostly novels about his own love
affairs, erotic lyrics, and epic poems on national themes. But with
his arrival in Florence and residence at the Capponcina, the house
he rented at Settignano, the period of dramatic composition
begins. Political tragedies like *La Gloria, Più, che l'amore,* and
La Nave, with national and international themes, mark the passage of the aesthete to the tribune and the warrior. The theater
always has a wider, more popular audience than the book; and
D'Annunzio himself described the great mass appeal of the stage,
". . . the great mob of the audience, unanimous and anonymous,
whose smell he had smelled, and heard their clamor under the
stars. . . ."

He had made one or two tentative ventures, such as *La Nemica,*
into drama before. But like many poets and novelists, before and
since, he had found it extremely difficult to break into the theater.
It is a closed circle, run by managers, impresarios, critics and
prima donnas, male and female, who resent intrusion, unless an
author's idea of "originality" happens to tally with their own. But
it clearly had possibilities for a man of D'Annunzio's histrionic
temperament, susceptible to the influence of women, particularly
actresses. He had said that he saw the actress "loaded with the
desires of all the mob" as she moved on the stage. And he had
written, ". . . the more the thing a man possesses awakens envy
and cupidity in other men, the more that man enjoys it . . . herein
lies the fascination of the ladies of the stage. When the whole

theater resounds with applause, is alight with desire, the man who alone receives the smile of the *diva* feels drunk with pride, as from a cup of strong wine. His reason wanders. . . ." In *Il Fuoco,* the novel about an actress which he wrote later, there is this passage, ". . . his desire was mingled with cruelty and jealousy . . . he wished he had possessed the actress after one of her stage successes, when she was still hot from the breath of the mob. . . . How many men, he wondered, had lusted after her in this way? The desire of thousands had entered that womb, if only figuratively. . . ."

He had heard of the Duse, of course. She was now at the height of her powers. D'Annunzio had referred to her in his Roman gossip column, in the *Tribuna,* many years before. He speaks in an almost unflattering way as she drives in her carriage in the Pincio, ". . . it is extraordinarily difficult to bow becomingly from a carriage. Signora Duse is too artificial. The way in which she bends her neck is too affected. . . ."

The meeting between the two artists was arranged by friends, who thought it might be advantageous to both of them. For the Duse, too, had reached a difficult point in her career, owing to the repetitive nature of the roles available to a prima donna. Her situation has been described extremely well by Miss Harding in *Age Cannot Wither.* "Nineteenth-century heroines ran to a single pattern. Other actresses, like Sarah Bernhardt, when confronted with this problem, were saved by their technique. But technique was not a quality the Duse employed. She obtained her effects entirely by her unusual personality, quickly identifying herself with the role, catching the cliché, the banality of the author's conception—in the emotional triangle dramas of Marco Praga, or the curtain-raisers of Gallarati-Scotti. Ibsen had, it is true, provided something new in Italy; but he was not enough on his own, and few of his plays had been translated. She needed something novel, preferably native."

She had heard of D'Annunzio, too, and did not like what she heard, as she says in one of her typically disjointed and actressy

letters, "the other evening I went to hear *Falstaff*—may God forgive me—but it seemed such a sad thing, that *Falstaff*. You may
be as loftily scornful as you like. But—there you have it. . . . And
another thing! That infernal D'Annunzio! All of us think—poor
things—that it's we who have found all the words. . . . That
infernal D'Annunzio knows them all too! I'd rather die *in a hole*
than love such a soul. Every great *test* of courage—every heroic
attempt *to put up with life*—all the great agonizing sacrifice which
is *to live* is destroyed in that book. No! No! No! Be as scornful as
you please but neither *Falstaff* nor D'Annunzio—that is, no—I
detest D'Annunzio. . . ."

The Duse was the personification of the acting muse. She once
told the actor taking the part of the villain who does not come on
the stage until the third act, not to approach her behind the scenes
during the first two acts, or she might lose the spell she was under
about his villainousness. She immersed herself so deeply in her
parts, that she shocked Parisian audiences on one occasion by really
kissing Armand a long and passionate kiss on the mouth. Realism
had never gone so far.

She had a most exacting standard for her own work, attributing
to her acting, to every movement she made on the stage, a sense
of eternity. She would go on the stage only when she felt in full
possession of all her "creative faculties." A small indisposition,
the rain, the snow, the view of a new American town which she
found ugly, an unheated room, were enough to make her "inspiration" vanish. Then, at the last moment, everything had to be
changed, postponed or canceled, regardless, of expense. Thus, the
manager of a theater where all the seats had been sold was
shocked, when she said she would not act that night.

"You are ill?" he asked.

"No."

"Why then . . . ?"

"I feel I can't act today in the way I should. Send the public
away."

"But it's impossible!"

"Why?"

"We've already taken 12,000 lire."

"Ah, so the public has spent as much as that!" she reflected. "Well, if the public has such faith and enthusiasm, it has the right to good acting. And I tell you, I can't today. I don't want to rob the public."

"But the seats, Madame! The expense!"

"That doesn't matter. I'll pay for all the expenses."

"But, Madame, don't you realize that the emperor's sister is coming specially from Bonn?"

"She's a member of the public, like everyone else. She'll go home like everyone else."

"No, really, Madame, you must act. . . ."

"All right then, I will. But I warn you, by tomorrow evening I shall be so ill, that I shan't act for fifteen days. And so you'll lose much more."

He insisted. She acted (marvelously); and fell ill the next afternoon. She remained in bed for two weeks.

This was the woman whom D'Annunzio met in Rome at the Grand Hotel in 1897 (not, as is often said, in Venice, in a gondola). It seems that the conversation immediately turned to the question of artistic collaboration. The Duse announced to her friend, Matilde Serao, a few days later, "Here at last is my dramatic poet! From now on, I shall work for my own Italian theater, in which only the highest and noblest art will flourish." D'Annunzio, equally enthusiastic, reported to his friends, "I have my heroine at last! She will give life to my unborn creations!"

Physical attraction cannot have played much part in D'Annunzio's feelings at the beginning, for the Duse was not a beautiful woman. A French journalist, Huret, has described her in these words, ". . . dressed in a dull, dark costume, she looked like the complete *bourgeoise,* without any sense of taste. There is nothing to say that she is even an actress. Only her black hair, dishevelled and drawn back in disorder, gives the impression of the female intellectual. She wears no rings. At first, she seems to emanate only sweetness and serenity. But as one examines her more closely, one is aware of an expression of determination. . . ." Renata Montanarella, D'Annunzio's daughter by his mistress, the Gravina, also tells how she first set eyes on the Duse: "I was unimpressed. I had expected the great Duse to be beautiful and elegant. Instead, she had gray hair, a faded, even common face. . . ."

The Duse quickly began to share D'Annunzio's belief in his mission as the announcer of the new Italy. When she heard that his difficulties with the Princess Gravina, by whom he had just had another child, were preventing him from working, she determined to save him. "His creative genius must be supported at all costs," she told a friend. "He must be taken from the destructive influences around him, so that he can create in an atmosphere of peace. I shall look after his work. . . ." She was warned by her friends about his reputation, but she heard "only the voice of her heart." Indeed, the Duse had always obeyed only "the voice of her heart." She had left her husband and child some years before on account of it, and her husband had written bitterly, "Eleonora is not bad, she is simply half-mad. Her mind is unhealthy, drunk with the stage, with the unhealthy reading of the lives of Rachel, Desclée, Bernhardt. . . ."

In July 1897, immediately after her return from Paris, she left her comfortable palazzo Volkov apartment in Venice, and went to a small villa at Settignano, to be near D'Annunzio. To her sister she wrote, "I have rented an old house near Florence among the olives, simple but poor, hidden but not too far from the city. One arrives by a long path as if to a convent, and the door is hidden among mulberry bushes. Swallows fly round the roof, and up the walls climb vines and wisteria. . . . Roses are everywhere, and there are orange trees in front of my window. . . ."

This house was irreverently christened La Porziuncola by D'Annunzio.[1] Here for some years, in the intervals of her frequent theatrical tours, she spent a large part of the time with D'Annun-

[1] The name of St Francis' little chapel inside the church of Santa Maria degli Angeli near Assisi.

zio. From contemporary reports, we see her sitting on a stool beside him at the Capponcina while he wrote, taking from his hands the sheets with the ink still not dry, and reading them with "devoted felicity." [1] On the days when D'Annunzio refused to be disturbed even by these silent attentions, she would come up in the evening from La Porziuncola, and stand outside the door, motionless and silent, almost without breathing, listening with an enraptured expression, as the goose-quill slipped over the paper. Legends and rumors about their relationship quickly multiplied, some more picturesque than true. It was said, for instance, that every morning when they were on holiday by the Adriatic, D'Annunzio, stark naked, used to ride his sorrel into the sea, and then swim ashore to where his "friend," the great actress, would be waiting for him, holding a purple mantle to receive him. It was reported that the pair of them drank strange brews together out of a virgin's skull, by the light of the moon.

The Duse was undoubtedly intoxicated with her poet. She not only demanded nothing of him, but gave him her all, money, inspiration, companionship, advice. Her admiration for his genius, her ambition to contribute to his fame as the great dramatist of the new Italian theater, were inspiring. When she went to America in 1903, she did not take her usual repertory of well-known plays, the *Dame aux Camélias, Odette, Fernande, Nori,* which the American public knew and could follow, even in Italian. Instead, she asked them to listen to the difficult dialogue of D'Annunzio, full of weird harmonies and obscure images. The American theaters were never more than a quarter full, but she continued pouring money into the venture, determined to represent her poet abroad; and she even sent him money which the plays had not earned. She also founded a company to tour with his plays in the Italian provincial cities, where her reputation ensured them at least a hearing. And she planned a special open-air theater at Albano, to be created by his pen and her acting. It would be built on Greek

[1] In Palmerio's *Memoirs:* he was D'Annunzio's veterinary surgeon at the Capponcina.

lines, and only the highest literary art would be performed, expressing the Italian genius in a new national theater. She would act the roles she had dreamed of, and he would create them for her. Ironical remarks were made in Rome about this last form of co-operation. The Marchese Guiccioli wrote, "the new aesthetic cult of D'Annunzio idylls is to be transferred to the lake of Albano. The noble ladies and their intellectual acolytes will end by coupling like fauns and nymphs beside the lake."

At the beginning, D'Annunzio was unknown as a playwright, and the audience whistled and threw cabbages. But both he and the Duse remained unperturbed, smiling after the performance, bowing gratefully to those who applauded, however few they might be. The first performance of *Francesca da Rimini* at the Costanzi theater in Rome was a complete fiasco. The audience were infuriated, less because they could not understand the play, than because they were almost killed by it. D'Annunzio, ever in search of new stage effects, had insisted that a genuine bombardment, with catapults for the medieval siege, should be enacted; and a large stone completely demolished one of the walls of the stage. A thick, choking smoke, which a chemist friend had assured D'Annunzio would give the appearance of gunpowder fumes, blinded and asphyxiated the spectators, who left the theater, not hissing, but howling. It is said to have been a night unique in the annals of the theater.

The early period of their friendship coincided with the writing of a play, *La Città Morta,* based on D'Annunzio's earlier Greek trip. It is a kind of ancient Greek tragedy set in the nineteenth century, concerned with incest and murder in the ruins of Mycenae. Only to read a few pages of this play is to be overcome with a vague sense of malady which becomes more and more oppressive. A brother, who adores and worships his sister as something almost sacred, is suddenly shaken with a hideous passion to mix his blood with hers. However much he fights against the temptation, he fails until, because of some nervous psychological aberration, he murders her.

This play fascinated the Duse, who longed to act the murdered and violated sister. Unfortunately, D'Annunzio had planned this play some time before for Sarah Bernhardt. He had always believed in going to the fountainhead of power. He hoped the French actress would accept it for Paris, and thus introduce him to the most important and critical theater public in Europe. This rivalry played an important part in persuading the Duse to attempt a Paris "season."

Until now, she had avoided the French stage, believing that Sarah Bernhardt was in an unassailable position.[1] The Duse had always operated in easier international atmospheres, America, Germany, the Balkans. In Italy, she was undisputed queen. But her manager, Schurmann, was anxious to make an assault on Paris and dislodge the aging Bernhardt, before she crumbled on her own. D'Annunzio supported Schurmann's theory, that the Duse might well supplant the French actress, who was fifteen years older. The Duse replied that she would do so if he would write a play for her, which she could use in her opening program in Paris. D'Annunzio agreed, and he produced in a remarkably short time, not *La Città Morta* (which he wanted to keep for Bernhardt, if the Duse failed), but the new *Sogno di un Mattino di Primavera*. The problem was to interest the Parisian audience in Italian drama, for to most of them, Italian theater was no more than a series of Sicilian puppet shows, or Punch and Judy boxes in the gardens of the provincial towns. Moreover, the French were well provided with their own playwrights.

Il Sogno di un Mattino di Primavera was the first play ever written specially for the Duse, and she was delighted that its author was, she considered, the greatest living Italian writer. Schurmann, her manager, has described the state almost of inebriation, which possessed her when she received the manuscript. She rushed into his room waving it.

"It's here!" she cried ecstatically.

[1] The problem of the French stage is also very well described in Miss B. Harding's account of the Duse in France: *Age cannot Wither*.

"What do you mean?" he said. "What's here?"

"D'Annunzio's play, of course! The one he has written specially for me."

"You have read it, I trust?" said the skeptical impresario.

"Not yet," she replied. "But it's bound to be a masterpiece."

The following day she left for Paris with the play in her case, determined that it should establish her name, as well as its author's, in the first theatrical city of the world. She read it on the way, and discovered that it centered round the story of a mad woman, a kind of Ophelia, a character she had always felt well suited for her particular genius. The other plays selected for her programme in Paris were the well-known *La Femme de Claude*, *Magda*, *Cavalleria Rusticana*, *La Locandiera* and *La Dame aux Camélias*.

Sarah Bernhardt was astonished at the effrontery of the Duse in trying to defeat her on her own ground, in roles which the French actress considered her own. If the Italian actress wanted to study foreign roles, why did she not select writers other than Dumas and Sudermann, whom the Bernhardt considered her own preserve? The Duse's program seemed a piece of studied provocation. Meanwhile, eminent French critics said that by acting *La Dame aux Camélias*, the Duse would destroy herself, for no one could act this like Sarah Bernhardt. They even contended that the wily Bernhardt had urged the Italian with clever compliments to attempt it. Other journalists gave publicity to the fact that here, at last, after many inconclusive skirmishes in other countries, the two greatest actresses in the world were to meet in the same arena, at the Renaissance theater in Paris.

The audience for the first night contained most of the Parisian theatrical and artistic world, with a sprinkling of *monde*. The well-known critic, Sarcey, who could make or mar the success of a play, was there. Around him were a number of smaller critics, anxious to watch his reactions (for it was fatal to be caught praising a play which Sarcey condemned). Miss Harding, who has clearly had the report from eyewitnesses, says that Sarah Bernhardt, who had come to watch her rival, sat in her special box, through which a steady stream of visitors filed before the curtain went up, greeted by the rippling laughter for which the great Jewish actress was famous; then sent on their way with a tap of her diamond-covered fingers. At last, the bowing and hand-kissing stopped, the admirers left for their seats, the Bernhardt turned to face the stage. The hum of conversation died, and from the stage came the three measured knocks, the signal for the curtain to rise on *La Dame aux Camélias,* with Eleonora Duse in the title role.

It was at this point, when everyone was looking at the stage, that Sarah Bernhardt moved. All she did was to bend forward, quietly but visibly, resting her elbow on the velvet cushion of the balustrade, cupping her little chin in her open palm—in a posture of rapt attention. But to attain this position, she had to clear her throat, and at the same time she closed her great ostrich-plumed fan with a snap. Immediately, a sea of white faces veered up in her direction, forgetting for a moment the rising curtain and the actress behind it. . . .

La Dame aux Camélias that night was not a success. The great Sarcey said the next morning: "Eleonora Duse did not strike me in any way as remarkable. Her gesticulations are more expressive than varied. She keeps her eyes lowered and frequently repeats certain mannerisms, such as passing her hand over her brow . . . either from conviction, or because she is incapable of grasping the dramatist's intention. The Duse's courtesan is a pathetic little soul . . . whose lover might be ruined by keeping her supplied with macaroni—a gentle being who needs to talk with Armand for only a few moments, before she loses her heart and becomes incoherent. . . . This is not the sort of woman who callously dissipates the fortunes of successive gallants—but a creature who would spend her life at the feet of the man she adored. . . ." He then made one or two extenuating compliments, but the general impression was that the French actress had won the battle.

D'Annunzio's play, *Il Sogno di un Mattino di Primavera,* was no more successful in the Duse's hands. The speed with which he had composed it revealed its structural defects, and the politest remark about it in the French press was, *"un experiment italien."* D'Annunzio always displayed an Olympian indifference to critics, favorable or unfavorable, and on reading the notices he tore them up. But he had judged the degree of the Duse's failure in Paris, and was determined that his most important play, *La Città Morta,* should not fall into her hands. He accordingly began negotiations for a French translation, which he later sent to Sarah Bernhardt. To his delight she accepted, sending him this typical telegram, *"Admirable! Admirable! Admirable! Admirable! Admirable! De tout mon coeur reconnaissant. Sarah Bernhardt."* She may have calculated that this would be a further setback for the Duse, who was already known as D'Annunzio's mistress; she may even have liked the play. Actresses regard plays in a special way, as vehicles for their own performance, and the incest female lead may have attracted her. Its unusual quality, as in all D'Annunzio's plays, lies in its ornate language. Here again, the French actress may have been attracted by new demands on her voice. But she did not remain enthusiastic for long. The play was a failure in Paris; only her reputation saved it from complete disaster. Its French title, *La Ville Morte,* was dubbed by the critics, *La Ville à mourir.* D'Annunzio abandoned France, for the time being, and returned to make some alterations in the Italian version of *La Città Morta,* with a view to handing it over to the Duse, who was still anxious to play in it in Italy.

The last word on the Duse's Parisian début must belong to the Bernhardt; it reveals as much of the French as of the Italian actress. In her memoirs, the Bernhardt says, "the Duse was nothing more than a brilliant mimic, she could not associate her name with a dramatic character and *make it entirely her own* . . . she planted flowers where others planted trees, she put on gloves, but put them on inside out. . . ." Actresses are probably unkinder about one another even than writers are about their colleagues.

The relations between the Duse and D'Annunzio during this collaboration, and while they were forming plans for a new Italian theater at Albano, are best known through D'Annunzio's semi-autobiographical novel, *Il Fuoco*. He was so accustomed to writing novels about his own love affairs, that it was only a question of time before the Duse became one of his heroines. When the subject of *Il Fuoco* became known, there was a great stir in Italian literary circles. Friends, publishers, editors and *quid-nuncs* of all kinds became immensely excited. D'Annunzio was always skilful with his publicity, and by refusing to allow certain friends to see the manuscript, he increased the general interest.

The only person who was not attracted by the idea of this novel was Schurmann, the Duse's manager. He obtained a proof copy from the publisher, and realized how much it would damage his client's reputation. The heroine, Foscarina, is depicted not only as a kind of sexual Gorgon, but many years older than the hero. The differences in their ages was, in fact, six years; but D'Annunzio has made it twenty. He gives her a sagging chin, crow's-feet and black rims round the eyes. The hero is shown with her in a gondola in Venice, not admiring the perfection of her skin, but counting its wrinkles. The theme of the novel is that this older woman has an attraction for him because of her age, and he is continually asking himself how many lovers she has had before— in particular, whether they have been able to satisfy her immense erotic capacities as efficiently as he can.

The indignant Schurmann rushed round to the Duse with the proofs of this book, and asked her to use her influence with D'Annunzio, if not to prevent it, at least to modify it. The Duse requested twenty-four hours to think this over. The following day she sent Schurmann this reply: "I had been informed about the novel you brought me, while it was being written. I know all about it, I even gave the author permission to publish it, whatever he felt impelled to say. All my sufferings, grave though they may be, count for nothing, when it is a question of adding one more masterpiece to Italian Literature. I am forty—and I am in love. . . ."

A number of rumors now circulated about the book and its heroine. It was said that the Duse had bought the manuscript from D'Annunzio, to prevent publication, with money obtained from the sale of her jewels; and that D'Annunzio had broken his word and was going ahead with the publication, having pocketed the money. Another story told of how she threw the manuscript in the fire, and D'Annunzio had to write the whole book again, at great speed, having already accepted, and dissipated, a large publisher's advance. Most of these stories are apocryphal. The Duse was, simply, a woman who believed in one thing, Beauty in Art. It was her only law, and she felt she had no right to hinder the creation of a work which such an artist as D'Annunzio was feverishly writing. Between December 1899 and February 1900, when he was working on it, she asked and obtained permission to be near him, "not only materially but also spiritually."

There was nothing Schurmann could do now but to await its publication. This took place on March 5, 1900, and was the signal for an almost international literary explosion. Within a month, the whole of Europe was in possession of the most intimate details of one of the great love affairs of the day. If its immediate effect on the Duse's reputation was doubtful, the publicity D'Annunzio gained from it was certain. Until now, his novels had been appreciated only in Italy, and by a limited number of French readers. With *Il Fuoco* he suddenly had a European, a world, reputation. Financially, too, it was his greatest success, translated into six languages, and published in America.

These three quotations give some idea of the writing, as well as of its autobiographical flavor:

" '. . . to have believed in the great strength of your genius since its dawn," [says the heroine to the young hero,] "never to have taken eyes off you during your climb to success, which I accompanied with vows as sincere as my morning and evening prayers. Silently, fervently, to have encouraged my own spirit in its search for beauty and harmony, and so to render it more worthy of approaching yours. How often have I, on the stage before an enthusiastic audience, pronounced one word of yours that thrilled me—so that later I think back to that moment when, through my mouth, you gave it to the world. To have worked unceasingly, trying ever to attain to an art which is simpler, more intense, aspiring ever to perfection. These were my goals. Afraid that I might not please you and be unequal to your dream. To have loved my own fame only so that it might be of service one day to yours. . . . To have made of you my heroic ideal, the symbol of all things good, strong and free. . . . Stelio! My Stelio! . . .' "

The second passage describes D'Annunzio's sensuality. Here he shows the hero in a labyrinth, getting down on all fours to identify himself with nature, becoming half-animal, half-Pan:

". . . beneath his knees he felt the dead leaves, the soft moss, and as he breathed among the branches he palpitated, excited by a new form of pleasure. Communion with the vegetable life became closer . . . he became transfigured, according to the instincts of his blood, into an ambiguous form, half-animal, half-divine, the Spirit of the Fields whose neck was swollen with the same glands that hang about the neck of a goat. He then desired a creature that resembled him, a prey to capture, a violence to accomplish. . . . At this moment Donatella with the slender haunches appeared before him . . ."

Whatever may be said about this as prose, it is a clear comment on the situation in which Eleonora Duse now found herself. Many of her friends who read the book hoped that it would at least cure her of her insane passion for D'Annunzio. But this was to remain with her forever. This woman who understood so well the meaning of the word "passion," which she had depicted so often on the stage, found herself in the grip of a more destructive passion than she had ever portrayed. Passages like the following in *Il Fuoco* intoxicated her:

". . . she had become in a flash a beautiful creature of the night, wrought on a golden anvil out of passions and dreams, a

breathing semblance of the immortal fates and of eternal enig-
mas. The sweetest, the most terrible, the most magnificent soul
inhabited her body, gave her life, shot lightning through her
eyes, breathed through her lips. . . . Thus Life and Art, the
irrevocable Past and the eternal Present, endowed her with
depth, with mystery and with a manifold soul. They magnified
beyond human limits her ambiguous destinies. They made her
the equal of temples and forests. . . ."

Il Fuoco is not really a novel at all. It is a book of poetry and a
treatise on aesthetics, seen in the story of an exceptional woman
who sacrifices herself, and in the setting of a city like Venice.
Both woman and city are treated in the same way, both autumnal.
The evocative names of Venice are used, it must be admitted,
with such poetic effect that the places and *palazzi* seem more alive
than the characters. The book, it has been said, might well replace Baedeker as a guide to Venice. The reader moves along the
canals in the lovers' gondola, less interested in their flowery conversation than in the balconies of tracery flanked by marble lions,
the slippery corners of the walls and façades of dogal buildings,
the ancient shields reflected in the glitter of the lagoons.

D'Annunzio later told Hérelle that he intended to do in this
book what Zola had attempted in his novel, *L'Oeuvre:* to analyze
what goes on in an artist's mind when he is composing. "Zola,"
he said, "failed, perhaps because he didn't observe carefully
enough what he wanted to describe, perhaps because he had insufficient knowledge of himself. I, while working, have taken many
notes on myself. I intend to do better."

The last extract, below, shows the self-confidence bordering on
peacock vanity with which D'Annunzio viewed his relations with
women. In this passage, the lovers are wandering aimlessly about
together, when they come upon the labyrinth:

" 'Have you ever been in a labyrinth?' he asked her.
" 'Never,' she replied.
"They lingered on, to admire this deceptive plaything which

an ingenious gardener had thought out for the delectation of
their ladies and their *cicisbeos* in the times of the crinoline. But
neglect and age had made it wild and melancholy and transformed it into a solid, inextricable tangle of brown and yellow
leaves.

" 'It's open,' said Stelio, feeling the gate giving under his
weight as he leaned against it. He flung open the rusty gate, and
made a step as if to go in.

" 'What are you doing?' asked his companion in instinctive
fear, and she stretched out her hand, as if to hold him back.

" 'Would you rather we didn't go in?' She felt confused. But
the mystery of the labyrinth drew them both on.

" 'And if we should lose ourselves?'

" 'But look! It's quite small. We'll easily find the way out.'

" 'But if we can't get back again?'

"He laughed at her childish fears. 'Then we'll have to keep
going round and round in there forever.'

" 'There's nobody in sight. No, no, let's go back.'

"She tried to pull him back, but he escaped with a laugh and
vanished.

" 'Stelio! Stelio!' She could not see him, but she heard his
laughter ringing from the wilderness of bushes.

" 'Come back! Come back!'

" 'Come and find me!'

" 'Stelio, come back. You'll get lost.'

"A wild fear ran through her, confusing her mind and preventing her from seeing that his action had been committed on
a passing impulse and without forethought. The terror which
hid at the root of her hopeless love broke out now, took possession of her and blinded her. The trivial and insignificant incident assumed for her all the appearance of deliberate cruelty
and scorn. And she still heard that laughter ringing from the
wilderness of bushes.

" 'Stelio!'

" 'Find me!' he laughed back, invisible.

"She flung herself into the thicket to find him, making towards the sound of his laughter. But the path turned aside, a
wall of bristling box rose before her and barred her way, im-

penetrable. She followed the deceitful windings, but turning followed turning, and every turn looked the same; and this going round and round seemed as if it would never end.

" 'Find me!' the voice called again in the distance.

" 'Where are you? Where are you? Can you see me?'

"She searched here and there for gaps in the hedge, so that she might be able to look round for him. She saw nothing but the inextricable barrier of branches. The box and hornbeam grew together in confusion, the evergreen leaves mingling with the fading ones, the dark green with the pale, in a juxtaposition of health and decay, in an enigmatic union which intensified still more the terror of the panting woman.

" 'I'm losing my way. Come to me!' Again his young laughter echoed through the thicket.

"Now the sound came from the opposite direction. . . . She turned back, ran on, kept going round in circles, tried to break her way through the walls of branches, pushed aside the leaves, broke off a branch. She could see nothing but the manifold and uniform maze. She listened, waiting; but she only heard her own panting and the throbbing of her veins.

" 'Stelio! Where are you?'

"There was no reply. She waited in vain. The minutes seemed like hours. 'Where are you? I'm frightened!'

"There was no reply. A mad desire to yell, to sob, to throw herself on the ground, to strike something, to hurt herself, to die, overcame her.

" 'I see you!' said the laughing voice quite unexpectedly and quite close by. With a violent start she turned and leaned towards it.

" 'Where are you?'

"He laughed among the leaves, like a sly faun without showing himself. The game excited him, his limbs glowed and rejoiced in the exercise of their agility, and the mystery of the wild wood, the contact with the earth, the smell of autumn, the strangeness of the unforeseen adventure, the agitation of his companion and the presence of the marble divinity, mingled something of antique poetry with his physical well-being.

" 'Where are you? Oh, don't trifle with me any longer! Don't laugh like that, I've had enough!'

"He had crept bareheaded on all fours into the undergrowth.
He felt under his knees the rustling leaves and the soft moss,
and while with beating heart he knelt among the branches, held
fast there by all his senses, his life seemed to grow into closer
community with that of the trees. . . . Now he longed for some
creature like himself, for a young bosom with whom he could
share his laughter, for two nimble legs, two arms willing to
wrestle, for a prey which he could seize for himself, for a virgin
to ravish. . . .

" 'Enough, Stelio! I can't stand any more. . . . I'm going to
sink into the ground!'

"Foscarina gave a cry, for she felt a hand out of the hedge
gripping the hem of her skirt. She bent down and caught a
glimpse of the face of the laughing faun in the shadow between
the leaves. He sent his laughter straight at her, but it did not
carry her away, it did not sweep away the torturing distress
which closed her in. She only suffered the more at the contrast
between his gaiety and her dejection, between his ever-renewed
joy and her inescapable unrest, between his facility in forgetting
and her burdensome scruples. . . ."

The incident continues like this for another three pages, a kind
of hide-and-seek in a maze, until the unfortunate woman is res-
cued by one of the keepers, "her face white and staring, her eyes
startled, her lips compressed. . . ." Stelio takes her home, and she
"lies stretched out on the floor of the carriage, her cloak covering
her to the chin, while at intervals convulsive shudders ran through
her. He took her hands and held them in his, trying to warm
them; in vain, she remained motionless, she seemed deprived of
life."

The way in which D'Annunzio treated the Duse at the end of
their relationship is revealed by many people who came to the
Capponcina. Tom Antongini relates that one afternoon, before he
was engaged as D'Annunzio's secretary, he had come for an interview. When it was over, he said good-bye to the poet and went
back into the hall, to wait for the carriage that was to take him

back to Florence. He was smoking a cigarette, when he heard a sound of footsteps in an adjoining room. He turned and saw, outlined by the light behind, a slender and completely naked young woman. Before he could recover from his surprise, she had hid her face with her arm, in a gracious and cautious gesture which, though it could not conceal her charms or confusion, was enough to preserve her incognito. It was not the Duse.

In the course of the next twenty years as D'Annunzio's secretary, Antongini was to become less and less surprised at such visions. He says that the explanation of many strange events in D'Annunzio's life, his unexpected decisions, sudden renunciations and improvised journeys, can be explained by this. D'Annunzio was a sexual maniac whose life, work and every action could be tracted at some stage to the influence of a woman, and always a new woman.

The exceptionally cruel, even anatomical, manner in which he views women is well described in the following passage, where he depicts a girl sleeping on the beach:

"There was a clear harmony between her breathing and the movement of the sea—giving a further charm to the sleeping girl. She was lying on her right side, and her long, supple body had a serpentine elegance. The sleekness of her lips made her look like an adolescent youth. The yet unproductive belly still had its primitive virginal purity. The breasts were small and firm, as if sculptured in delicate alabaster, a violet-colored rose at the ends which were extraordinarily erectile. All the back part of her body from the neck to the knee made one think of a Grecian *ephebe*— one of those fragments of the ideal human type, which nature sometimes throws among the quantities of mediocre imprints by which she perpetuates the race. But the most precious thing about her was, to George, the coloring—the flesh had an indescribable color, very rare, very different from the ordinary color of brunettes. To compare it with alabaster gilded by an interior flame would not give an idea of its divine subtlety. It seemed as if a diffused impalpable gold and amber enriched the tissue of the body, speckling them in varied marbles, with the harmony of music; darker in the channel of the loins, lighter on the breast and the groins, where the skin has its most exquisite suavity. . . ."

His behavior to the Duse over the play, *La Figlia di Jorio*, showed how he treated women when they were no longer of use to him. This play, perhaps his best, was written expressly for the Duse in the title role. It is a moving drama of peasant life, based on an experience he and his painter friend, Michetti, had had years before in a small Abruzzi village, Tocco Casauria. Here they came by chance in the *piazza* on a disheveled woman being chased by a mob of drunken reapers, intoxicated with the sun, wine and carnal desire. The painter immediately depicted this and it was on seeing Michetti's painting some years later, that D'Annunzio decided to write the play. At the height of the excitement over its production in Milan, an announcement was made that the leading part would be played, not by the Duse, but by Emma Gramatica. Everyone had understood that the play, not only the part, had been written expressly for the Duse; and the official explanation—that the Duse was suddenly ill with her old complaint, tuberculosis, in a Genoese hotel—was not believed. The illness, it was said, was "diplomatic." D'Annunzio wished to give the part to another woman, presumably a new mistress.

Matilde Serao, a friend of the Duse, describes how she visited the Duse in the Genoese hotel, and found her really ill in bed with a recurrence of her old complaint, but suffering from a greater mental complaint owing to D'Annunzio's behavior.

" 'The play is mine! Not that woman's!' she cried, and she pulled a copy of *La Figlia di Jorio* from under her pillow. Then, raising herself on the cushions, she began to read aloud the part of Mila di Codra, which he had written for her. Her voice became hoarse with emotion, her face changed color, she recited as if she had been on the stage, in front of a thousand spectators. I tried to stop her, for she had a high fever and was coughing blood. 'No! No! Let me go on!' she cried. 'It is good for me. It cures me to read these lines.' She took up the thick

manuscript and began from the beginning, half in the bed, half
out. She read not only *her* part, but the whole play, acting, de-
claiming, sometimes in half-tones and whispers—just as D'Annunzio had envisaged it—giving to each part its character, to
each voice its expression. I sat back spellbound at hearing not
one voice, but all the voices of the pastoral drama. I seemed to
see all the scenes. I was in the house of Lazaro di Roio, at the
leave-taking on the mountain, beneath the big tree. All the characters appeared, from Candia della Leonessa to the blonde Vi-
enda, from the Saint of the Mountains to Ornella, all created,
interpreted, by the one voice and person of Eleonora Duse! On a
sick bed, in the room of a Genoese hotel! She was wearing a
long nightdress with broad sleeves closed at the wrists, and
sometimes she actually stood on the bed. Once, when I tried to
push her back, she obeyed and got under the sheets. But then
rising, with a stronger arm than mine, she pushed me away
again. She went through the entire play, and finished on the
famous words at the end, where the heroine is being led to the
stake, 'The flame is beautiful! The flame is beautiful!' Physically
exhausted but mentally, it seemed, cured, she fell back on the
bed. I kissed her, for I was now in tears.

"In this way," says Matilde Serao, "I saw the first performance of *La Figlia di Jorio*. It was acted for me alone. By the
Duse. The second performance took place a week later, at Milan,
with Emma Gramatica in the part of Mila di Codra."

D'Annunzio wrote characteristically of this play he had written
for the Duse, and given to another, ". . . it seems to me that the
work has not been fashioned by my hands at all, but has come
from a very distant past, immemorial and national, and that I
have merely been observing a kind of vision which has surged up
from the past. The profound things which ancient hereditary blood
has displayed—I heard them in my own attentive silence. But in
expressing them, I seem to have repeated sincerely and faithfully
what was dictated to me by an immense and imperious voice. That
is why it is sweet for me to confess humbly that everything in me
which is strongest and purest belongs to the people of Abruzzi. . . .

Beauty, which is to me Art's brother, sees with its own miracu-
lous eyes. The beauty which I hear and sing in the intervals of my
rhythms is immortally mixed with the substance of the spirit. We
artists are only the astonished witnesses of eternal aspirations,
which help raise up our breed to its destiny. . . ."

Here God is speaking to Moses. A man who could take himself so seriously, easily became the target for satire; and his plays
were parodied in Rome. D'Annunzio's *La Figlia di Jorio* has this
elevated dedication: "To the Land of the Abruzzi, to my Mother,
to my Sisters, to my exiled Brother, to my buried Father, to all my
Dead, to all my People between the Mountain and the Sea—to
them, I dedicate this song of antique blood."

A parody appeared in Rome, called *The Son of Jorio,* with this
dedication: "To the land of Pipe, to my Creditors, to my friend
Mascagni, to my friend Tenneroni, to my Heroes, to my Ships,
to the Sea, to the Sky, to the Moon, to Michetti and Giuseppe
Treves, to Mahomet and Fra Jacopone, I dedicate this song of
antique blood."

D'Annunzio's novels also lend themselves to parody. One of
the great weaknesses of his prose is its servile faith in the syno-
nym. D'Annunzio clogs up his narrative with heavy descriptive
passages, under the impression, apparently, that the moment he
has compared something to something else, the passage is eternal.
Here are examples of (a) D'Annunzio's prose from the *Novella
della Pescara;* (b) from a contemporary parody.

(a) ". . . the great sandy *piazza* was shimmering as if strewn
with powdered pumice stone. All the houses around, whitened
with chalk, seemed like the great ruined walls of an immense
furnace about to be extinguished. In the background, the pillars
of the church reflected the radiation of the clouds, becoming rough
like granite; the glass windows glittered almost as if they contained the flames of some internal fire. . . ."

(b) The parody runs: ". . . through the April air spread a
smell of marine and sylvan marriages. The sparrows flew in twos
across the Adriatic, their naked sides tattooed by the salt, and the

sea looked up at them from below, frothing with light blue desires. The plants crawling up the walls began to squeeze their old surface, and as a result, being damp with dew and lichen, out from their cracks came lizards. The Pescara river lay supinely in its large bed, the water flowing, as it were, from the luminous palpitations caused by the fish which were swimming in the current. . . ."

A scurrilous "obituary" notice also appeared:

"*Gabriele D'Annunzio*. Born at Pescara. Extremely precocious. Wrote, at the age of three, *The Loves of Oedipus and Jocasta*. At twelve, was already known in all the elegant pastry shops of Rome. At thirteen, committed first adultery and bought first *objet d'art*. To cover these expenses, wrote 6 novels, 14 dramas, 3 'dreams,' 2 opera librettos, 4 volumes of lyrics, 6 volumes of Praises, 2 volumes of songs of antique blood. Although the material for these works belongs to other authors, the subject of all is the same—incestuous adultery combined with mystic sadism. Ransacked the dictionaries and photographic albums for vocabulary and imagery. Is said never to have spoken a word or made a gesture which did not exist in the best texts and pictures. An elegant provincial man. Dissolute by design. Dunned by old clothes dealers and shirt-makers, took refuge in France, and wrote a further 22 works in Old French, but always on the same theme—incestuous adultery combined with mystic sadism."

The fact that he was so widely satirized is some measure of the position he had now attained in Italy. He was becoming the best known literary, perhaps even public, figure. A comment on his power over almost all classes of Italians is given by Luigi Barzini in his study of the Italian aristocracy. "In Italy, D'Annunzio now enjoyed the sort of fame which only 'the divine Aretino' had had. Every word, image, gesture, and love affair of D'Annunzio's resounded in the lost, uncertain, and discontented souls of countless people. The young noblemen became his fervent followers and adopted his ideals, even going so far as to model themselves after his characters, to speak, write, live, and dress like him. Women of great noble families fell desperately in love with him, risked scandal and dishonor to have affairs with him. Hordes of other women adored him from a distance, dressing like the heroines in his novels and throwing themselves into decadent love affairs in the provincial towns. They forced their lovers to behave like D'Annunzio's heroes, speaking in a lyrical language composed of archaic, incomprehensible words; and they decorated their houses with rubbishy bric-à-brac, just as D'Annunzio did, and continued to do, until his death. Greyhounds and horses became fashionable. The Duke of Aosta, the King's cousin, husband of Princess Elena of France, even wrote his letters in a handwriting almost identical with that of the poet, on large sheets of hand made paper adorned by Renaissance engravings and sibylline mottoes."

It was not until 1904 that the friendship between D'Annunzio and the Duse ended, and she left the little house near the Capponcina. She probably had no presentiment of the end, for she had just returned from a theatrical tour on the French riviera, composed and invigorated, looking forward to a rest in the house on the hill of Settignano. Few women longed more for their home than did this actress who was always on tour. Her letters written before her many departures from the Porziuncola, always tell of regrets and unhappiness at leaving. It was perhaps inevitable that someone who had never had a home, born the daughter of wandering players, who had wandered and played all her life, should know such nostalgia.

But when she returned in 1904, the situation was already critical. D'Annunzio, although working hard, was increasingly pressed by creditors. Not even her attentions, which were if anything more tender, seemed to soothe him. Palmerio describes one of the many incidents which ended their relationship. One day, towards the middle of May 1904, while D'Annunzio was in Livorno, the Duse telephoned Palmerio urgently to come immediately to the Capponcina. He pressed her to say why, but she refused; he felt, from the mysterious way in which she spoke, that something serious had happened. On arriving, he found her in the music-room, lying on the sofa, with the look in her eyes of a medium who has just come out of a trance. She leapt up crying, "Palmerio, you must help me! We must set fire to this house immediately. It must be burned down!"

He asked for an explanation. "The temple," she said, "has been profaned. Flame alone can purify it. You are a good and faithful friend of Gabriele. You shall be the witness of this unhappy sacrifice. It must be. . . ."

He tried to calm her, but she became more excited. "Fire! Fire! Quickly!" she cried, and began rushing round the room with the intention, apparently, of finding a box of matches. He took her firmly by the arm. "Calm yourself, Signora! If you try to set fire to anything here, I shall call the police. Let us go outside. Perhaps the fresh air will calm your nerves."

She stared at him for some seconds, and then followed him out. When she was a little calmer, he said, "Now tell me what this is all about." The Duse, without saying a word, opened one of her hands which she had held, until now, closely shut, and revealed two small golden hairpins, such as are worn by women with blonde hair. She had found them in the "guest room."

The blonde "guest" who had been staying there was Alessandra di Rudinì; she was shortly to take the place of the Duse as D'Annunzio's mistress. Palmerio pointed out politely that fire is something which, even if it purifies, can also damage irreparably. He suggested that it would be better to wait until D'Annunzio returned, before purifying the house. There might be some explanation. He knew this was unlikely, but he succeeded in quieting her; and later she relieved her pent-up feelings in tears. Within a few hours she was perfectly calm again, and she spoke gently to D'Annunzio when he returned.

D'Annunzio's attitude to any woman he had been living with for long had been summed up in a letter to Hérelle, about an earlier mistress—words which apply equally well to the Duse, or indeed to any of his mistresses.

"I am supposed to have a bad reputation," he wrote. "People who know me only from my books imagine I am immoral, unscrupulous, capable of any crime to satisfy my desire, or even simply my curiosity. But those who know me really well are aware that I am fully aware of my responsibilities. Now, in the matter of women, my responsibility is great, I admit it. . . . Nor do I pretend that I am not the cause of her downfall. . . . That I am aware of, and *that* is why I continue to live with her. And yet, you must know, living with her for me is a hideous torment. I no longer love her. Last year, before I left for Venice, I went through hell; June, July and August were sheer torture. She was mad, with a kind of bestial jealousy. And to the jealousy was added an insatiable sexual appetite, which was really endangering my health and reason. I found my energy dissipated, my intelligence numbed. Sometimes I felt that the best thing that could happen to me was to have a stroke. . . . I have work to do. I carry in myself, I know, something important. And it would be cowardly and selfish to abandon it to secondary considerations. To accomplish my work and destiny, I am ready to dare everything, to suffer everything. And one of the hardest, but most necessary, things I must do is to get away from women. But I don't see how I can, or even when I can. I simply await my deliverance, by some stroke of luck of which I have not the least notion." [1]

The Duse, determined not to be dismissed openly in favor of another woman, took her leave without bitterness. This leave-taking is described by D'Annunzio's daughter, Renata, in her memoirs, written many years later. She was a small girl, and happened to be staying at the Capponcina on holidays from school. "I remember my father having to go away for three days, and during that time I slept in the room of Eleonora Duse. One night I heard her crying desperately in bed. She was sobbing. I wanted to go to her, but an inexplicable timidity kept me back. . . . My father returned, gay, young, exuberant. But the Signora Duse only became paler and more sad. It made me suffer too. I used to

[1] This was the Principessa di Gravina, an early mistress.

leave the house and go for long walks with the dogs. On my return from one of these walks, she was no longer there. 'She has left us and will never come back,' said my father placidly, unaware that I was suffering too on her account.

"A few days later he took me to see the Duse, who was staying in a Florentine *pensione*. Timidly, I entreated her to come back to the Capponcina. 'It is impossible,' she said firmly. And I shall never forget the look of anguish on her face. I never saw her again."

When it was all over, years later, the Duse displayed her magnanimity and comprehension of the poet who had left her. She wrote this comforting letter to a friend, the singer, Emma Calve, who had also been abandoned by an artist she loved. ". . . whoever possesses a voice which is unique in the world, composed of all the colors of the rainbow, as pure as a mountain stream, has no right to complain. What presumption and pride to suppose that a mind and heart of *his* kind can belong to one for all one's life! Such a thing would be to chain the liberty of a human being! To become his kindest, his best friend, that is the only kind of vengeance which a woman he loved can have. So, my poor girl, come to me when you are in too much torment. I know your suffering. Two of us can bear it more easily. . . ."

To another friend she wrote much later, in her characteristic hyphenated style: "Who listens in the morning to the bells of dawn—it is the one with insomnia—all night as I lie with my eyes open, and dawn seems never to come to deliver me from my obsession—I know what it is to be a prima donna—poison—and being an apostle too is . . . futility! And He, the Genius for whom we all live—what need has He of us?—He who possesses the gift of Beauty in his Art—while of Truth we possess but one sole Truth—in another five, another ten, years His work will be known, and by 'the mob' too—— But you, poor Duse, then you will be no more than a blade of grass. . . ."

10

Nationalism in the Theater

D'Annunzio's love of the classical world has been seen in his trip to Greece, and in the *Laudi,* which are his poetic vision of Mediterranean grandeur. Nearly all the plays he wrote express this view, based on a revival of classical tragedy, but treated in the twentieth century manner. In the preface to *Più che l'amore* he says, "I recognize the truth and purity of my modern art, which moves with its inimitable step, with its own movement, belonging essentially to it and to it alone, but always on a road studded with the monuments of the 'Father Poets.' " The Father Poets are the Greek tragedians, and his plays, *Fedra,* and *La Città Morta,* are actually set in Greece. Others, like *La Gloria,* are constructed round themes which have been taken from ancient Rome, to express his idea of Italian greatness. He looked on these plays as classical. But there are important differences between classical and Dannunzian drama.

Classical tragedy aims, according to the Greeks, to excite terror and pity in the spectator, through the *peripetia,* which show the characters struggling with their destiny, and the results of their passions. This, D'Annunzio indeed does. Fear and horror are there perpetually. But—again according to the Greeks—their expression must be discreet. Only the passions of the characters are in rivalry; motion, their gestures, movements, the concrete happenings of their lives, must not be shown on the stage. The European followers of the Greeks, the great French tragedians, observed this faithfully. Corneille is most careful not to show the duel between Rodrigo and the Count on the stage, so as not to distract the spectators' attention by the rattling of swords, nor to offend them with the view of a corpse. Racine, instead of bringing onto the stage a blood-stained Hippolyte, freshly killed, informs us how he died, through Théramène's famous speech.

But D'Annunzio, in spite of the long abstract ruminations of his characters, is always introducing concrete happenings onto the stage. In *La Figlia di Jorio,* Lazaro di Roio is killed by a blow from the axe of his son, Aligi. At the end of *La Nave,* Basiliola refuses the unpleasant death suggested to her, of being nailed to the prow of a ship; she prefers instead death at the altar, to which she is tied. In the same play, Orso Faledro and his four sons are blinded and have their tongues cut out, at the orders of Mario Gratico. The presence alone of these blind-mutes on the stage is enough to make the spectator shudder.

In *La Gioconda,* there is the hideous spectacle of Sylvia Settala's mutilated arm stumps, which are crushed while she is trying to save a statue from falling. In *Francesca da Rimini,* Malatestino brings the newly decapitated head of his enemy onto the stage, and he later has his own eye gouged out. Gigliola di Sangro, in *La Fiaccola sotto il Moggio,* places her beautiful hands into a sack of asps, and thus commits suicide before us. Even when D'Annunzio does not present these concrete happenings, he hints at them in speeches which are intended to be so horrifying, that they are sometimes ludicrous. Fedra in the scene with Ippolito cries, ". . . here, between the shoulder blade and the throat strike me with your sword! Cleave me with all your force to the waist—so that you may find my naked heart all trembling, all burning for you. . . ." To avoid bathos here, tragedy must be great indeed.

But it appears, as most foreigners admit, that, at the theater, the Italians need to *see* things more than the French. They are a visual race, whereas the French are more *raisonnable;* like the Greeks, the French are content to hear about events from a messenger or eye-witness. *L'Horrible concret* is the term employed by the French to describe "action." They prefer not action, but the *reasons* for action. There is a story told of a performance of Racine's *Phèdre* in Paris, at which there must have been some

Italians in the audience. The play has arrived at the great moment in the second act when Phèdre, seeking death, tries to take Hippolyte's sword away from him, to kill herself. She cries:

> *A défaut de ton bras, prête-moi ton épée,*
> *Donne! . . .*

At this tense moment, a female spectator could not restrain her enthusiasm. *"Brava! Brava! Brava!"* she applauded, revealing her nationality. *"L'instinct italien avait emporté sur la bienséance,"* as a Frenchman said. Brought up in the Racinian tradition, the French dislike tragic gestures which seem excessive. They do not want to see Grand Guignol at the Comédie Française.

Violence, by its very nature, is unlikely to give a writer much opportunity for expressing subtlety and shades of opinion. Generally, he uses it as a culminating point towards which his action moves; as an excuse to examine his characters under stress. But in D'Annunzio's plays, violence is not a culminating point. It is the continual state in which the characters live. His particular form of tragedy is based on a primordial violent quality in human nature, which seems to have obsessed him. If in his novels, the background is one of civilized decadence, in his dramas he goes back to earlier times, to give full play to instinct rather than reason. For with all his elegance and acquired urbanity, D'Annunzio always remained the son of a semi-barbarous people. Coming into contact with the more sophisticated world of Rome, D'Annunzio had absorbed it rapidly, summarily, and with inevitable dissonances—from which come the cruder, more brutal elements in his work. Stelio Effrena in *Il Fuoco* expresses this, ". . . from far, far away came that torpid burning inside him, from his most remote origins, from a primitive bestiality, from the ancient mystery of sacred libidinous desires . . ." This "ancient mystery of sacred libidinous desires" is not just a piece of Dannunzian rhetoric. It describes perfectly D'Annunzio's native patrimony.

The notion of profanation, or taboo, which D'Annunzio had

received as an ancestral gift, belongs also to the *fin de siècle* decadence he had found in Rome—just as that cruelty in love which
the French use as a stimulus to languor belongs quite naturally to
the Abruzzesi. For both the extremely civilized and the extremely
barbarous are cruel, the second by instinct, the first by a kind of
mental erethism. The lack of humanity in so much of D'Annunzio's work derives from this, that he was at once a barbarian and a
decadent. The intermediate area which most people possess, called
loosely "humanity," was lacking in him. This explains, too, why
he was later to prove himself a warrior. Most people expect a
voluptuary, an intellectual and a decadent, to be a poor soldier,
with unreliable nerves. This was far from the case with D'Annunzio.

A glance at the settings of D'Annunzio's plays, in time and
place, shows that he deliberately preferred primitive and barbarous
civilizations. *Fedra* is an evocation of legendary Greece, heroic
and Homeric. *La Nave* shows the Venetians at the beginning of
the second millennium, when they were waking to their new
maritime power. *Francesca da Rimini* is set at the moment when
medieval barbarism gives way to Renaissance civilization, and
there were sanguinary internecine struggles between Guelphs and
Ghibellines. Even when D'Annunzio takes a religious theme, as in
Le Martyre de Saint Sebastien, it is incipient Christianity at its
most primitive he portrays. In the character of Saint Sebastian, he
does not show the divine serenity of the believer who, through all
his tortures, sees always ahead Salvation. He shows a masochist
saint with a crude, atrocious desire to see his own blood, who cries
out to the archers, "Oh archers, if ever you loved, let your love
be known through your steel. I pray you, I beg of you—he who
wounds me most deeply, that man loves me most deeply." As the
arrows penetrate his body, the saint cries, "More! More!" and the
archers bend their bows in a kind of savage desperation.

The theme of blood always obsessed D'Annunzio. In *Il Sogno di
un Mattino di Primavera,* the heroine has seen her lover die in her

arms, and "the vision of his blood had remained always in her mind." When much later a lady-bird alights on her hand in the garden, she thinks immediately of blood and her murdered lover. She can talk of nothing else. "Blood is all over me. I am covered with it. Look, see, my hands, my arms, my chest, my hair . . . I am suffocated with his blood . . ." The author's vision from the start is of a mad woman, despairingly tied to the bloody, nude body of her lover.

The action of *La Gloria* takes place in Rome during a time of popular revolution, of civil fever and drunkenness, when all restraints of rights have been abolished. This play was thought to have been in part inspired by the Italian statesman Francesco Crispi, the Founder of the Triple Alliance. But Ruggero Flamma, the hero, was more likely simply a mouthpiece for D'Annunzio, from which to attack the corruption in modern Italian politics which, he maintained, could be overcome only by revolution. He ingeniously let it be known to a reporter, however, that Flamma was meant to be Crispi (and he then openly denied it), and the theater was filled.

When D'Annunzio was working on these plays, he became almost savage himself. He confesses how he worked,[1] ". . . always something carnal akin to carnal violence, a mixture of ferocity and drunkenness accompanies the act of generation in my brain. . . . When the sparks fly from me, I feel the thick stuff of which I am made. My whole being is in commotion, aroused, to the extent that there is no wild heartbeat or instinct which does not seem to rise from the depths within me. . . ." And there is no doubt that his play, *La Gioconda*, about a sculptor, is autobiographical, when the artist cries in fury, "Goodness! Goodness! Do you think that light and life are likely to come to me out of goodness? And not from that profound instinct which moves and precipitates my spirit towards the most superb apparitions of life? I was born to carve statues. When a form has come from my hands with the imprint of beauty on it, the office designated to me by nature has

[1] Article in the *Corriere della Sera*, August 20, 1911.

been fulfilled. I am no longer under law, I am beyond Good and Evil." Here was the direct statement of Nietzsche's superman.

D'Annunzio's theater then is based on brutal and savage forces, uncontrollable instincts and irrational impulses. He deliberately chose barbaric periods of history when, in the general civil, social and moral disorder, with the absence of a proper legal system, men behave like savages. For savages are not subject to moral restrictions; they recognize no control of their behavior save greater force. Their actions are anti-social, egotistic, without piety, without any notion of defense of the weak, or of chivalrous love. Conquest, rapacious desire for women, possession, domination—these are the subjects and feelings D'Annunzio plays upon in his dramas. He seems, in these plays, to be preparing himself for the events between 1914 and 1919, in which he played a prominent part; as well as for those between 1923 and 1943, of which he was the false prophet.

The *Gran Signore*

The house where D'Annunzio wrote most of his plays, and where he lived with the Duse next door, was called the Capponcina. It was an old country villa which had once belonged to the de Capponi family, about two miles outside Florence, not far above the Ponte a Mensola, halfway up the green hill of Settignano. It has leafy battlements, massive walls, and there is something conventual about it. D'Annunzio said that he came here because he wanted to get away from the noise of the city, to be on high ground, hidden among foliage. He selected Florence for a reason which would hardly mean anything there today—because "great art can only be produced where great art has been." He had rented La Capponcina furnished, but he offered the surprised owner a higher rent—to take away his furniture and leave it empty. A host of workmen and craftsmen then appeared; smiths, carpenters, bricklayers, stonemasons, glaziers, floorlayers and decorators. Among these men D'Annunzio moved, altering, arranging, creating, ever fertile with new ideas. He immediately set about transforming the house, so that it would be suitable for this art, in the style we now call Dannunzian.

The walls were painted in various shades of gold, the shade depending on the room, whether for study, music, meditation, repose or physical exercise. The windows had delicate stained glass from the late fifteenth century, or small round panes, thick, uniform and yellow like alabaster, through which a cathedral light seemed to filter. In the center of each glass was a bigger circle with a lighter background, on which was written in red, *Per non dormire,* encircled with branches of laurel leaves. This motto,

D'Annunzio's favorite, was repeated all over the house; on the architraves, friezes, majolica vases, on the woodwork, even printed on the great pieces of vellum on which he wrote his plays.

The Dannunzian style may best be described by saying that every object must be decorated with another object. On a chest will be a bust; on the bust, a jewel; on the jewel, a flower. On a table will be a piece of old velvet; on the old velvet, an embroidered stole; on the stole, a coat of arms; on the coat of arms, a glass cup; in the glass cup, an hourglass; in the hourglass, some grains of incense. It is like D'Annunzio's prose style, in which each noun is decorated with a number of adjectives which are, in turn, decorated with adverbs. Damasks, velvets, cushions, jewel-cases, plates, vases, engravings, plaster-moulds, tapers and bronzes tumbled over one another. In one fourteenth-century marble recess was a sixteenth-century gilded iron screen, and behind it a thirteenth-century triptych. In the drawing-room, stood two mummy's feet behind a crystal urn, a lectern, a missal and a convent bell, while above them was a stucco skull with some large marble gaming dice beside it, with a reproduction of the Delphic charioteer. The entry of the library was marked *clausura,* and of the study, *silentium.* Here hung the death mask of Richard Wagner, the profile of Sigismond Malatesta, and huge photographs of the greatest pieces of classical sculpture in the world. On a shelf at one end was a bust of Dante (who had produced the other long Italian poem).

Here D'Annunzio lived for ten years, with twenty servants, thirty greyhounds, two fox terriers, one spaniel and more than two hundred pigeons, spending at least ten times more than he was earning. We see him at the height of this Capponcina period, as the *Gran Signore,* dressed in elegant pajamas, seated in front of a roaring fire, in a beautiful room full of statues, bibelots and richly bound books, into whose presence a creditor is being ushered by a black-coated butler.

D'Annunzio could stand great heat, and he had this house heated for all but two months of the summer. He did this for a most ingenious reason—to protect himself from creditors and importunate callers! When he knew that a difficult guest was coming, he would order the big stove to be fully lighted in the drawing-room, and he would then retire to his own room. The unwelcome guest would spend twenty minutes in the drawing-room, waiting for D'Annunzio, until the sweat was streaming down his face. When D'Annunzio came in, he apparently found the temperature quite bearable and he talked affably. But the guest, after attempting for five minutes to stutter out his grievance or homage, could stand it no longer and left.

D'Annunzio also had a servant, Rocco Pesce, who was skilled in protecting his master from such visitors. He was an Abruzzese too, and he kept visitors away by the simple device of speaking Abruzzese with foreigners, and French of his own fabrication with Italians.

"*Voulez-vous bien m'annoncer à M. D'Annunzio?*" a guest would ask.

"*O signurine sta durmenne . . .*"

"*Que dites-vous? Je ne comprends pas.*"

"*O signurine riposa. Nun ce penza, nun pozze . . . e in vere, crideme . . .*"

When the unfortunate visitor left in despair, Rocco Pesce would say, "*E christe, e nato ca se ne va!*"

D'Annunzio treated importunate letter writers in much the same way. Hundreds of letters now arrived daily (for he was the best known writer in Italy), asking for interviews and reviews, or simply conveying admiration. He was particularly annoyed by those with *urgente* written on them. Rocco Pesce, when he was a newcomer, would bring them in excitedly, "But look, *signore!* It is *urgente!*"

"I'm sure it's urgent for whoever sent it," D'Annunzio would say, "but not for the person who receives it"; and he would throw it away.

He had also added a sports section to the Capponcina, to cultivate his physical as well as his mental side, with fencing and dumbbell exercises, its walls decorated with swords, sabers, bows and arrows. He considered that sport was essential to his work. "I could never have produced my plays," he told a friend one day, pointing to the dumbbells, "had I not hoisted those things every morning." To this friend, Hans Barth, he described a typical day in his life at the Capponcina. ". . . It is quite untrue that I am a Sardanapalus," he said, "I get up at seven o'clock, take a bath, do my gymnastics, fencing, a gallop on my horse. I go in for exercise. Not until ten o'clock, do I sit down to my table. And I don't budget from it till nine in the evening. I eat at my writing-table. In writing, I follow my inspiration. If I feel like it, I jump on a horse and off I go to the hills, without any plan, wherever the spirit leads me. Before settling down to work, I think about it for some time. Only when an idea has become my lifeblood, can it lead to good work. I never sit down at the table, unless I know I can work for ten hours at a stretch. When I write, a sort of magnetical force takes hold of me, like an epileptic, as if some mystery is going on in my brain. I wrote *L'Innocente* in three and a half weeks in an Abruzzese convent. A peasant brought me food, bread, eggs, fruit. If anyone had disturbed me, I should have shot him. . . . When I have finished a novel or play, I allow myself every form of relaxation. I forget my work to the point of not recognizing it. For example, I can now remember nothing of *La Nave*. It is as if someone else had written it. . . . During the day, after a rest, I allow my body to live on its own, abandoning itself to its ardor, its violence. Above all, I do not allow myself to think of the work I am preparing, so as to leave the brain at rest and receive impressions during the night, *when the Gods descend* [sic]. . . . All I need are 20,000 sheets of my special paper made for me by Miliano di Fabriano, plenty of ink, the sight of 500 quills which have been specially collected for me from geese stripped alive. All this gives me an extraordinary desire to write. As I have a very heavy hand, I put a lot of force into the act of writing, and no steel pen could stand up to it. But the quill of a goose is flexible. I have used as many as 20 or 30 a day. . . ."

He also claimed to have learned the art of writing from a Japanese, standing upright, with the pen held away an arm's length from the desk, not using the support of the elbow. A salamander used to sit on his work table, because he was superstitious. Indeed the salamander, personification of Fire, had a special cult in his workroom, and he even had an altar to it. He suffered greatly from the cold, and he could not work unless he was in a specially heated room. For this reason, he looked on Flame as a necessary companion to his work, and he had the tag "and what would I want it for, unless it burn?" placed above the fireplace.

The Capponcina, like all D'Annunzio's dwellings, possessed the personal imprint which he was able to give even to a hotel bedroom he was temporarily inhabiting. But these places never had anything intimate about them. None of his houses was what the English mean by a "home." There was no favorite corner, where the poet liked to sit, nor among all the *objets d'art* any photograph or painting of a friend or relation; nor the familiar things to be found in most houses, rich or poor, a clock, a calendar, a barometer inherited from a grandfather.

It was during the Capponcina period that D'Annunzio began contracting his big debts. He was earning large sums from his novels and plays, but he had no idea of how to handle money, and when he received a sum from a publisher or manager, his chief concern was where to put it. Sometimes he would put it in a trunk, or between the pages of a book, or even underneath the pedestal of a statue. He often forgot these hiding places. He had no notion of modern banking methods. On being told by his secretary that a current account was "an amount deposited in a bank, against which sums could be withdrawn as required," D'Annunzio said, "Well then, if it is to be withdrawn, wouldn't it be more sensible not to put it in?" His secretary explained that the bank paid interest on such "current accounts." Whereupon D'Annunzio roared with laughter and said, "How do you expect the bank to pay interest, if the money can be withdrawn at will?"

In spite of this, he was persuaded to open a banking account, and was even given a check book. After learning how to use it, he went round with it for days, as happy as a child with a new toy. But within two weeks, he had signed all the checks, and withdrawn the entire sum. After that, he kept clear of "current accounts," regarding them as a doubtful joke.

This childish side, which contrasted with his otherwise sophisticated behavior, revealed itself in many delightful ways. He never understood, for instance, railway timetables. The mere thought of arranging a journey filled him with grandmotherly fear. His secretary, Antongini, says that he used to have conversations of the following kind with D'Annunzio, when there was question of a railway journey.

"D'Annunzio: I have decided that I must go to Brussels. How can it be arranged?

Secretary: One tells the hotel porter to book seats, and the train leaves at 8:32 P.M.

D'Annunzio: How do you know?

Secretary: I know because everyone knows. In the timetable.

D'Annunzio: But how can one be sure? And then . . . you know . . . the time table . . . ?

Secretary: But of course you can be sure! It's the same train the Marchese Origo took only three days ago for Brussels.

D'Annunzio: But then . . . where are we going to stay in Brussels?

Secretary: We shall telephone from here to a hotel before leaving, and book rooms.

D'Annunzio [roaring with laughter]: Telephone! But you're mad! To Brussels? It's impossible.

Secretary: But of course! It's the easiest thing in the world.

D'Annunzio: That's what *you* say!

Secretary: I say it because everyone knows it. [Pause].

D'Annunzio [at length]: Huh! we'll think about it then. After all, it's not urgent. We'll arrange it some other time.

And so, says Antongini, the projected journey would be shelved, forever, as it was on several occasions to England, America, the Middle East. . . .

It was with the arrival of Alessandra di Rudinì, who replaced the Duse in his affections, that D'Annunzio's already crumbling financial edifice received its final blow. This aristocratic lady had none of the Duse's peasant sense of economy; nor was she concerned with the quietness and tranquillity necessary for a writer's work. A woman of great beauty, tall, vigorous, full of passion, she had fallen in love with D'Annunzio suddenly, tempestuously, after cordially hating him for years. She was the most masculine of his loves, a foot taller, wearing a gentleman's riding-habit and top boots. She also cracked her riding whip like a huntsman, to the great scandal of the more modestly skirted female riders. She was a morphinomaniac.

Life with her, a Marchesa in her own right and the daughter of a cabinet minister, demanded a more rigorous etiquette than had life with the Duse. Mario, D'Annunzio's eldest son, describes them in the house D'Annunzio took at Marina Pisa. "We would sit down to lunch at two o'clock. Even though we had been bathing before, everyone had to be now correctly dressed, because the Marchesa was a stickler for etiquette. The liveried servants were on duty in the dining room, and when they had served us, they assumed military positions, snapping their heels together in a sort of position of attention, at opposite ends of the room. They had been instructed by the Marchesa, who was the sister-in-law of an ambassador [sic], and who not only claimed to know about these things—but who really knew about them."

To D'Annunzio, love was no more than a long novel, always to be continued, with further pages to write, necessary as material for his work. He and the Marchesa did not, his secretary says, *spend* money; they threw it away. Orders and counter-orders for the Rudinì's riding clothes and horses followed one another with no regard for expenses. The number of servants in house and stable quadrupled. The Rudinì had special riding habits made for her in Paris, at £80 each. When the secretary pointed out that this was an unnecessary extravagance, in view of D'Annunzio's debts, she said she had frequently worn more expensive clothes. D'Annunzio's daughter by an earlier mistress, the Gravina, was sent to the most aristocratic school for young ladies, the *Istituto della Santissima Annunciata* at the Poggio Imperiale. D'Annunzio himself behaved in a luxurious, even effeminate manner, bathing, redressing and spraying himself with scent two or three times a day. He used, it was said, on an average, a pint of *eau de Coty* a day; and a bottle of scent lasted him only four or five days. *Mousse de Diane, Chypre, Borgia,* and *Toute la Forêt* were the titles of some of the scents he had mixed for himself. He had a hundred suits. Only the Chevalier d'Orsay is said to have spent more than D'Annunzio at the height of his extravagance with Alessandra di Rudinì. Rumor had it that their horses slept on Persian rugs.

Alessandra di Rudinì had Russian blood in her veins; and so it is not surprising that one day, at the age of 34, she suddenly left home, horses, dogs and man, and became a nun.

When warned about his debts by his secretary, D'Annunzio adopted a fatalistic attitude worthy of a Moslem. "Never fear! Be patient. All will pass," he said. ("As if," writes the secretary indignantly, "the debts were *mine,* not his!") For after two years with Alessandra di Rudinì, the Capponcina had become a sort of Mecca for creditors. Every day, they labored up the hill from Florence; and the secretary became an expert in using delaying tactics with them. Sometimes D'Annunzio, coming down from his Olympian height of art and love, would have a suggestion to make. Once, he told the secretary to pay a debt with two lire which he had put on the top of the wardrobe. When the secretary looked, he found several hundred lire which had been lying there for months.

Instead of writing books, D'Annunzio engaged in frivolous pastimes, such as inventing scents which he believed could be a commercial proposition. Like Balzac, he suffered from the hallucination that he could make money in business to relieve his literary debts. He wrote to a friend, "I hope that next year *Acqua Nunzia* will permit me to write poems and tragedies for my own personal pleasure." *Acqua Nunzia* was a scent he had invented.

He contended that it would revolutionize the perfume industry, and he sent samples to the big scent manufacturers. His secretary tells how he used to search the shops in Florence for its ingredients, jasmin, rose-water, which he would mix conscientiously for hours at the Capponcina. But the big scent manufacturers thought nothing of *Acqua Nunzia,* and it was never patented.

Not long before his bankruptcy, D'Annunzio met an Argentinian gentleman called del Guzzo, of Abruzzi origin, who offered to liquidate all his debts on certain conditions. Del Guzzo, who was a business man, sent him a telegram, "Sincere admiration your vast output makes honor to our native land, propose tour Latin-America, there affirm in opulent distant lands force and virtue of Abruzzese race and culture . . ." In short, he suggested a lecture tour in South America which he would finance, and at the same time pay D'Annunzio's debts.

When the two men met, D'Annunzio appeared delighted at a plan which would relieve him of his embarrassment. "Everyone in Italy," he said to del Guzzo, "knows of my financial difficulties. I do not intend to conceal them, certainly not to anyone who is prepared to liberate me of them. I must tell you, I am in debt for some millions of lire. But this is not the moment to say how this happened, relating something which harasses my mind, and which makes me see mankind through a very smoky glass. It is enough to say that I have always tried to pay my debts, and that in paying them, I have incurred further debts. But now, these methods of borrowing to pay debts have unfortunately been exhausted, because the circle of my creditors has enlarged considerably. You will agree that I, as an artist, do not deserve such a fate? But inhuman humanity has always been the same. Interest alone rules the human race. Selfishness alone makes men move. However, I have always had the presentiment that Providence would not abandon me. And now I see someone who comes forward to relieve me of these difficulties. And this someone is you! In whose face I can read the goodness of your soul. . . ."

Hearing this paean, del Guzzo became almost as lyrical himself, and the two Abruzzesi fell on one another's necks. "This is not the time to be dismayed," said del Guzzo. "The past is past. The future is ahead. From this moment, you can count on me as on your own brother. The little I have is at your disposition."

To which, the poet replied, "I do not doubt you. I had read between the lines of your noble telegram. I knew I was not mistaken. That is why, from this moment, our spirits are linked in a sacred bond of friendship. Gone from now on between us must be every kind of formality and pretension . . ." So saying, D'Annunzio took a copy of his latest book, *Forse che sì, forse che no,* from his pocket, and wrote the inscription: "To the Messiah Invoked! And now met! To Giovanni del Guzzo! With Hosannas! Gabriele D'Annunzio." He then invited del Guzzo to dinner in the best restaurant.

Del Guzzo tells how the waiters fell over themselves to serve the man who always tipped them so generously. He ate a vast and varied meal; but after, D'Annunzio said, "I am sorry to tell you I have no money, and I must ask you for a small loan to pay the bill. With you, you see, I do not intend to be mysterious. Therefore I shall not ask you to excuse me."

"Of course not! How much do you want?"

"A thousand lire."

Unfortunately, this admirable solution to D'Annunzio's financial problems, which seemed almost fool-proof, for D'Annunzio had only to go to the Argentine and talk endlessly—an occupation he adored—did not succeed. D'Annunzio claimed later that del Guzzo did not provide him with the financial advance he had promised. He had also learned that del Guzzo expected him to go to two big receptions daily and give a speech at each; to visit the offices of all the newspapers in the Argentine; to compliment the presidents of innumerable Italian local societies. Lastly, he was to visit all the Italian wine establishments in which del Guzzo had interests. "And I do not drink wine myself," D'Annunzio said. He did not like the idea of America anyway, either north or south, and he later said that the mere thought of going there made him ill. "Why should I go to America for a packet of cigarettes?" he said.

It would seem that, much as D'Annunzio grumbled about his debts, he had a strange liking for them; for this was not the only means by which he could have liquidated them. He had become interested in flying, and a Bergamo impresario offered him a large sum to give a series of lectures on aviation in the big northern cities of Italy. D'Annunzio agreed, and gave about three. But he then became offended, either because the audience was too small, or because the lecture rooms were inadequate. When the taxi taking him from the station at Genoa to the lecture hall some miles away at last approached the sea, D'Annunzio said, "Do they expect me to address the fishes?" Finding the hall half-empty, he was so annoyed that he read most of his speech. The next day he broke his contract.

It is more likely that D'Annunzio did not employ any of these methods of liquidating his debts for the very good, and very honest, reason, that he could never bring himself to do what he disliked or despised, however lucrative it might be. Not long after this a further opportunity arose of making money easily, with the newly invented cinema. He was asked to lend his name to a film script which had been written as a Greco-Roman subject. All he had to do for 50,000 lire was to give it his paternity, and rewrite certain directions. But he had great scorn for the cinema, a scorn which was to last all his life; and although he accepted the offer, he could never bring himself to write even the stage directions. "It is not worth bothering about," he wrote to his publisher. "I would never forgive myself if I associated my name with such vulgar trash." About this time, too, the Tribunal of Milan condemned him to a fine of 12,000 lire, for taking money from a film company the year before, signing a contract to produce six films for them—and producing none. On the few occasions he entered a cinema, he said he had felt nothing but "profound disgust for the stupidity and coarse character of the spectacle." "A poisoning of popular taste," was his description of the celluloid world.[1]

Another likeable factor which contributed to D'Annunzio's bankruptcy was his generosity. Whenever he entered a shop accompanied by a friend, or even a simple acquaintance, to buy something, he never failed, after buying what he wanted, to ask his friend, "And what will you have?"—rather as one might ask a friend in a bar, "And what will you have to drink?"

If the friend did not take the offer seriously, D'Annunzio would insist. This would happen not only in the florist, the patisserie or the restaurant, but also in the leather-shop, at the tailor, or even in a furniture store. Antongini relates that once in Paris, they went into a shop to buy some garden furniture. After buying it, D'Annunzio turned and put the usual question. Antongini did not possess a garden, but he saw a wardrobe for sale. "I would like that wardrobe over there," he said jokingly. D'Annunzio took this quite seriously, and immediately bought the wardrobe, not considering for a moment that it was odd for a man who lived in a hotel to buy a wardrobe.

Some hours later, Antongini returned to the shop and explained the situation to the shopkeeper, who said he would take the wardrobe back and give Antongini the money. When Antongini later confessed to D'Annunzio, D'Annunzio roared with laughter. "You see what a good psychologist you are! I would certainly not have given you a present of 500 lire in cash. But in the form of a wardrobe, you have had it all the same. . . . Now we are both pleased with what we bought you!"

Mario, his son, points out how all D'Annunzio's theatrical works were written under the threat of this bankruptcy. At the time of the *Figlia di Jorio*, he wrote this letter to his mother (it is a great tribute to his filial devotion that, even when he was

---

[1] In spite of this he did, later, make the film *Cabiria*, on a suitably heroic scale. It takes place in the third century before Christ and depicts Hannibal crossing the Alps, and Archimedes setting fire to the ships.

deeply in debt, he managed to send her money): "Dear Mamma,
I have finished an Abruzzi tragedy, and I hope to have done
something worthy of my native land. At the moment, I am fin-
ishing the second volume of the *Laudi*. As soon as I regain breath,
I shall try and come and see you. I have sent you 150 lire from
Rome. Forgive me! I am in a state of great financial distress."

To his son at the same time, he wrote: "I must have *Francesca
da Rimini* finished by the end of August. All my hopes repose
on this work—the only way to solve my financial problems. If it
fails, my ruin is certain. I see from your letter that you too are
getting into the same state as we all are . . ." (He here refers to
the forced sale of his mother's Villa del Fuoco outside Pescara.
Her husband having died bankrupt, this was the only way she
could free herself of taxes and mortgages.)

Financial disaster could not be far away at this pace. He wrote
several letters to his publishers, Treves, asking for more money;
and when these loans were used up in liquidating his debts, he
took refuge in an even more luxurious life, going to Rome, where
he gave a series of sumptuous dinners to ladies of the aristocracy.
It was at this point, too, when the creditors were almost besieging
the house, that he had a serious fall from a horse. Great publicity
was given to this in the papers, which insinuated that the poet,
surrounded by debts, had tried to commit suicide.

On April 1, 1911, two Receiver officials appeared before the
door of the Capponcina, to declare the poet bankrupt and his pos-
sessions confiscated by the state. The door was locked because
D'Annunzio had already fled, and his lawyer, Coselschi, had taken
away the key. In spite of the objections of D'Annunzio's faithful
servant, Rocco Pesce, the door was forced by a smith, and the
officials entered to take possession. The Capponcina, with all its
contents, was put up to auction.

Much has been written about this auction and the "brutal and
callous behavior" of Giolitti's government in not supporting Italy's
greatest poet in his moment of disaster. Antongini, the secretary,

refers to "the ignoble sale of the Capponcina, where D'Annunzio had patiently collected so many lovely things and written so many masterpieces." "An idiotic and irreverent pillage," he called it. In fact, D'Annunzio had gone bankrupt for several million lire; and when people go bankrupt, they are seldom allowed to keep their houses, however full of masterpieces they may be. Brutal, callous tradesmen stump in, and take over these masterpieces, and sell them in a brutal, callous way. But if you are different from other men (so apparently runs the argument), you are entitled to entirely different treatment from that granted to other men. This argument is eminently Italian. Not only had D'Annunzio expressed it frequently in his works, but an even more eminent authority had countenanced it, some centuries before. Pope Paul III, when asked for the head of Benvenuto Cellini, because the artist had committed murder, replied: "Please understand that men who are unique in their art, as is Benvenuto Cellini, must not be subject to laws." This argument did not avail D'Annunzio. Giolitti did not imitate Paul III.

The auction lasted ten days, while crowds of antiquarians, friends and enemies thronged the Capponcina, to take away some souvenir of the *magnifico signore*. One of the features of the sale was the quantity of religious and theological objects this irreverent man had collected. People were astonished on the first day to find dozens of painted wooden statues and statuettes for sale; male and female saints, altar-tables and missals, psalters, lecterns, bibles and breviaries. In the words of Ojetti, who was present daily as a journalist, "One might have been present at the sale of a rich prelate, not of a very pagan poet. Every instant, the auctioneers were announcing: A seated Virgin! . . . a wooden Virgin! . . . A Virgin with child! . . . tabernacle with Saint and Virgin! . . ." In this way, unknown hands took away a Dominican Saint, a Saint Anthony of Padua, a Saint Mark, a Saint Ambrogio and a Saint Peter. Among this hagiographical bric-à-brac was a statue of Saint Onofrio, which was of special sentimental value to D'Annunzio. He had found it when he was a boy, in the Abruzzi, where his countrymen consider Onofrio as a *portafortuna* or lucky charm. If D'Annunzio was not religious in the orthodox way, he was always superstitious, and he had even taken this statue to Rome at the beginning of his career, to keep it near him in the early days of his marriage. Its sale at the auction was a greater blow to him than that of the more expensive works of art. Another example of his superstition appeared in the sale of a large Gothic chair, which he used at his writing desk. It had carved on the back the motto *Angelus Domini nobiscum,* a reference to the protecting presence of his namesake, the archangel Gabriel, while he wrote.

The proceeds of this auction, which included not only his house and goods, but all his animals, horses and dogs, realized only a fraction of his debts. To remove himself from the danger of further lawsuits (in particular the one which del Guzzo was threatening), he decided to leave the country and live in France, until the scandal died down. That spring he arrived in Paris, for a stay which was to last five years.

His parting statement was typical: "My troubles are due to the fact that I have behaved in keeping with what I am—a *gran signore,* a Florentine *signore* of old, whose tastes are sumptuous and disorganized. I live in an entirely disinterested manner, for I care nothing about wealth. But sometimes, my disproportionate tastes, my love of the beautiful have caused deplorable delusions. This, however, is not of the slightest importance. Misfortune and exile are necessary, mentally enriching—above all exile which restores the mind. My house which I so loved in Florence is now a morgue. If by chance I should ever return there, the memories of the past will crowd in from every corner and fill me with despair. But now I need to get away; I need space, air, a new country, where my spirit can expand, where I can survey new horizons. Everything in life depends upon the eternally new. Man must either renew himself or die."

This courageous statement was not unconnected with the fact that he was already well known in France.

12

French Exile

D'Annunzio's long absence from Italy pleased many Italians. A man's greatness can, it is said, be measured by the number of his enemies; and D'Annunzio had every class and description of enemy. His works had been put on the Index: *omnes fabulae amatoriae, omnia opera drammatica;* and all good Catholics were pleased to see him go. Almost all married men approved. Ladies to whom he had failed to make love were pleased; so were those to whom he had made love, and forgotten. Hundreds of creditors in Florence, Rome and northern Italy hoped that they might now salve something from the wreck of the Capponcina. The happiest band of all were the writers of Italy. Their hatred for D'Annunzio was, naturally, boundless. He had encouraged this dislike, it is true, by refusing to have anything to do with them, even professing not to know their names. A story of the times tells of D'Annunzio replying when asked about his famous contemporary, Fogazzaro, "Yes, he's, I believe, from Verona." He said Fogazzaro's work was like "a cup of *café au lait* taken in a church vestry." Most of the writers hated him as much for his literary success as for his outstanding versatility, turning from novels to politics, from politics to plays, from plays to airplane flying—which literary men considered frivolous. When the poet, Arturo Colautti, heard that D'Annunzio was writing a libretto for an opera, he cried to his friends, "So the cad's writing an *opera* now! This man does everything! He's a bloodsucker! A hydra! He's our *flagellum Dei!*"

It is remarkable perhaps, less that literary men should hate one another, than that the less they earn, the greater is the hate. There is a word in Italian, *"Il rospo,"* meaning "the toad," but which is used figuratively to mean "an insult." D'Annunzio was so well hated in Italy, that he anounced one morning, "Alas, no toads for breakfast today!" For he used to receive with every mail insults, threats, "toads" of all kinds—offensive articles, calumnious letters, grotesque portraits of himself, depicting his alleged vices which, we have seen, ranged from arson and simony to sodomy and incest. Indeed, he became so accustomed to "toads" every morning, that they even became dear to him. He used to say that without *"un bel rospo"* for breakfast, he could not work. He shared this appetite with the French writer Zola. Both employed agencies to send them offensive press cuttings, pasted onto cards. They came from all quarters of the globe, and D'Annunzio's worktable in the morning often looked like a country lane after a heavy shower. "Toads" of all kinds pullulated on it, big and small, green, yellow and brown.

D'Annunzio never liked literary cliques. Although he proudly called himself a poet first and foremost, he preferred the life of a lover and fashionable companion to unattached duchesses. In Paris, he found them even easier to acquire than in Rome. That he was a libertine was as well known as that Manzoni was a good Catholic, or Napoleon a good general. One famous critic had used the word *lussurioso* 148 times in a long article about D'Annunzio. The Parisians had accepted him too, long before, in 1896, when Sarah Bernhardt had played *La Città Morta.* All the doors therefore opened, as much to a fellow citizen by adoption as to a famous foreigner. He lived in France for five years, at first under the pseudonym Guy d'Arbes, so that the initials on his suitcases would tally. He changed this for some reason to Guy d'Ardres, and finally to Gérard d'Agaune.

Paris at this time, when thrones had not fallen in the rest of Europe, was the only capital which could offer as well as "good society," another sort of "society," which lived its own excitable life—a world of Papal Countesses, false marchionesses, doubtful Polish princesses, ambitious homosexuals and innumerable *nouveaux riches,* prepared to undergo any form of social baptism in a society where royal assent was no longer necessary. Among these people, D'Annunzio moved easily and confidently. He frequented particularly the actresses. He had often proclaimed the hold the ladies of the stage had over him; and in Paris there was no shortage. Every day, some female group would invite him to a party or reception, where he would talk interminably, with the born conversationalist's skill, knowing that the women had come not only to hear him, but also the reflection of their own imagined brilliance. Diego Angeli has written, "The most famous singers, immediately he entered a room, would select for his benefit their finest songs. And the *midinettes* of Paris, as well as the great ladies, all saw themselves in the role of Ippolita Sanzio or the Foscarina." He had to tell many stories about himself, true or imaginary, knowing that only in this way could he satisfy the vanity and curiosity of his charming listeners. It was said that the women of Paris had such a hold on him, that it was impossible at a reception for a man to approach him.

Arthur Symons has described how he would give a poetry reading to *le monde:* ". . . it was like one of those readings in the days of powder and peruke, when poets were still elegant, and a part of society's amusement. D'Annunzio, small, blond, at once eager and discreet, with the air of a perfectly charming bird of prey, his eyes full of bland smiles, his mouth, with its uplifted moustache, poised in a keen, expectant smile, had indeed the air of a court poet as he stood in the anteroom greeting his friends as they entered, before he made his way to the dais, draped at the back with crimson cloth, where he sat down at the table on which were his MSS and a Bible. Once seated, the reading once begun . . . you saw the artist who, as he told me, was well content if twelve hours' work had given him two pages; for his own words vividly absorbed, possessed him; he never lifted his eyes from the paper; he read all that chanting prose as if he were reading it, not to the duchesses, but to the unseen company of the immortal judges of art.

"It had been announced that the conference was to be held by someone else; and one careful mother went to the host, and asked if he thought her daughter might remain. A French abbé, who had come to hear the unexceptionable Costa, quietly disappeared on seeing D'Annunzio. Neither the abbé nor the mother need have been alarmed. D'Annunzio first read the parable out of the Bible, then his gloss upon it. The gloss was full of color and music. Then he read one of the most delicate of his poems, *Villa Chigi.* Everyone was charmed, D'Annunzio and all his hearers—and then the duchesses went . . ."

He was not always so delicate. He knew too how to impress his elegant audience by *outré* remarks. At one smart Parisian dinner, in the middle of some rather prosaic talk about the tenderness of cooked meat, he suddenly observed that the flesh of newborn babies very much resembled lamb. Some of the ladies gave signs of perturbation at this confession of cannibalism, particularly as it was announced with such an embarrassed smile. "You frighten some of us," said one of them. "It can't be true! Where did such a frightful thing take place?"

"In Africa," said D'Annunzio, dropping his head sadly, "a very long time ago."

Most of them laughed, but a vague impression of discomfort remained.

His skill with women is summed up by the American dancer, Isadora Duncan, whom he knew well in Paris. "I remember a marvelous walk I had with D'Annunzio," she writes. "In a forest. We stopped and remained standing silently. Then D'Annunzio exclaimed, 'O Isadora, it is only with you that one can be alone in the midst of nature. All other women destroy the landscape. You alone are part of it. You are a part of the trees, the sky, you are the supreme Goddess of Nature!' " ("What woman," asks Isadora Duncan, "could stand up against such flattery?") "For many years," she adds, "I was against him, on account of his treatment of the Duse, and I refused to see him. When a friend came and said, 'I can take you to D'Annunzio,' I replied, 'No, if

I see him, I would be rude to him.' All the same, my friend came one day with D'Annunzio. Although I had never seen him before, when I set eyes on this extraordinary being, all light and magnetism [sic], I cried, 'I am delighted you have come. You are really kind to come and see me.'"

Another French lady, the actress Simone, has also described the charm he exercised over her sex. "He bowed over my hand with a charming gallantry, and with his flowing compliments surpassed even the praise I am accustomed to receive from my own countrymen. . . . I listened to these exaggerated remarks, spellbound at such a display of verbal pyrotechnics—while he emphasized them by fluttering his little white hands and fingers, on one of which were two emeralds set in gold. He was dressed most elaborately, in a close-fitting suit, a silk shirt and jewel cuff-links, black and white shoes. He disconcerted me as much by this feminine coquetry as by his smallness, the shoulders less broad than the haunches, the minute feet, a feeling of fat arms and legs which was almost bisexual.

"His head, on the contrary, revealed the virile bust of the antique sculptor. Indeed, beneath the fingers of a sculptor, the fine forehead, powerful nose and well-balanced mouth, would have become objects of individual beauty. But alive, deprived of the faultless unity of marble, their nobility was lost, owing to D'Annunzio's deplorable coloring. His scanty hair, of washed out color; the protruding eyes, without eyelashes or eyebrows, had the bluish green of soapy water. The pallid lips revealed funny little crenellated, unhealthy teeth. While his thick skin covered unequally a face which ended in a Valois beard.

"Have I not drawn a portrait of a man whose physical qualities should disqualify him for women? Yet how many beautiful women have not renounced their homes and husbands, destroyed happy marriages, forsaken children, when this man decided to seduce them? How can one explain his conquests except by his extraordinary verbal power, and the musical timbre of his voice, put to the service of exceptional eloquence? For my sex is susceptible to words, bewitched by them, longing to be dominated by them. . . ."

To follow D'Annunzio in all his amorous adventures in Paris would be difficult and tedious. He found amorous life even easier than in Italy. It was enough for a woman to live with this "magnetic" man only a month, for her to start thinking of herself in Dannunzian language. After a short spell with him, the female American painter, Romaine Brooks, wrote this about herself, "Romaine, you are a great artist. All your powers and all your thoughts are in your art. . . . How comes it that you are descending from your throne, to mingle in the intrigues of the crowd? Romaine, you are the elect of the Gods, and yet you become an ordinary female, and concern yourself with things that the least tart in the street knows better than you. Climb back quickly, dear artist, and realize that love affairs are not for you. . . ." D'Annunzio is also said to have dropped his handkerchief at a party, and to have remarked to the hostess who picked it up for him, "You may keep it."

His method with women during this period, of his "great debauch," as he described his French stay, is illustrated by a gift which Antongini gave him. It was an onyx cameo representing Venus and Mars, in that special posture which Roderigo Borgia, the cardinal, described as "a dreadful sin, but a most ingenious and intelligent combination of two people." After admiring it for some time, D'Annunzio accepted it, saying that he always used "scabrous objects" to attract women. "Most useful," he said. "These are my working tools."

With such working tools and his own charms, he quickly seduced not only Romaine Brooks, who wanted to live with him forever in a villa at Arcachon in southern France, but a Russian lady, Natalia Victor de Gouloubeff, who also wanted to live with him forever, in another remote villa. She is worth comment among his ladies, for she belonged to the class of Slavonic female whom the Russian novelists had recently popularized in the West. D'Annunzio called her his "Caucasian Diana"; and later, in the *Libro Segreto,* he said, "She was mad with the blackest of black Slavonic madness."

No one knew where the passionate Russian came from. It was typical of this kind of "society" in Paris, that she claimed descent from a governor of the city of Kiev. Her mother, we know, had the charming name of Zoé de Pélican. She also claimed to have been brought up in a college of the nobility, where she and her classmates were followed everywhere, "by the melodious march birds who frequented the lakes around the aristocratic college." Russians in Paris were less certain. "No one knows where she comes from," said one of them.

"How can you say that?" said another. "It is well known that she is the daughter of the celebrated Admiral Makaroff, who blew himself up with his ship, rather than fall into the hands of the Japanese."

"But you are muddling her up with her charming sister-in-law."

"No, it's much simpler. She comes from Riga. She is the daughter of a piano tuner."

To other ladies in the capital who were fascinated, D'Annunzio sent enigmatic but poetic telegrams. (The ladies were generally titled.)

"*A Madame la Comtesse de Maupeou, 184, Boulevard Haussman, Paris, La mélodie des marées berce mes regrets. Tout est lointain et tout est proche. Au revoir. L'Exilé.*" Or, "*A Madame la Baronne Lippe, rue Greuse 40, Paris. Vous n'êtes pas un tombeau mais une trompette. Je vous écrirai, cependant. Je n'oublie pas les heures charmantes. Au revoir. Votre frère.*" (The ladies were not always discreet, apparently. Instead of being a "tomb," this lady had behaved like a "trumpet" about their liaison.)

To most of these ladies, he gave the affectionate pseudonym "*piccola,*" and they all signed with this name, not knowing that other women were using the same signature. Tom Antongini, his secretary, quotes telegrams like the following:

"Monsieur Guy d'Arbes, Villa Caritas, Moulleau, Arcachon.

Gabri, how I wish I were with you now! Feel you should come away to me. Promise you the greatest peace in my house. To work, will leave you unmolested. At Versailles then, await you, *Piccola.*"

From another lady:

"Monsieur Guy d'Arbes, Moulleau, Arcachon. Gabri darling, Bring a good oil lamp when you come. Light bad here. Come soon as possible. *Piccola.*"

An even more exalted lady felt she must be in the literary fashion, the Duchess de Grammont who wanted him to join her at Bordighera. She and a friend sent the following telegram: "Guy d'Arbes, Arcachon. Come soon to Beatrice and Maria, Hotel Cap Ampeglio, Bordigera."

One feels that he made fun of all these ladies rather as, today, Picasso makes fun of art collectors. Perhaps his most interesting female friendship was with the Jewish dancer, Ida Rubinstein, who claimed to have the most beautiful legs in the world. His play, *Le Martyre de Saint Sebastien,* was written in French, for her in the title role; and when he had finished it he sent her a telegram, "Play finished. I kiss your bleeding legs." He signed it, "Sanae," the name of one of the archers who killed the saint. The musical accompaniment was by Claude Debussy, the décor by Bakst, and Ida Rubinstein's interpretation satisfied D'Annunzio completely. But the Archbishop of Paris, scandalized that a Christian saint should be represented by a ballerina, and a Jewess, instructed good Catholics to boycott the performance. Both D'Annunzio and Debussy were most offended, and D'Annunzio wrote indignantly to the Bishop, that *Saint Sebastien* was a highly religious, deeply-felt play. "In it," he said, "I have exalted the most ardent defender of the Faith. And the interpreter I selected for him is pure in her manners and gestures—as pure as a Perugino painting of Saint Sebastian. A woman, it is true . . . and a ballerina . . . but in the same way that the Madonna della Seggiola by Rafael is the Foscarina. Madame Rubinstein is, in a certain sense here, asexual. She is Androgyne. The shape of her body awakens no sense of the voluptuousness of love . . ."

That Ida Rubinstein also had similar sub-lunar notions about him, may be interpreted from her descriptions of D'Annunzio talking French. "When Gabriele talks, he throws back his head, as if listening to some internal music. In fact, it *is* an internal music, profound and moving which flows from his lips, a music whose sense surpasses that of the words themselves, and brings the speaker nearer, giving him a new soul as it were, an unaccustomed courage, and some of that temerity which is the supreme virtue in the eyes of the poet. . . ."

But this could not satisfy the Bishop of Paris, who recalled that during the last diocesan congress, all Catholics were earnestly required to abstain from the dramatic representation of anything which might offend the Christian conscience. This, he said, applied as well to "written dramas which display in the most indecorous circumstances, the life of one of its most glorious martyrs." To the objection of D'Annunzio and Debussy, that they "glorified not only the admirable athlete of Christ, but all Christian heroism," the cleric replied, "Today, a sacred drama no longer has a mystic or religious meaning; it is given simply to divert and delight the spectators. The ancient notion is profaned. More than that, the conditions of the modern theater are such as to allow of no mystical quality. The saint is here played by a female dancer; a representation of Christ's Sacred Shroud is shown. And there is an irreverent scene called *Paradise*. . . ."

Some observers agreed that D'Annunzio had made nothing of the dancer's voluptuousness and famous legs. Indeed, to obtain the correct religious atmosphere for the play, he claimed that he had shut himself up for weeks, not with Ida Rubinstein, but with reproductions of all the Saint Sebastian paintings and religious statues that had ever been painted or sculptured throughout the centuries. Certainly, the epilogue to his play is treated in a highly, one might almost say exaggeratedly, Christian manner. It shows the archers on the stage shooting at Ida Rubinstein, who is half naked and tied to a tree. The arrows cannot kill her, however, although her body is bristling with them, until suddenly, one arrow flies off at a tangent, and goes up into the sky. Everyone watches it rising and rising, as if carried by an invisible force. It goes on up until is disappears—in Heaven, where it actually hits God in His empyrean, and wounds Him! It is only then that Saint Sebastian can feel his wound. Only his love of the Divinity can wound him to death!

The parochial quality of the play is described by Cocteau, in the fatuous simile language of the period: "Madame Rubinstein strikes the ear as a primitive picture strikes the eye. There is the same noble awkwardness, the same precise breadth of treatment, the same shy charm, though I dislike comparisons of the sort (for if Madame Rubinstein recalls early Italian painting, it is because all impressive works of art are apt to have a family likeness). In any case, she suggests some saint from a stained-glass window who, suddenly called to life, and still trammeled by the thought of his translucent immobility, has not yet grown accustomed to the newly bestowed gifts of speech and gesture." The play was not a success, largely because Ida Rubinstein, like most ballet dancers who aspire to be actresses, was not good at pronouncing words.

There were other plays, too, which D'Annunzio wrote in French and which caused trouble, because he selected actresses who were not good enough for the part. In *Chèvrefeuille*, jealousy and quarreling arose among a number of women, to each of whom he had apparently promised the principal part. In D'Annunzio's own words to his friend Albertini, "Bargy and Berthe Bady were detestable over *Chèvrefeuille*. Out of jealousy, they did all they could to ruin every word they pronounced—jealousy against the poor woman Roggers, who alone understood, and alone was able to express with justice and force the essence of my tragedy."

Le Chèvrefeuille had a most complicated genesis. He had formally promised a play for the actress Madame Simone—*La Hâche,* written in French; and he had described the whole plot to her. But a little later, he tired of Madame Simone, in favor of another actress. In order not to offend Madame Simone he officially buried *La Hâche* and began writing a new play in Italian, *Il Ferro,* for the new actress. It was exactly the same play as *La Hâche;* but when translated into French he called it *Le Chèvrefeuille.*

He also wrote a play in French called *Pisanella, ou La Mort Parfumée,* in which a whore is smothered alive in a bed of rose petals.

He then became involved in the Mariano Fortuny theater, in which most grandiose plans were announced for a new revolutionary "ambulatory theater." "It will be made entirely of iron," said the announcement, "and it will take seven days to set up completely. It will contain 4,500 seats, placed in an amphitheater, adorned with flower baskets and with little boxes covered in velvet. The stage will be semi-spherical: a kind of balloon cut in two. The first night will be June 20, 1911, in front of the Invalides, or the Champs de Mars. The first performance will be of a mammoth collection of the verses of Gabriele D'Annunzio, with dances, choruses and songs. The orchestra will have 120 players. Over 700 actors will appear on the stage. The plan is to give three months of performances in Paris, after which the theater will visit other European capitals. In October, subscriptions for the shares in the enterprise will be open to the public— of which two-thirds have already been acquired by friends and admirers of the poet. The capital will be 2,000,000 francs. Isadora Duncan will take part in the first performance . . ." This ambitious project too, like the Lake of Albano theater, was never executed.

It is clear from this that D'Annunzio had in a few months conquered all the editors, publishers, critics and newspapers of Paris, and a large part of the fashionable world. Vogué, Maurras, Doumic and other well-known writers had acclaimed in him "The Latin Renaissance"; and Maurras had written before in the *Gazette de France,* "Nothing good has come out in the world without the help of some child of Italy." D'Annunzio's fame quickly crossed the channel to England, and to America, where editors inundated him with demands for articles. D'Annunzio replied proudly, "Yes, without Italy nothing can be done. What would Chateaubriand have been without Rome? Perhaps the place I shall occupy in the history of our prose will be the one which Chateaubriand holds in French prose."

On arriving in Paris, he had contrived to obtain an advance of 100,000 lire from his French publisher. But instead of returning to Italy to pay his debts, he preferred to remain in Paris—which, considering the way he was being treated, was understandable. He had now become so famous that even kings and heads of states wanted to meet him. Antongini, his secretary, describes several of these meetings, in particular one with the President of Brazil, which shows the extent of his fame. The President had said he wanted to meet D'Annunzio, so Antongini visited the President's secretary to arrange the meeting.

He went to the hotel where the Brazilian President was staying in Paris, and was about to introduce himself. But the President's secretary, assuming Antongini was D'Annunzio, had in a twinkling introduced him through the folding doors, into a drawing-room, where Antongini found he was in the presence of the exalted Brazilian himself. No sooner had he crossed the threshold than the President rose, held out his hand and, under apparently the same misapprehension, addressed most gracious words of welcome in broken French. Antongini was embarrassed. His first impulse was to correct the error, but while preparing to do so, he was surrounded by other distinguished Brazilians, and before he could say a word, the President had announced, "I hereby present to you the greatest of living poets, Gabriele D'Annunzio."

Antongini realized that it was now too late to retract so, commending himself to Providence, he decided to impersonate the poet. Compliments of all kinds were showered on him, and he was invited to visit Brazil, under the most splendid conditions. The President said he would place at his disposal the Brazilian battleship, *Minas Geraes*. Overflowing with expressions of gratitude and devotion, he finally took his leave and returned to D'Annunzio, to whom he explained what had happened. D'Annunzio listened with amused contempt, and then said, "You have done well. After all, you have stood proxy for me in what amounts to a marriage with a battleship."

In his amusing and often scandalous book, *Vita Segreta di Gabriele D'Annunzio,* about his years as D'Annunzio's publisher and later secretary, Antongini is the only Italian writer who has really brought D'Annunzio alive, and made him human. So famous had his master become in Paris, he says, that one day a well-known American professor of craniology wrote asking D'Annunzio if, on his death, he would leave him his skull for research. The craniologist said that Ibsen, Streseman, Barnum, Vereshchagin and other men distinguished in various walks of life had agreed to do this. Only the skull of a poet was lacking. D'Annunzio replied most courteously to the American craniologist, agreeing on one condition—that if by chance the craniologist should die before he died, he would leave D'Annunzio *his* skull, to be put on the poet's study-table. "It was not an excessive demand, was it?" D'Annunzio said to Antongini. "One good turn deserves another. But do you know—that craniologist never even bothered to reply!"

Antongini acted as a sort of bodyguard as well as personal secretary at this time of "the great debauch," and his main duty was to keep away inquisitive journalists and overanxious ladies. He says that when they arrived in Paris, D'Annunzio wanted to keep away from "smart" life, and rent a house outside the city. They were walking in the outer suburbs one summer day, when D'Annunzio stopped and said, "That's the kind of house I want. We'll see if they'll let it."

They rang the bell, but there was no reply. They went through the little garden, but found no owners, guardian, or dog. As there was still no reply at the front door, they went in through an open french window—to find a drawing-room full of flowers and *objets d'art*. "We then tried to summon someone," says Antongini. "At first quietly, then by shouting. It seemed uninhabited. Although this could not be so, because in the center of the room, on a table, was a tray with a steaming teapot on it, cups, saucers, cakes and sandwiches. Tired of waiting, we sat down and D'Annunzio took a sandwich. I did the same. They were excellent. 'How about a cup of tea?' said D'Annunzio. Without waiting, he poured out two cups, adding milk and sugar. This too was excellent. We ate some cakes, I lit a cigarette, and we chatted on until, as no one came after half an hour, we got up and went back into the garden, where D'Annunzio picked some roses. We left by the main gate. When we were in the road, D'Annunzio turned and looked at the house fondly. 'What a charming house!' he said. 'And what charming people! I never met nicer hosts!' "

Failing to find a house outside the city, D'Annunzio stayed at the Hotel Meurice, where his famous compatriot, Marconi, was also staying. The inventor of the wireless was of considerable value to D'Annunzio, because one morning something went wrong with the electric light in D'Annunzio's bedroom. The hotel electrician could not be found, and then D'Annunzio cried, "Why, the man for this is Marconi, of course!" and he went up to the higher floor where the great man was living. The great electrician was good enough to come down and mend the electric light, standing on a chair in his shirt-sleeves, with a screw driver.

It was while D'Annunzio was in France that the Great War broke out, and for nine months, until May 1915, Italy remained neutral. During this time, D'Annunzio obtained permission to visit the French front, where he had his "baptism of fire." He became enthusiastic about hostilities, and went to Reims, which was within range of the German guns, and where the Cathedral had been set alight. He spoke of the flames rapturously. "The Cathedral has never been more beautiful!" he said. "What a miracle!" These remarks hardly pleased the Bishop and his sacristans, who were trying to put out the flames. "But the Germans continue to bombard us all the time . . ." they complained indignantly. D'Annunzio again reassured them. "I assure you, the Cathedral reaches its perfection in flames," he said. "One longs to fall on one's knees before such a miracle . . ." And he added, to their stupefaction, "I trust you will take advantage of this unique occasion, to remove from your church some of the frightful paintings which deface its interior . . ."

He returned to Paris, determined to leave France as soon as possible and persuade his own country to enter the war, in which the Superman himself would take part.

Like many Europeans in 1914, D'Annunzio saw the war exclusively in romantic terms; his own notion of the old struggle between the Latins and Barbarians, together with the new idea of Right and Wrong. His poems written in France, where he had seen Soissons Cathedral, as well as Reims, in flames, were a call to Latin action against the Germans and their Austrian allies who, he said, intended to turn the Adriatic, and thence the Mediterranean, into a Teutonic lake. Hitherto, his writings had been novels, plays and poems of which only a small proportion had been both patriotic and topical. From now on, until his death in 1938, they are concerned almost entirely with the question of "For a Greater Italy," the general title he gave them. When he was asked officially to speak at the inauguration of Garibaldi's memorial at Quarto in May 1915, he seized the opportunity to return and start his campaign in Italy for intervention on the side of the Western Allies, with the celebrated lapidary phrase, *"Qui si fa l'Italia, o si muore."*

Six weeks before this, his tragedy *Fedra* was played for the first time at the Scala, Milan; and some friends had suggested that this would be a suitable moment to return to Italy, now that Europe was at war. To Albertini, the editor of the *Corriere della Sera,* he had written, "I consider that my turn should be reserved for a more patriotic day. I have already agreed to speak before the Thousand Monument at Quarto, on May 5. But perhaps I shall not be in time. Italy may already be at war. All the same, what an occasion this will be! The commemoration of the Thousand, with the heroes of the Argonne around the monument! A new reveille announcing a new departure! For a new Liberation!"

During the ten months of neutrality, while he was in France, he wrote a number of poems calling on Italy to support her "Latin sister." The *Ode for the Latin Resurrection* was published on August 13, 1914, in the *Figaro,* whose editor commented: ". . . the admirable talent of the author of *L'Innocente* and *La Gioconda* is here displayed in all its force and vigor. We are convinced that our great Latin sister will welcome with profound admiration this cry of fraternal heroism in honor of France from Italy's greatest living writer . . ."

The "force and vigor" the editor refers to seem today patriotic
rather than poetic:

> *Vae Victis!* The barbarous forces call us
> To combat without mercy.
> Oh Victory, shy harvester,
> I feel already on my forehead while I wait,
> The freshness of the Morning . . .

To this the French poet, Henri de Régnier, had already written a
grateful reply:

> *Fils illustre deux fois d'une noble patrie*
> *Et dont la fière main planta si fièrement*
> *En notre sol de France un lanrier d'Italie*

D'Annunzio now began to write every kind of frenzied national
hymn, in French and Italian: *To the Nation; To the Citizens; To
the Combatants; To the King.* He had already harangued Victor
Emmanuel III, in *Electra,* that part of *Laus Vitae* which acclaims
the great heroes—where the little king is incongruously placed
beside Garibaldi, Dante, Leonardo, Wagner, and Victor Hugo.
"Accompany your father to the tomb where his own father lies,
in the sublime temple which the strength of Rome has erected on
new granite columns. May the thunder of austere hymns ravish
your thoughts, like a whirlwind, and carry you towards greater
heights beyond the tomb, beyond the altar . . . May those great
thoughts, with Rome and its future fortune, be forever in your
mind! You will not sleep—if your heart is not worthy to be
consumed by a violent vulture. You will not sleep—if your eyes
are unworthy to contemplate the horizon that the Quirinale reveals to the man who can dominate it. You will not sleep—if
your hands are not ever ready for struggle and works, for the
sword and the hammer, to shape for your forehead another iron
crown made from the sufferings of another savior, on the anvil
of another altar. Reach your goal, and you will be the Savior of

Rome. . . ." The Mussolinian harangue was for the first time foreshadowed.

He then harangued the King's subjects: "Oh Italy, somnolent and inert, will you ever waken from your ignoble sleep? Too long have you lain stretched in the sun, in opprobrious servility, governed by old men who pollute you, who have made of you an easy bed for idleness, and of all your noble laurels have made only a rod to castigate your glory! Oh young King, do you not scent the odor of that death? You are now the Hero we await, the shepherd of the fiery race . . . Bend the bow, oh King! Light the torch! Destiny has chosen you for great events. For you know that Peril is the belt with which the heroes gird themselves. From purple blood may Dawn be born! The fortunes of Italy have arisen from the field of a lost battle . . . Bend the bow, oh young King! Light the torch! Strike, and with your blow re-animate the Latin race! Venerate the laurel, exalt the strong! Open the doors of future domains! If present shame and ill continue, when the hour is come you will find before you among the rebels, the one who now acclaims you. . . ."

In fact, nothing was more alien to the calm, retiring, essentially middle-class temperament of Victor Emmanuel, than the fiery eloquence and bloodthirsty glamour of these poems and speeches.

D'Annunzio was now aged fifty-two, and had he stayed with his plays and women in France, no one would have blamed him. Instead, having spoken in favor of war, he determined to fight in it himself. To Alfred Capus, the director of the *Figaro,* he wrote at the beginning of May 1915: "My dear Friend, I am leaving France for Genoa. The die is cast. What has not taken place under the sign of the Ram, will arrive under the sign of the Bull. That zodiacal beast has an even harder forehead, *frontem duriorum frontibus eorum.* From Genoa you will receive great news. Publish my poems in the *Figaro* on the morning of May 5. At that very moment, we shall perhaps have become Allies. . . ."

13

The Orator

Italy had a military alliance with the Central Powers in 1914, but, as is well known, she did not declare war on France and England. Giolitti, still the most influential politician, was convinced that she should disentangle herself from an engagement his predecessors had unwisely contracted. The pretext he suggested for this was that the Central Powers had ignored Article VII of the Triple Alliance, by which no alteration could be suggested in the Balkans without consultation among Allies. (Austria had delivered her ultimatum to Serbia without consulting Italy.)

The announcement of neutrality was made in August 1914, and was accepted with general satisfaction throughout the peninsula. The Socialists, who preached international co-operation, applauded the pacific decision. The Catholics, although in principle on the side of Austria, remembered that a Christian Church should, properly, not support warfare. The Radicals and Republicans, heirs to the Irredentist tradition of Venezia Giulia and the Trentino, were delighted at not having to enter the war on Austria's side. Only the nationalists, who were still in favor of German authoritative methods, and were discreetly Francophobe, regretted Italy's failure to fulfil her pledges.

But this neutral attitude lasted a very short time. The Nietzsche-Futurist idea expressed in the writings of Sorel, Corradini, D'Annunzio and Marinetti, had penetrated deeper than Giolitti realized. There was now a growing following for war, as an idea, throughout the country. Giolitti's veneration of the useful, the practical, the bourgeois was becoming despised by the middle classes themselves. Even Carducci had talked about, "the ignoble Italy, the pacific, the ridiculous Italy, with her Pope, her King and her constitutional democracy." And a contemporary writer Papini had written [1] "what Italy now wants is a warm bath of blood . . ." When D'Annunzio, in one of his interventionist speeches, said, "Italy is no longer a *pension de famille,* a museum, a horizon painted with Prussian blue for international honeymooners—but a Living Nation . . . !" the storm of applause lasted several minutes.

The question by 1915 was not, "Should Italy enter the war?"; but, "On whose side should she enter it?" If she joined England and France, she would obtain the Trentino and Trieste; if she joined the Triple Alliance, she would perhaps get parts of southern France. The politicians disagreed as to which was the better course; so Sonnino, the Foreign Minister, adopted the Italian solution of entering into secret negotiations with both sides at once. He had become Foreign Minister in November 1914, and had been at first in favor of the Triple Alliance and the sanctity of treaties. He had therefore started bargaining with Austria on the famous "compensations" clause in Article VII of the Triple Alliance, asking for the whole of the Trentino, as it had belonged to Italy before 1811; the eastern frontier, to include Gorizia and Gradisca; Trieste; some of the Dalmatian isles; and an Italian sphere of influence in Albania.

These demands were at first strenuously resisted by Austria; but as a result of German influence through Prince Bülow, who had been sent specially to Rome from Berlin, she gradually began to accept them, unwillingly, one by one. Italy might have obtained much in this way. But the entire British Empire was now in the war, influencing the Italian nationalists, who saw possibilities in the Mediterranean as England's naval ally. Hoping for Mediterranean concessions, these men, who had originally supported the Central Powers and were Francophobe, changed completely and proclaimed that Italy should now enter the war *against* the Central Powers. The Republicans, too, full of irredentist talk about the Trentino and Venezia Giulia, began sending "volunteers" to Ser-

[1] In *Lacerba,* 1st October, 1914.

bia, to fight against the hated Habsburgs. Other, but equally strong, motives affected the hitherto pacific socialists; the German invasion of Belgium and the brutalities committed in the occupied countries; the announcement of unrestricted sea warfare; the too great speed with which Germany appeared about to destroy France, the "home of socialism." All these groups had strong reasons for joining the western allies, and their views were made public through the most influential newspaper in Italy, the *Corriere della Sera.*

The only people who still wished to remain neutral were the well disciplined phalanxes of the Catholics, and a handful of socialists who had special reasons of their own (among them the editor of *Avanti,* Benito Mussolini, who announced that war was a hateful and imperialist thing); and a number of simple, ordinary folk averse to adventures of any kind, who looked upon Giolitti as their champion. The Vatican, calmly calculating for future centuries, kept out of the debate altogether. As late as February 1915, Giolitti summed up the feelings of all these people. "Italy can get a great deal without entering the war." But intervention fever was mounting, and his advice was ignored. On April 26, 1915, the secret Treaty of London was signed, and a week later Sonnino repudiated the Triple Alliance. A last attempt by the neutralists to bring Giolitti back to power failed; and on May 24, 1915, Italy declared war on Austria and Germany. In achieving this a considerable part was played by Gabriele D'Annunzio.

At the beginning of May, D'Annunzio left France and, when he came near the Italian frontier, he bound his eyes, lest the emotion of seeing his native land again after five years should be too great. At two-thirty on the afternoon of May 2, 1915, he crossed at Modane, and entered Italy. What moved him most, he said, was the reception of the soldiers at the frontier; above all, that of the Dalmatian exiles, who wanted to give him the copy of a Venetian lion from one of their cities. "You shall have the *real* lion back,"

he said, "when your towns are reunited with the mother country." To the first journalists he met on Italian soil, he declared,
"If Italy declares war on Austria, I shall never leave Italy again.
If she fails to declare war, I shall become a Laplander. I shall
take out Lap citizenship . . ." From Modane to Genoa his journey
was a triumphal progress. In every station, an immense crowd
gathered to acclaim him. In Genoa, the Socialist deputy and university professor, Raimondo, was about to give a history lecture.
But when he heard who was arriving, he recommended his pupils
to meet at the station, and to "live" history. At the Eden Palace
hotel, D'Annunzio made his first interventionist speech.

The next morning, the inauguration of the monument took
place at Quarto, the small port near Genoa from which Garibaldi
had set out fifty years before, on the conquest of Sicily and Naples.
The King and most of the government were to have been present; but at the last moment, the Foreign Office had insisted that
D'Annunzio's speech should be submitted for approval. After seeing it, they decided that the King must not come. The Royal presence would have implied government approval of war against
Austria immediately; and the final military preparations were not
yet complete. The King therefore sent this telegram to the Mayor.
"If cares of State, changing my desire to regret, prevent my taking
part in person at the ceremony, they do not keep me away in my
thoughts . . ." To this, D'Annunzio made an ironical reference in
the opening of his speech the next day. "To His Majesty the
King, absent but present . . ."

Unfortunately, this speech had also been sent to the press on
the same day, and although D'Annunzio had asked the papers
not to publish it until after he had spoken, the *Corriere della
Sera* printed the full text that morning. Thus the enthusiastic
audience, while listening to him speak, held the entire text of his
words in their hands. The speech had a poetical and mystical
flavor, ". . . aerial messengers tell us that Michelangelo's *Night*
has awakened in Italy, that his *Dawn* has forgotten her ancient sadness and is now moving forward in the sky, from the Alps to the

East. It is towards her, towards this Dawn that the heroes reborn in their tombs are striving. The wings of Victory will grow on her shoulders, and the winding sheets of our heroes' tombs will furnish the white of our flags . . ."

He then evoked in his hearers the notion of the beauty of sacrifice and the sublime temptation of peril, using biblical imagery. "See, he comes, the Lord I call. He makes the night bright." "Who then would I send, Oh Announcer of sacred things?" he asks. " 'Here am I, send me, Oh Lord,' I cry. I have no longer flesh or bones around my panting heart, to cross the rivers and mountains. Already on the frontiers, by the light of the Pleiades, I can read the ineffable name, and hear the neighing of the horses of the Dioscures. Oh Victory, wild as the horse which crops the asphodel in the Roman desert. . . . Oh desirable Victory, if ever there is one, I ask for its signs, from a people ignominiously clothed in peace . . ."

The speech finished with a modernized version of the Sermon on the Mount. ". . . blessed are they who, having yesterday cried against this event, today will silently accept the supreme necessity, and do not wish to be the Last, but the First! Blessed are the young who, starved of glory, shall be satisfied! Blessed are the merciful, for they shall be called on to quench a splendid flow of blood, and dress a wonderful wound! Blessed are the pure in heart. Blessed are those who return in Victory, for they shall see the face of a new Rome, its brow crowned again by Dante with the triumphant beauty of Italy. . . ."

This speech struck the imagination of the crowd most forcibly. They sang the "Marseillaise," cried out for war, and thronged forward to carry him away in triumph—while suddenly on the top of the monument, a large poster was unrolled, bearing the one word, TRIESTE. Garibaldi's son says that among the crowd were 500 young Garibaldeans, who each wore a red silk shirt under his bourgeois suit. That evening, D'Annunzio telegraphed to Maurice Barrès, "Our two countries have become one! From French Flanders to the sea of Sicily is one land. It is poetry which makes this marvelous gift of our militant friendship. *Fidem signemus sanguine.* Your brother Gabriele."

D'Annunzio was at last putting into practice the oratory he had depicted in his patriotic play *La Nave,* which might equally have been entitled *The Mob.* In it, a mob is worked up by a skilful orator from relative apathy to collective curiosity, and thence to organized frenzy. There is a passage in *Il Fuoco,* too, in which D'Annunzio describes the pleasure he obtained from addressing a mob: ". . . there is in the mob a beauty from which the poet and the hero alone can obtain flashes of inspiration. When, quite unexpectedly, that form of beauty reveals itself in the theater or the piazza, then a torrent of joy swells the heart of the man who has inspired it, with his verse, his oratory, or his sword. The word of the poet communicated to the mob is therefore an act, like the gesture of the hero, which creates in the obscurity of the soul an instantaneous beauty, just as a prodigious sculptor can from a block of clay reveal a divine statue. . . ."

D'Annunzio stayed a week in Genoa making speeches, and moved on to Rome, where the welcome was even greater. Crowds gathered round his hotel and he addressed them from the balcony, not hesitating to attack Giolitti personally. "There are traitors in Rome, in the City of the Spirit, in the City of Life," he cried. "In your own Rome, they are trying to strangle Italy with a Prussian halter held by that old thick-lipped hangman, whose fleeing heels know only the road to Berlin [this was Giolitti]. If I am the first to say this aloud today, you will be the first to thank me tomorrow. Your blood must cry out within you; rebellion must roar within you. With the stick and the blow, with the kick and the punch, we will protect ourselves against the littleness of these lickers of Prussian boots. Their servant mentality fears force and physical violence. I tell you, there is a stench of treason here. Treason is taking place right before you, here, in Rome! We Italians are being sold like cattle . . ."

"No! No!" roared the crowd. "It shall not be! Death to the traitors! War! War!"

Enthusiasm reached its peak when the sword of the Garibaldean hero, Nino Bixio, was handed over to the poet on the Capitol. "This sword of Nino Bixio," cried D'Annunzio, "of the man who was second of the Thousand, just as he was always first in battle. This sword which his heirs have offered to the Capitol—Oh Romans, I kiss it for you, I kiss it in the name of our victories. . . ."

Official, if tacit, royal approval was given to this by the presence of Queen Margherita, concealed behind a curtain on one of the balconies during his speeches.

The effect not only of D'Annunzio's oratory, but also of Sonnino's tortuous negotiations, were at last beginning to be felt. On May 19, D'Annunzio was summoned by the King to the Villa Savoia. It was his first meeting with the monarch he had so often harangued in print. "I met the King alone, in a shady avenue of the garden," he wrote. "He put out his hand to me—and I knew he was putting it out to the good fighter, who expressed the feelings of his people. With a gesture of noble pride, he stated on which side lay right and reason. That hand held out towards me as a poet was also ready to unsheath the sword." This was the King to whom D'Annunzio had addressed the inflamed epistle at his accession in which he praised, spurred, and finally menaced him. "If thou wilt not give greatness to the Italian people," he had said, "I shall be among thy enemies." Here, he thought, the King had at last satisfied his demand.

On May 23, 1915, the King signed the declaration of war against the Central Powers; and that night in Rome D'Annunzio celebrated the event in a restaurant with a group of friends. They stayed late, until the dawn. D'Annunzio then got up and made a speech. "Companions, here is the dawn. Our vigil is over. Our gaiety begins. The frontier is passed. The cannons fire. The earth gives forth its fumes, and the Adriatic is gray, at this hour, like the torpedo boats that cut through it. Companions, can it be true? After so much wavering, the incredible has happened. We shall now fight our war, and blood will flow from the veins of Italy. We are the last to enter the struggle, but will be among the first to find glory. Here, companions, is the dawn; here the knell. Let us kiss one another and take leave. What is done is done. Now we must separate—to find one another again. God will surely allow us to meet again, dead or alive, in a place surrounded by light . . ."

Immediately after war was declared, he stayed for some days at the Hotel Regina in Rome, where rich ladies deliberately took rooms, hoping they might meet the great poet who had brought Italy into the war. D'Annunzio's son, Mario, tells of a rich, tall and thin Argentinian who, unable to meet him through a proper introduction, used to stand about the corridors, and finally actually went up to introduce herself. D'Annunzio was very polite with her, and she began to send him flowers. But to her great distress, he did nothing in return. He told his son later that she was "too thin." Isadora Duncan also appeared in the hotel at this time, and gave D'Annunzio flowers. But she, on the contrary, received the honor of the orator's bed.

Mario says that another female admirer, knowing he was shortly going to the front, sent him a steel vest. But it was too heavy, and he left it behind with his son, Gabriellino, who wore it to the station to see his father off. But he too complained that it "was so heavy that he had to hire a carriage to get it home." When D'Annunzio left for the front, he said proudly to his sons, in his usual lapidary manner, "It is not I you salute, but the spirit that leads me, the love that possesses me, the ideas that I serve."

14

The Warrior

The propaganda for the Italian intervention was based on the supposed brevity of the conflict, which, it was claimed, would last at the most six months, and stop in 1915. For in May of that year, the Italian Army was neither modern, nor had it any traditions other than negative ones. As a national army, it had gained more defeats than victories; only among the Piedmontese aristocracy could there be said to be anything approaching an *esprit de corps*. Not even the local loyalties of the old Lombard Trained Bands or the Florentine *Caroccio* remained. At Adowa, corruption as much as inefficiency had defeated it. Mules for that campaign had been bought in Naples for 100 lire, and sold by the army contractors for 500. One of its Generals described the Army in 1915 as "a ship lost in the Dead Sea"; and the General Staff was completely misinformed about the Central Powers. Like all Europe, they believed that the "Russian steam-roller" would quickly roll over half of Austria-Hungary, leaving the other half to the Italians, if they were quick. When it was pointed out that German troops might also appear on this front, General Pollio, the Italian Assistant Chief of Staff, showed his scorn for the Austrian troops by saying: "Let the Germans come by all means! We can then at least gain *some* glory." People spoke of occupying Trieste in a matter of days, of marching on Vienna and provisioning the Italian Army in the Hungarian plain.

Yet, when hostilities were opened against the vast armies of Central Europe, the Italian Army had 112 field guns, 14 siege guns, 70 airplanes, and it was desperately short of munitions. Few soldiers knew anything about throwing grenades, and there were only a handful of officers to train them, giving an illusion of grenades with stones. The first waves of infantry thrown against the Austrian barbed wire were equipped with scissors which did not cut. Liaison between the different arms was so bad that the artillery regularly cannonaded its own troops. There were no sappers. The officers wore brightly colored trousers which could be seen for miles (like the red pantaloons of the French infantry). In spite of this, the High Command continued imperturbably issuing detailed instructions about minutiae. They became òbsessed at one point with the height of officers who might make Grenadiers, and even continued measuring candidates under fire. Officers in command of battalions in action would suddenly find themselves transferred to Rome for a promotion exam. The result of this, particularly with Generalissimo Cadorna's insistence on *frontal attacks,* was that in the first few months of the war Italy lost 50,000 dead, 180,000 wounded and 25,000 prisoners.

General Cadorna had complete power. He was a kind of military sovereign, more important than King or Government. His swollen HQ at Udine was a veritable state within a state, where he created ministers, informed the press, and corresponded directly with foreign governments. He gave his confidence to a small group of chosen staff officers, and was famous for his exemplary cashiering. From the beginning of the war, until he handed over command to General Diaz in 1917, he had, it was claimed, cashiered 217 generals, 255 colonels and 355 lieutenant-colonels. He shot many soldiers for retreating, including a number of volunteers, who had come over from the United States at their own expense. He was a kind of Louis XIV general resurrected in the twentieth century. At the head of a professional army, in which discipline is maintained by floggings, he would have been excellent. He saw the war as a gigantic siege operation, and thought it was a supreme honor for a regiment to resist indefinitely in a trench. He made the fatal mistake at Caporetto of trying to lure the Austrians into a trap. He opened the northeast door of Italy to them, and they poured in. Then he shut the door, intending to crush them in the little strong room he thought he had formed behind. But the opposite door of the strong room was not strong. The Austrians broke it down and poured like a deluge into more than half the region of the Veneto. They were stopped on the Piave by the younger recruits of the Italian Army, boys of eighteen years of age, who were taken directly from the barracks to the firing-line. Allied forces also came to support them, and the Italian Army was reorganized.

It was after Caporetto that Cadorna proved his metal, and with unbreakable serenity continued to issue orders for the formation of a new front on the Piave, when the Italian Army was in headlong flight. At this time, Marshal Foch came to the Italian Front for a hurried visit, to give advice. After a study of the maps in Cadorna's HQ, he said to the Italian Generalissimo, 'But artillery must be sent there . . .''

Cadorna replied, "It has been done."

"Reserves must be massed here . . ."

"It has been done."

"Fresh troops must be moved in here . . ."

"It has been done."

After a succession of "It has been done's," Foch rose and said irritably, "Why, everything has already been done!"

The Italian High Command paid little attention to the means by which an army submitted to the new trench warfare may be kept in good heart. The commissariat was irregular, the guns deficient in numbers and weight, the facilities for amusement and education[1] behind the lines, so lavishly provided on the other fronts, almost non-existent. The Italian soldier in his rare intervals of leave would return from the scorching limestone plateau of the Carso, to find his family starving on an insufficient allowance from the state. In such circumstances, his will to victory faltered and he listened to the priests if he were a Catholic, to the

---

[1] The army in these days was still extraordinarily illiterate. G. M. Trevelyan reports that, during the War, he found two Italian solders drawing water from a fountain just under a prohibitory notice, and saying to them, "Can't you read?"—and being effectively silenced by the quiet reply, "No, we can't."

Soviets if he were a Socialist. From each of these very different sources he learned that the war should be stopped.[1]

The immediate strategic effect of the Italian intervention was to open a new front for the enemy in the Trieste area and on the high ground of the Carso. Although the Italian plan to march straight through to Vienna failed, they fought a long and on the whole not uneven battle with the enemy in this area, losing in all nearly 800,000 men.

Not since the Crusades had there been such a war of Right against Wrong. The Allied slogans spoke of Civilization and Barbarism, of Democracy and Militarism. But beneath these terms was a deeper, more strongly felt, motive—that the Allies faced an ultimate trial against warfare as a means of solving problems. The hope arose that when victory had been won, war might end forever. Every soldier who fell was a Christ who died that others might live, a Redeemer, while freedom and brotherhood were promised to victor and vanquished alike. These general ideas were in line with popular Italian humanism, and D'Annunzio wrote a quasi-religious poem. It was called "The Reborn," and it depicts Jesus fighting in the trenches, where He is heroically killed.[2]

But D'Annunzio never had any real religion, and his true feelings were better expressed in a speech he made about the Piave, where the fighting was thickest. "Are there today in our country any other waters, other rivers, than the Piave? Tell me if there are. Is there today any other place where all Italians wish to be? Tell me if there is. Are there any other living rivers in Italy today? If so, I do not wish to know them. Are there names of other streams? If so, I do not wish to know them. Soldiers of the peasantry, from the cities and from the countryside, laborers, artisans, men of every Italian province, forget today all else. Remember only that this water from the Piave is regenerative water—as the

[1] See H. A. L. Fisher, *Europe*.
[2] It was not the first time that D'Annunzio had depicted Christ. In the sensual *Poema Paradisiaco* he had described Him being baptized by John the Baptist in the Jordan.

water from a baptismal font. If near your cottage at home a stream passes, it contains the water from the Piave. If a rivulet marks the end of your field, it contains the water from the Piave. The Piave is today the richest vein of our national life, in the body of our country. If it is severed, our heart will cease to beat. Every part of it which is darkened with enemy blood, each one of us must be ready to redeem with his own blood . . ."

D'Annunzio's love of war was not only patriotic. There was a psychological side of it, which has already been revealed in his writings. In *Forse che sì, forse che no,* the hero says he does not know which pleases him most, "to spill sperm or to spill blood." In the romance of war, all D'Annunzio's strongest instincts appeared, heroism, egoism, violence, sensuality, his interest in blood and wounds. But there was also in D'Annunzio the other, ambitious side, of the man who intends to excel in everything, as we have seen, in all forms of human activity. "At the height of Pindar's lyrical power," he wrote in *Notturno,* "the Greek poet could cut the cords of his lyre and suffocate his song, because he knew that he could also fight, and dare . . ."

After D'Annunzio's death, a book called *Les Deux Masques,* by a Frenchman, Paul Saint-Victor, was found in the library at the *Vittoriale.* It had been carefully annotated by D'Annunzio, with many passages underlined, including a most revelatory one about the poet Aeschylus, the author of seventy plays—*but who also fought at Marathon.* The words underlined are, ". . . with literary genius went also physical courage, he acted what he sang . . ." Other passages underlined show Aeschylus as the soldier rather than the writer, with particular reference to the wound he received at Marathon, and the epitaph he wrote on himself, in which he commemorates his military, rather than his poetic, prowess.

Death to D'Annunzio was not a religious thing, in which the poet sees the world being eternally renewed, from earth to man, and man to earth. In one of the books he wrote in France, about the death of a friend, *Contemplazione della Morte,* there are pages which sound extremely spiritual: "Jesus was never nearer to me, never has the spectacle of death given me such a tragic feeling, I have never felt so powerful, and so miserable . . ." But these pages, if examined closely, are really deprived of all spirituality; he examines death in its purely exterior aspect, with all the visual, aural and oliferous details. He wrote of a corpse, "There the dead man lay, newly dead, suddenly without *our* air, the air we breathe, but already with his own air, the air of the tomb. . . ."

1915 marks a break in D'Annunzio's career. It divides his life into two parts. Until now, from his adolescence to 1915, his writing has been concerned mainly with Art; in the second period, from the war until his death in 1938, he is concerned almost exclusively with Patriotism. In the second period he continued writing; but from his pen came no new novel, drama or lyrical poem. Instead, there were orations, diatribes, messages, condemnations, poems inspired not by women, but by the Fatherland. They form a set of writings of considerable importance in understanding his character; but they add nothing to his artistic stature. From the Quarto speech to the departure from Fiume in 1920, Italy alone occupied every thought, every action, almost every hour, of the life of Gabriele D'Annunzio.

He has been accused of being a "decadent"; and it is true that his literary work has all the blemishes of the "decadent," pretentious and obscure, intended to shock, full of incongruities, of "subtle sensations and gorgeous exotic colors." But with the war, D'Annunzio changed. The change is best illustrated pictorially, by contrasting the portraits of him in his "decadent" period, with those that were painted in the war. In the earlier ones, the general effect is tender, the eyes a little downcast, with a vaguely melancholy smile; the Victorian notion of the lyrical poet. In the wartime paintings, such as the one by Romaine Brooks, the features are firm and hard, the mustache is curled ferociously at the ends, like the Kaiser's; the small pointed beard is menacing, the eyes aggressive, the eyebrows knit. This is the first portrait of D'Annunzio as a warrior. His career as a man of action developed gradually, until it reached its climax at Fiume, when he put into practice all that he had written.

He did not find it easy to join the army at the age of fifty-two. He had to spend some time in Rome before getting to the front. From Rome he had written to his friend, Albertini, of the *Corriere della Sera*. "You cannot imagine how hard it has been to arrange everything—the number of strings I have had to pull. But at last, I have received a letter from General Cadorna telling me that I am to be called up as an officer in the Novara Lancers, in the Duke of Aosta's army. At the same time, I received a letter from Admiral Viale allowing me to go to Venice and follow the naval operations. I am wondering how I can reconcile these two, on land and sea. . . . I have started my first war poems, but it is essential that I now *take part in action myself*, if I am to continue writing. . . ."

About his uniform, he wrote enthusiastically, "I have now been in uniform two days, already feeling like an old soldier. This morning, I went to the Farnesina barracks to look for a mechanic, and I was treated to all the military honors! A strange sensation, to be saluted and have arms presented to one! The cowl admittedly does not make the monk, but a new spirit is quickly created by putting on a uniform. One seems already to belong to a caste, to an accepted system. Cap, general service; leggings, general service; great-coat, general service! What important things these have all suddenly become to the author of the *Laudi* . . . !"

He was a little short-sighted, and on several occasions in Rome he saluted ordinary *carabinieri* on guard, mistaking them for superior officers. Once he was with Marconi, the great electrician, who had also been commissioned, and who was wearing uniform for the first time. He had only one eye; and the pair of them smartly saluted a man who was sergeant of the guard outside the Finance Ministry.

When difficulties were raised about his taking part in action on account of his age and his value as a poet, D'Annunzio wrote

indignantly to Salandra, the President of the Council, ". . . you
know with what impatience I have requested the honor of serving
my country. You know that all my life I have been waiting for
this hour. If the hour of great achievements has struck for the
Italian people, the hour of blood has struck for me. Although new
literary work is expected of me, I am unable to compose a line
today. I now have a horror of all sedentary work, of the pen, the
inkwell, the blank page. All these things have suddenly become
vain and futile . . . I am deeply shocked and offended that Admiral Cutinelli has forbidden me from taking part in 'dangerous
enterprises.' How can people talk of my 'precious life,' and other
commonplaces? I am not the traditional 'literary man,' in slippers
and a skullcap. I am now a soldier. I intend to live like one. By
that, I do not mean sitting about in cafés and at mess tables—but
fighting. I beseech you to raise this ridiculous prohibition. . . ." [1]

Salandra at length complied, and D'Annunzio, from the base
which he established in Venice, took part in over fifty actions. His
oft repeated claim, to be a Renaissance figure, was now justified.
In earlier times, in the Middle Ages, it was unusual to find a
cavalier who manipulated, with equal skill, the sword and the
pen. This quality, which distinguished the men of the early

---

[1] It was while he was waiting impotently in Rome to get to the front that he
had his main contact with the English—a race of whom he had a poor opinion.
The ambassador had asked him to lunch—to thank him for all he had done
for the Allied cause in bringing Italy into the war. D'Annunzio accepted, but
on the day in question he forgot to go. The English ambassador telephoned to
his secretary, Antongini, who made excuses as best he could. But unfortunately
the next day, when D'Annunzio and Antongini were coming out of a hotel,
they saw the English ambassador coming towards them, his face livid with
rage. D'Annunzio whispered to Antongini, "You must say you forgot to tell
me."

Antongini shrugged his shoulders, but like a good secretary he stoically accepted the unpleasant task. He apologized and then, in front of the ambassador,
he came in for such a rating, and such abuse, from D'Annunzio, that finally
the ambassador himself intervened, accepting the apology. The matter passed
off, and when they were alone, Antongini said to his master, "That was a bit
unfair. And what reward do I get for it all?"

"You certainly deserve one, and you shall have one," said D'Annunzio. "I
shall tell the ambassador exactly what happened. The Truth. And he will give
you the Victoria Cross."

Rinascimento, appeared again in D'Annunzio, in the twentieth century.

Venice before the war was the center of a brilliant cosmopolitan life, such as had not been since the days of the Doges. English, French, Germans, Hungarians, Russians and Americans, inhabited hotels, restaurants, beaches, gondolas and café terraces in a kind of orgy of luxury. Music, carnivals, international exhibitions of art and ladies' dresses, together with much private hospitality, entertained the millionaires and monarchs (the film stars had not yet arrived). Kaiser William himself appeared from time to time, to take out the beautiful Countess Morosini in his yacht. A large foreign colony existed, with princes and poets, diplomats and painters, students of art and history, romantic and extravagant visionaries of all kinds, filling their days with esthetic-peripatetic conversations and visits, suppers and serenades, displaying the same enthusiasms for an object found in an old antiquarian's shop, or for an unknown garden, or a new *osteria,* a Byzantine tile, or the façade of a falling *palazzo.*

But suddenly, with the sound of the first cannon, they all disappeared. The revelry ended; the city emptied in a space of days; the hotels shut; the port was closed; the lagoons were rendered unnavigable by mines. When D'Annunzio arrived at the Danieli hotel in July 1915, he found the city already in arms, having had three air attacks—during one of which a destroyer had been sunk in the harbor. A black-out had been imposed; the exterior canals were blocked; the monuments were swathed in sandbags. On the belvederes were AA guns.

The military authorities, with unusual acumen, realized that his oratorical powers might be used to inspire the troops and raise their morale. He was therefore allowed to transform himself at will into a cavalry lieutenant, an HQ officer, an infantry officer, a sailor and, to his great delight, an aviator. His first thought was how to get into action. His friend, the editor Albertini, had advised him that these war years should be a period of saving, or restoring his finances. "Luxury," said Albertini, in a letter to him, "is distasteful to most people these days. You can now save. Work, act, speak for the nation. Be all spirit, and no flesh!" To which D'Annunzio replied, "Yes, indeed I shall speak, and even write. But not until I have had my baptism of fire. The tone of my muse will depend on the artillery batteries of Opcina, and the machine gun boats that go up the valley of the Muggia. I must take up a piece of shrapnel in my hand. I must pick it up, as if it were a shaft of celestial fire. Perhaps very soon, tomorrow evening, you will know that I am a great poet again. . . ."

His superiors soon lost track of him and his exploits. Indeed, his career thereafter is like that of one of those paladins in Ariosto's poem, whose whereabouts remained unknown to the Emperor Charlemagne himself, although they were doing doughty deeds for him. D'Annunzio delighted in a kind of individual enterprise in which, together with some chosen Ulyssean companions in a motorboat, he would glide into an Austrian harbor by night, and fire off torpedoes, at shipping or at the shore. Or in an airplane, he would fly over enemy cities dropping, instead of high-explosive, hundreds of leaflets couched in his own high-sounding prose. Officially a commissioned officer in the army, he adopted on his own authority a naval title, *Comandante*—perhaps because, when literally translated into Latin, it sounds like *imperator* i.e., one who wields supreme command. He fought in the air, on the sea, on the land, and was finally decorated with one gold medal, five silver ones, a bronze medal and the officer's cross of the Savoy Military order. His theory was that fear is natural to the body, and that courage to control it belongs to the mind. He always liked to tell the old story of the Great Condé before a battle. Even this famous *foudre de guerre* knew fear, and was trembling. But to his physical self Condé said, "You'd shake a lot more, you old carcass, if you knew where I was going to take you."

During the first phase, between D'Annunzio's flight over Trieste and the time when he returned to the Casetta Rossa in Venice with the damaged eye, he took part in ten exploits. Once, he had to go up to 14,000 feet (a tremendous altitude in those days), to avoid the AA fire. It was seventeen degrees below zero, and shouting to the pilot gave him laryngitis. On August 7, 1915, he flew over Trieste dropping tricolor flags and india-rubber sacks containing this message: "To the people of the very Italian city— 'Courage brothers! Courage and fortitude! To be free sooner, let us fight quicker. There is no enemy that cannot be destroyed by our courage. There is no impertinent lie which cannot be deflated by Italian bayonets. We have already taken more than 20,000 prisoners. The Carso will be ours by force of arms. I tell you, I swear to you, my brothers, our victory is certain! The flag of Italy will be planted on your Great Arsenal, on the hill of San Giusto. Courage! Constancy! The end of your martyrdom is at hand! The dawn of your joy is imminent. From the heights of heaven, on the wings of Italy, I throw you this pledge, this message from my heart . . .' "

A few weeks later, he dropped the following message and package on Trent, "Today Rome has consecrated for you in the Forum an urn filled with water from its sacred fountain, and a bough of laurel picked from the Vestal Virgin's garden. I throw you this because I know that no other water will quench your thirst, no other garland will console you . . ." To Zara, in Dalmatia, he said in another message dropped from the skies, "Oh Zara, for your Venetian grace, for all your Italian beauty, believe in the promise, believe in the joy of your second spring, when the Corinthian acanthus will flower again around your Latin columns, and your Lions of St. Mark above your doors will roar again at the sacred entry. He would like to live till that day, worthy to sing your coronation, who today from on high has felt the strong beating of your great heroine's heart . . ." On his airplane he had painted the motto "The lion roars again," surrounded with seven stars and a tongue of blue flame.

It is easy today to forget the courage required for all this flying. His flights, including many over the Alps, took place over forty years ago, when flying was in its infancy, and an obstacle like the

Alps seemed insurmountable. Unpleasant incidents occurred on most attacks. On one raid, he had eight bombs, and after having satisfactorily dropped seven, he found that the eighth had stuck in the undercarriage. Every effort to dislodge it failed, and the danger of having to land with it still hanging and liable to explode on contact had to be faced. It was finally dislodged by making a skimming landing over water.

So penetrated was D'Annunzio's mind with the air, that he sent a despatch to the Generalissimo Cadorna himself entitled *"Bomber planes and how to support infantry with them."* Even books he read for relaxation back in Venice are full of military jottings in the margins, as if his mind was fulfilling two roles at once. In his library at the *Vittoriale* today is a most unwarlike book, which he must have been reading at this time. It is called *Dictionnaire de la Fable,* by Victor Verger. Notes of this kind are scribbled in the margins, in his handwriting:

'(1) [Inside the binding]. Cut off Susac bridge by demolition.
(2) [On one side of the illustrations]. S.V.A. velocity 220. Bomb load 250 kilos, deliver at 0020 hrs from 30 metres at distance 4–500 kms. 2 Vickers machine guns.
(3) Maurice Pagliano, died on Coneglian territory, 28th Decr. 1917.
(4) [Near the frontispiece, in red pencil]. Myriomorphis, the witch doctor. Luigi Gori, both legs split, died the following day.
[Pagliano and Gori were two of his aviator friends].'

When the Americans came into the war, he wrote a poem, *All' America in Armi*—lofty verse, sixty stanzas of it, ranging from the past glories of American history, to the present battle of the Piave. He was tactful enough to choose the Civil War rather than the War of Independence, so as not to offend their ally, England; and he ingeniously praised both South and North equally, as having the same heroism.

Because the Austrians had put a price on his head, he decided to reply to it with a *beffa,* or joke. He organized what he called the *Beffa di Buccari,* entering Buccari harbor by night with a group of *Mas,* or small torpedo boats; he torpedoed a merchant ship, and left rubber containers in the water, each containing one of his own harangues written in indelible ink.

On January 16, 1916, he was returning from a flight over enemy territory, when he was thrown sharply against his machine gun as the airplane landed, and his right eye was seriously damaged. So bad was this accident that he temporarily lost the sight of the eye, and it was thought that the vision of the other had been impaired. He had to remain in bed, in the dark, for several months, with his head lower than his feet, until the vision healed. Fortunately, he was able to retain his blinded eye, and was thus spared the disfigurement of a glass one. He was told not to fly again, and thus endanger his other eye; but he ignored these instructions. He returned to the air on May 23, and in the general attack he gained a silver medal. He then came down and attacked by land (he was present at the battle from Castagna to the sea). He was with Randaccio's battalion in the big assault, where Randaccio was killed.

It was during the healing of his eye, when he was tended by his daughter, Renata, that he wrote *Notturno,* 10,000 words on large cards, each containing two or three lines, because he could not see to write properly. This monograph is generally considered his *De Profundis,* not because it contains any trace of piety or repentance, but because D'Annunzio has been here compelled, for once, by the sheer force of circumstances, to look inside himself, instead of reveling in the outside world. In it, he speaks of the loss of his eye with a serenity which was not cynical, nor even stoic, but with a pride in the heroic circumstances of the loss. "I have lost one eye," he said. "Of what importance is that? The other will suffice. Cyclops can do his work in any smithy." He then goes on to say how he longs for death. "Death appears to me nothing more than the final form of perfection. I shall thus become young again, in the marble of my tomb . . ." He claimed that he was inspired during his convalescence by the memory of Foscolo, who was wounded in the attack at Cento, and who afterwards took refuge in a monastery, under the assumed name of Alighieri. In *Notturno* he also gave a detailed description of one of his torpedo attacks in the Adriatic.

It was during this period of enforced inactivity that his famous relations with the Countess Morosini flourished. She was one of the most fashionable ladies of the day, of great beauty, an ex-mistress of the Kaiser. D'Annunzio had already begun to pay court, before his accident, in the intervals of his martial exercises. His letters and *billets doux* to her combine perfectly amorous sentiments with an aviator's ardor. D'Annunzio generally wrote novels about his love affairs when they were over, but here the novel preceded the love affair. His aviation novel *Forse che sì, forse che no,* written in 1909, dealt with a man of mature years, of vigorous intellect, caught between a woman of violent passion and his desire to be in the air. The heroine, Isabella Inghirami, was meant to be the "new woman," equally at home behind the steering wheel of a racing car, in the cockpit of an airplane, a kind of Latin Amy Mollison.

The Morosini was not quite up to all this, it is true, but her enthusiasm for the air seems to have matched his. She lived in a palazzo just across the Grand Canal from his home, the Casetta Rossa, and he wrote: ". . . each morning I feel the influence of your beauty across the canal in the form of an increase of light. . . . I hope to come this evening and rest in the light of your eyes [the Morosini prided herself on her eyes], which float in the oil of Nepenthe, that drug which produces forgetfulness of grief. . . . Where do you obtain your mysterious and constant renewal of life and beauty? I kiss your forehead between those two stars with my eyelashes. . . . I adore your eyes . . ."

These flowery compliments completely conquered the Morosini. But on other occasions the letters he wrote to those eyes, far from being couched in such language, read more like a general's war despatches:

"Dear Friend, During the nights 2-3 I bombed the port of Pola with excellent results. The action took place before the first quarter of the moon. We stayed out every night with our machines loaded with bombs, watching the sky, listening for the messages of our observers. I cannot describe to you my impatience when the weather was unfavorable. Uncertain of the weather one morning, I went out to bomb the valley of Chiapovano, so as not to leave one single day *sine ictu* . . . Wednesday. A clear, serene morning. I don't think I ever looked at the sky with such excitement. Every woolly cloud, however small, made me shudder with apprehension. My airplane (of which I send you this small photograph) took off at 1 a.m. on Thursday. We were over Pola at 2:33. I sent down ten bombs on the Rock of Olivea and Santa Catarina, coming down to 2,000 feet. I cannot describe to you my emotion when the whole crew, in the sudden silence, let out our new war-cry—Alala![1] . . . Your sublime gift of a *Florilegium* as talisman enriches my day. . . .
Always your, Gabriele."

His later letters to the Morosini begin to show the elliptical quality for which his work at the end of his life is notable:

"My dear, dear Friend, I *have* what I have *given*. Never before did those ascetic, little known words have more meaning to me. 'And what would I want it for unless it burn?' My greatest joy after fighting and *feeling* is to know 'burning within me' my faith in you as my companion. I have acquired, in faith and war, a companion with the most beautiful eyes in the world. I am therefore your most grateful, Gabriele D'Annunzio."

[1] It was during the flight over Pola that he invented the war cry, *Eia! Eia! Alala!* corresponding roughly to the British *Hip! Hip! Hooray!* which he considered "barbaric." "Are we not Latins?" he said. "Should we not have a Latin cry?" He ordered his pilots to utter the *Alala!* as they dropped their bombs—a war cry clearly inaudible to the enemy around the target, but of great moral value to the airmen.

He often crossed the canal to the *palazzo* where she lived. "My dear Friend," he says in one letter. "In a day or two I shall again think of crossing to the fairy on the other side. This recalls one of my own lines, *la gioia è sempre all'altra riva.* But too many troubles and difficulties of all kinds have prevented me from testing the truth of my poetry. Until tomorrow then . . ." She would come over to him at the Casetta Rossa, to dine or listen to music with friends. One of his notes reads, "Tomorrow Tuesday, Maestro Giarda is playing the organ for me in the Sala del Liceo Marcello at 9 p.m. Would you like to come? He will play some of the most pathetic pages from my *San Sebastiano,* set to music by Claude Debussy.[1] We shall be few, we shall be close . . ."

Dollot, the French consul in Venice, relates that the other aviators took him and his love affairs rather as a joke, particularly as the Casetta Rossa where he lived was anything but austere and suitable for a warrior's HQ. "An exquisite *bon-bon* box," Dollot calls it, "a boudoir rather than a Major's sleeping quarters—with its complicated toilet articles, high candelabras, Murano vases and silver-edged mirrors."

Other women of course assailed him in the Casetta Rossa. There were frequent evening parties, and often too many people tried to come at once. He therefore introduced a rule to keep down the numbers. Ten o'clock was the "hour of violence." Anyone arriving after it tacitly admitted that they would be the object of any liberty the other sex might care to take. Even this did not sop the influx of the ladies. If the sanctions were applied, they were evidently enjoyed.

Being near D'Annunzio in Venice did not always have advantages for the Morosini. The Austrians had put a price on D'An-

[1] One of D'Annunzio's most curious ideas about survival after the war was connected with Debussy. He admitted that he hoped to be killed in action—that he would be prepared to survive *only* if Debussy were still alive. He had planned to write an opera with the French composer. When he received the telegram announcing Debussy's death, he was about to set forth on an aerial mission over enemy territory. He said that none of his companions were aware of his strong feeling at the time that he would not return.

nunzio's head, and they tried to bomb the Casetta Rossa. Like all Venetian palaces, at the smallest bomb, it would have opened up like a pomegranate. But they missed and dropped the bomb instead on the Morosini's palace. The poet composed a plaque on the wall to commemorate it. BOMBA AUSTRIACA—7 SETTEMBRE 1917—LA SPADA DRITTA DEL PELOPONNESIACO—PROTESSE.

After his famous flight over Vienna at the end of the war, he sent the Morosini as a souvenir a bracelet, on which was reproduced the number of his airplane motor and the date—*From the skies of Vienna—9 August 1918—Gabriele D'Annunzio.* "My dear Friend, Here is the living souvenir of a long flight, the plaque of the faithful motor, with the image of the Ibis, the sacred bird, the destroyer of reptiles. I am happy to be able to offer it to the person who gave me fortune on my first flight . . ."

The flight over Vienna marked the zenith and the culmination of his war career. At 5:30 that morning at the end of the war, he set off from Treviso with eleven airplanes. They crossed the Julian Alps and reached Vienna at 9:20, where they dropped this pamphlet, written by D'Annunzio:

"VIENNESE!

"Learn by this to know the Italians!

"We could now be dropping bombs on you; instead we drop only a salute. The salute has three colors, the colors of Italy, the colors of Liberty! We Italians do not make war on women and children. We are making war on your Government, which is the enemy of your national liberty. We are waging war against a cruel and bigotted system, which gives neither peace nor bread, which nourishes you only on Hate and Illusion!

"VIENNESE!

"You are known to the world as an intelligent people. Why then do you put on the Prussian uniform? You have turned the world against you.

"If you wish to continue the war—continue it! You will thereby commit suicide. What have you to gain? The decisive victory promised you by the Prussian generals? Their decisive victory is like Ukrainian bread. You will starve waiting for it . . ."

So successful was this flight, from which all but one airplane returned, and the propaganda value it had in Austria, that D'Annunzio became mesmerized with the possibilities of flying over capital cities, delivering messages from the air. The French consul in Venice, M. Dollot, says that he then suggested flying over Paris, and dropping victory pamphlets. When the French Government replied politely that the time was not ripe for this (the French thought after Caporetto, that Italy was not doing all she could in the war), he proposed similar flights over London and Berlin, crossing the Alps not over Mont Cenis, which he considered beneath his dignity, but over Mont Blanc, the highest mountain in Europe. After London, he would fly over Berlin, where he would drop not pamphlets, but high explosives. The end of the war overtook him planning this ambitious exploit.

He had by now gained the reputation of the first fighter in Italy. He was an international hero, who had amassed a formidable array of medals, from all the Allies, as well as from his own country. The British had given him the MC for his attacks in the Adriatic on the Austrian fleet; and foreign medals and decorations now began to fall on him like ripe cherries—as they do only on high commanders at the end of a successful war. His swelling chest assumed the colors of the rainbow. Only France, Serbia and Belgium were remiss, and he instructed his secretary "to rouse these sleepers." In a letter to him, he said, "I had been led to expect the Serbian gold medal, which all the others have received, and also the Belgian Order of Leopold—particularly after the fine words their King spoke to me when he visited our squadron on the Lido. Belgium is forgetful. Do see to it! . . ."

Towards the end of the war, he made a statement which was often to be repeated in the years to come by the Fascists, who used it to prove that he was really one of them. "Whatever happens, one thing is certain after this war. The future will bring something quite new to us, such as we have never seen before. Something stronger, more beautiful, will be born from all this blood and sacrifice. All forms of art and politics will be overthrown; the new ones will be healthier. I believe that we are entering a new era, whose transformation will surpass that of the Renaissance and the French Revolution. Happy are they who shall see this new world; happy, too, those who, like us, have announced it, foreseen it, prepared it . . ."

15

Disillusion

When the war finished, the Yugoslav nation had been created and her irregular troops had occupied the whole of the Dalmatian coast as far north as the Austro-Hungarian port of Fiume, which she was also proposing to invade. The Yugoslavs had fought well, and President Wilson wanted them to be rewarded with this territory at the Peace Conference. Unfortunately, England and France, anxious to bring Italy into the war on their side, had already signed the secret treaty of London (in 1915) in which they had promised Italy large slices of the Dalmatian coast including, the Italians claimed, the port of Fiume. At the Peace Conference, therefore, President Wilson was in the embarrassing position of offering Yugoslavia territories which his allies had already given to Italy.[1]

In fact, Italy had done extremely well out of the war. All her war aims seemed satisfied. Austria, her main and hereditary enemy, had disappeared completely, replaced by a cloud of little states. France was weakened by 1,500,000 dead—over double the number of Italian dead for an equal population. Italy was now surrounded on every side by weaker states; she had military security, almost insularity. Menaced by none, cherished by most, she seemed at last heading for the spiritual glory which had inspired her in the nineteenth century.

Her hatred of the Slavs made her forget all this. The new nation, Yugoslavia, was to her merely a castle of cards put together by Wilson and Clemenceau, together with some English journal-

---

[1] The terms of this secret treaty were not known until the Bolsheviks, having obtained control in Petrograd, ransacked the archives. The contents of the document were then sent to English newspapers.

ists and one or two Italian traitors—a country without roots in history, language or religion, and doomed to crumble at the first puff of wind. In the Dalmatian coastline, Italians saw only the the Venetian past, the lovely Venetian churches and palaces; in its towns and villages, they heard only the echoes of the soft Venetian dialect. They were unaware that these remains were fossils of a long extinguished empire, no more significant than the Genoese stones in Constantinople, or the Roman remains in Britain. Instead, they now considered that they were morally, as well as ethnographically, entitled to them.

A further, and more understandable, reason for their Adriatic nationalism was that, in 1917, the Western allies gave the impression that they might make a separate peace with Austria. Little has been said about this since then in England, but to the Italians it naturally sounded like treachery—as they had entered the war for the express purpose of beating Austria and retrieving the "irredentist" lands. Fearing this, they had drawn up the Pact of Rome with the exiled Serb and Croat leaders of the oppressed territories under Austrian domination; it was aimed at opposing a separate peace with Austria. D'Annunzio later coined the phrase "the mutilation of Victory," for the way these territories were withheld from Italy at the peace treaty.

There was in Italy, it is true, another, less belligerent, school of thought about Dalmatia, identified naturally with Giolitti (who had passed the war in retirement), and the present Prime Minister, Nitti, who was anxious for a pacific settlement at all costs. Nitti, like Giolitti, was almost everything that D'Annunzio and the nationalists were not. He was a well trained civil servant, a Treasury expert, a book reader, a don. He had played a respectable, if somewhat lukewarm, part in the war, counseling caution and moderation, in favor of an honorable peace rather than a glorious victory; and he had opposed the victorious campaign of 1918, thinking it might repeat the disaster of Caporetto. He was therefore accused by the nationalists of high treason. Nor did they approve of his voice and manner. He was fat and bourgeois in appearance, and his voice had a soft Neapolitan cadence, to which he added a lazy intonation of his own, the half-conceited, half-sarcastic manner of the Donnish man of intellect confronted by the mere man of action. War seemed to him futile, and the desire to continue it, when it was manifestly over, excited his irony rather than his indignation. His sarcastic and literary jokes seemed unsuited to the circumstances; and when he did speak of politics, he made dark and gloomy forecasts about hunger, isolation and national insolvency. An avowed democrat, he felt more distrust in opposite theories than belief in any theory of his own; he preferred to disbelieve in nationalism, rather than to believe in the League of Nations. He realized that the Anglo-Saxons now owned two-thirds of the globe, and anyway, as an economist, he rather admired the English and Americans, who were now being abused by D'Annunzio. Lacking that faculty of emotion so necessary in a Latin country, he saw everything in terms of figures and equilibriums of force. In short, Nitti the Prime Minister had nothing to offer a Latin people, who saw in the end of a victorious war, the beginning of a new Roman empire.

One of Nitti's spokesmen, Bissolati, gave a conference on the question of Fiume at the end of the war, in the Scala Theatre, Milan. He argued that this port was essential to the Southern Slavs; that the Dalmatian coast was populated exclusively by Slavs; that Fiume, even if its inhabitants were largely Italians, would be of little further use to Italy, who already had the excellent Adriatic ports of Trieste, Venice and Bari. He invoked Mazzini, the builder or modern Italy who had always advocated friendship with the Southern Slavs (or Jugoslavs as they were now called). Here was the moment, he said, for Italy to make a noble gesture to her new neighbors.

While he was speaking in the Scala, a band of young men rushed in, shouting that he, Nitti and Giolitti were traitors, that the frontiers of Italy were along the Velebit range, that Fiume was Italian, had always been Italian, and would always be Italian. When he attempted to reply, he was drowned in shrieks, whistles, howling, drums and trumpets. These were the first *Fasci di Combattimento,* a new political movement, supported by the *Popolo d'Italia,* a newspaper of limited circulation and doubtful influence, edited by one Benito Mussolini.

This revolutionary man had only met D'Annunzio once before, but he had read with pleasure his strictures on the western democracies and his admiration for Nietzsche, particularly his contention that the Superman could be a southerner of dark complexion. He disliked Anglo-Saxons, and applauded D'Annunzio's witticism that President Wilson's mouth was, "full of false words and false teeth."

There was every reason why D'Annunzio and Mussolini should collaborate (although until the Great War, Mussolini had been a pacifist socialist). As late as 1911, he had been attacking the "miserable war of conquest in Tripoli masquerading, thanks to government propaganda, as a Roman triumph." He had organized strikes against it and, during one of his piazza harangues, had been arrested and imprisoned. But then he suddenly changed. Mussolini, editor of the notorious anti-war *Avanti,* suddenly founded the pro-war, *Popolo d'Italia.* It was anti-Marxist, anti-clerical, anti-Giolitti, discreetly anti-monarchical, and violently anti-foreign—all qualities shared with D'Annunzio.

D'Annunzio was now an unemployed reserve officer who, just before the Armistice, had been heard to say, "I smell the stench of peace." He had had, as we have seen, a most unusual war, reaching all the military as well as nautical and aeronautical peaks; and he was not at all anxious to divest himself of his uniform, on which were pinned three rows of medals. His patriotism about Dalmatia was combined with a scorn for the mediocre men who were now ruling Italy, and with an Abruzzese's enthusiasm for the Adriatic. Having been born on the western shore of that sea, he felt he was entitled, more than most Italians, to be interested in its eastern shore as well. In *Faville del Maglio* he had written of it, ". . . all my ardent Italian passion is here, *crucified* at not being able to send an armada against this 'fourth shore.' In my play *La Nave,* how gladly did I long to place upon the Admiral's prow a Victory made, not of bronze, but of some new unknown metal from an untried mine. . . . Destiny demands that this play be acted in Fiume, in that Fiume which, to my childish imagination, has ever been mysterious, since I first saw her loaded brigantines and schooners comging into Pescara harbor . . ."

About the "mediocre men who were governing Italy," he wrote, "It is shameful that men like Giolitti and Nitti should still be speaking in Parliament. They represent Decomposition. They are without education or culture . . ." He recommended a "national action to overturn Parliament." "I have been thinking," he said ironically, "for some time of bombing Montecitorio." He also composed a set of three poems entitled *The Three Hand Grenades*. The first was addressed to Giolitti, imploring the Winged Victory to take off her wings and come down to earth, "to plant her feet in the mud and dung of Montecitorio," and bury Giolitti alive in it. He said that Nitti should have, "a punishment as direct as a flame-thrower."

When the war finished, he wrote to Albertini, the director of the *Corriere della Sera:* "I live in a mixture of joy and unhappiness. The Allies have defrauded us of the ships in Pola which should yesterday have been floating in the lagoon of St. Marks. For this we must thank our 'friends' [France and England] whom you rightly fear more than the Quaker and those 'born yesterday' [President Wilson and the Americans]. I saw our Admiral crying. Nor have I the courage to go to Trieste, where there is too much shouting and too many intruding people. Already those who have persevered and fought, already the 'pure' (and I am one of them) have been thrown back behind the agitators and the profiteers. Too many ignoble tongues are yelling 'Long Live Italy!' I hope we shall fight again and that I can bomb Berlin from a new Bohemian front."

In his *Letter to the Dalmatians,* he wrote, ". . . When we took up arms three years ago to save France, and the world, I and my companions in arms made an act of pure devotion, before all the

altars of Dalmatia, before the cities of Fiume, Zara, Sebenico, Spa-
lato, Trau, Ragusa, Cattaro, Perasto. We fought for that pledge to
be redeemed—a pledge placed between us and the foe, between us
and the Adriatic, between us and that huddle of Southern Slavs
who, beneath the mark of youthful liberty and a bastard name, still
aim, as ever, at our disarray . . ."

Such was his fury with the "ungrateful French," that he sent a
joint letter to Poincaré, President of the French Republic; Clemenceau, President of the French Council; Pichon, the French Foreign
Minister; and Dechanel, President of the French Parliament. This
forensic letter was to be borne across the Alps by his friend, Captain Palli, in an airplane (in those days, to fly across the Alps had
great symbolic value). In this open letter to the French called
Aveux de l'Ingrat, he referred to their ingratitude for Italy's wartime sacrifices. "A million dead, a million wounded," he said,
"together with the ruin of our finest provinces of the Veneto. Into
the furnace of war we threw three-quarters of our national wealth.
Now, having borne the yoke of war, we bear the yoke of peace.
But if need be, we will assault the rogues who plan to take Fiume
from us—in the manner of the old *arditi,* a bomb in each hand, a
knife in the teeth . . ." Unfortunately this airplane to Fiume
crashed on its way across the Alps, killing its pilot; and the messages had to be delivered to their august destinies, by the more
humdrum method of the French post.

The statements D'Annunzio now made were attractive to many
Italians, for other reasons than simply patriotic ones. As in all the
European countries, there was the problem in Italy at the end of
the war of demobilizing soldiers who, in economic terms, are simply large masses of men accustomed to receiving food from the
state. There was the difficulty of converting war industry to peace
uses. There were strikes; the devaluation of the currency; a civil
service still partially disorganized; a housing shortage. Ex-soldiers
always remember the advantages of military life, when the war is
over—the regular salary, the jolly companionship, the songs, the
stars on the sleeves, the gun at the belt, the feeling of Power.

Moreover, one of the great Italian maladies has always been *reducismo,* soldiers returning from some great enterprise which has made the state, and who now believe they can unmake it. The Rubicon has never really been forgotten in Italy.

Discontented and unemployed, these men were looking for a leader; and General Badoglio, the Chief of Staff, warned the Prime Minister, Nitti, ". . . a kind of fever has invaded the younger elements of our army due, it seems, to a dislike of ordinary, gray, everyday life and the constituted order; a scorn for goodness and saving, for the family, tradition, religion . . ."

This feeling increased when the Versailles peace settlements were announced. Orlando, impotent in the hands of Lloyd George and "Tiger" Clemenceau in Paris, seemed to have gained nothing for his country. Italians of all classes, whose fathers, sons and brothers had shed their blood, felt that Italy had been cheated. It was at this moment, when insurrectionary feeling ran high, that D'Annunzio turned his eyes on the port of Fiume.

16

Fiume

Fiume is one of those disastrous places, like the Polish corridor, Transylvania or Alsace, for which all claimants can put forward perfectly reasonable arguments. The Slavs, Hungary, Austria and Italy, have all claimed, and possessed, it at one time or another. Even to the traveler arriving by sea today, the first view of Fiume is somewhat bewildering. On every side, a range of hills stretches down to the sea, enclosing in a large semicircle that body of water known as the Carnaro. The hillside is bare, rocky, almost completely without vegetation; but on it, a number of buildings can be seen, and near the shore they seem to encircle the gulf in one long continuous line. A closer view reveals groups of small towns and villages; and on the map, one reads their names in a jumble of languages, Italian, Croatian and Magyar—Lovrana, Ika, Icini, Abbazia, Lipviza, Fiume, Volosca, Cantrida, Castua, Susak, Martinscica, Kraljevica. It is difficult to tell where one ends and the other begins.

Still more confusing is the information that this natural geographical disunity has often been shattered by artificial and political divisions. The towns of Cantrida, Fiume and Susak, for instance, lie adjacent to the bay. Yet under the old Austro-Hungarian regime, Cantrida formed part of Austria, Fiume part of Hungary, and Susak part of Croatia. How this could happen requires a historian's understanding not only of the Holy Roman Empire, but of the tortuous politics of Maria Theresa, the Dual Monarchy and the treaty of Vienna—in short, of that ingenious slogan which the Habsburgs adapted for centuries, for their own purposes, *divide et impera*. But they divided too much, linguistically, ethnographically, pragmatically—and ruled too little; so that the inhabitants of their empire lived in a curious condition, for which only the Greek language really has a word, *stasis*. It means more or less permanent civil strife, without hostilities ever actually breaking out.

In the archives of Fiume is a document which is at the base of the 1919 troubles—the famous Hungarian-Croatian compromise on Fiume in 1868, the *Kriptic*. Not even a Byzantine diplomat could have produced anything so equivocal. It was submitted in that year, in both the Hungarian and Croatian translations, for approval by the two Parliaments, the Hungarian in Budapest, the Croatian in Zagreb (both of which then belonged to the Habsburg empire). The Hungarian translation stated quite simply that Fiume belonged to Hungary; the Croatian one, equally simply, that it belonged to Croatia. And yet, when these documents, which the two parliaments had separately approved (each ignorant of the different nature of the other), went forward for final signature to the old Emperor, Franz Joseph, over the Croatian one a thin strip of paper had been pasted, the famous *Kriptic* (now on view in Zagreb), bearing a translation of the Hungarian text. Thinking all his subjects were satisfied, the short-sighted and well-meaning old Franz Joseph signed. This was the falsification on which the claim of Hungary to Fiume was founded, and afterwards upheld against the Slavs by superior forces.

In these circumstances, one can easily understand how Fiume gradually became a Hungarian colony, of the strangest character, a city on the Croatian coast, hundreds of miles from Hungary (the nearest Hungarian town was 350 kilometers away), overflowing with Hungarian officials, yet whose population was almost entirely Slav. It was impossible for the Hungarians to introduce their own colonists in large enough numbers from so far away, to balance the racial preponderance, so they adopted a most ingenious method— the help of the old enemies of the Slavs, the Italians. What could be more natural than to make them allies of Hungary, offering attractive privileges, if they came and lived in Fiume? So, the strange colonization began, towards the end of the nineteenth century.

From the nearest provinces of Italy, thousands of Italians were induced to emigrate by the promise of a large share in the government offices, and other municipal appointments. The Italian notion that service under the Government (whatever government) is eminently respectable, was encouraged and exploited. Besides the naturalized Italians, there were many others, who did not become citizens, but who were encouraged to carry on business in the town. The Croatian language was proscribed, and a knowledge of Italian was in itself a key to advancement. It was sufficient for a man to understand and carry on a conversation in Italian to stamp him as *italianissimo,* and therefore a member of the ruling classes.

Osbert Sitwell, one of the few Englishmen to visit Fiume after the war, puts forward the novel and typically aesthete's view that Fiume is Italian, "by right of landscape." "It belongs," he says, "to the same order as Genoa or Naples. With its spur of hills sinking into the opalescence of the far sea, and the quivering, misty outlines of the islands, the traveler feels that he is once more in Italy—whereas Trieste is a different, and an alien, bay."

At the end of the war, the polyglot city was occupied by an Allied commission who were to rule it with French, English, American and Italian troops, until its fate was decided at Versailles. A good description of this twilight period is given by Giovanni Comisso in his book, *Le Mie Stagioni.* "Fiume was a city of victory, of continuous victory celebration. The troops fraternized, and the city was full of beautiful girls, the shops and restaurants full of food and goods. In the restaurants, we ate cakes and fruit syrups, whipped cream and delicious *zabaglione* served by obsequious waiters. The inhabitants invited the Italian officers every evening to parties in their houses, lasting till dawn. Eating, drinking, dancing —this city with its irrepressible, overflowing vitality seemed Italy's prize for all our efforts. We soldiers felt we had earned it . . ."

The Italian who first thought of the seizure of this place by force while the Allies were arguing about it, was a Grenadier Major called Rajna, a native of the Veneto who, like Comisso, was in the Italian contingent of the Allied troops occupying Fiume. This contingent had been withdrawn in June 1919 by Nitti, with the laudable intention of lessening Italo-Yugoslav tension in Fiume, and thus leaving only French, English and American troops. For feeling was running high, and thousands of supporters came out daily to applaud the Italian troops whenever they marched.[1]

D'Annunzio, who seemed intent on trouble, had now gone to Rome, to address public meetings about Fiume. Mobs would collect outside his hotel, just as they had in 1915, calling for speeches and assurances that Fiume was to be Italian. He would come out on the balcony, make a speech condemning the Government, invoke the glorious Latin Past, and then arrange an appointment with the same mob for the next day. On one occasion, he summoned them to the Augusteo; on another, to the Capitol, where he tied a piece of black crepe around the Italian flag, proclaiming that it must remain there, "till Fiume became Italian." Once, he threw a glove as a gage to the crowd.

At the Augusteo, he spoke as he had in 1915, "Our hope lies only in our daring. *To Dare not to Plot*—that must be our motto (*Ardere non ordire*). Down there on the roads of Italy, on the roads of Dalmatia, roads that are all Roman, do you not hear the tramp of marching feet? Of the Legions? The dead march faster than the quick . . ." Under his influence, the crowds quickly learned the names of two small towns in Dalmatia, Sebenìco and Spàlato—which were supposed to be large Italian communities enslaved by the Jugoslavs, yearning to return to the motherland. They even learned to put the accents in the right places (they had previously called them Sebènico and Spalàto). On May 24, the anniversary of Italy's entry into the Great War, D'Annunzio was again to speak in the Augusteo. But this time the government forbade the speech, on the pretext that D'Annunzio, as a reserve officer, was recalled to his regiment.

Two generals were even sent to see him in his hotel, to per-

---

[1] The first disorders took place in Fiume when some members of the French contingent pulled the Italian tricolor off a young Fiume girl. The incident was known as "the Fiuman vespers." Nitti tried to keep it out of the Italian press.

suade moderation. He was in his suite writing, wearing only pajamas when they came in. They should have announced their arrival, or at least telephoned from the hall—but in those days immediately after the war, Generals could do anything. D'Annunzio was so embarrassed in his *négligé* that even his argumentative skill failed to impress them. But at a certain moment, profiting by the fact that the Generals turned towards the window, he managed to retire into his bedroom—from which, within a minute, he emerged fully dressed, with all his medals. His confidence now restored, he began arguing with the Generals; and very soon he had convinced them entirely by his case for Fiume. They left with changed minds. (This incident is related by his son, Mario D'Annunzio.)

D'Annunzio was supported in all this by a number of well-known people, including the futurist Marinetti, who addressed obscene and threatening insults to the Prime Minister, Nitti, from the columns of the popular press; while Keller, the aviator ace, threatened Nitti from the skies of Rome, and later parachuted a chamberpot full of carrots on to the Parliament buildings. Nitti became so frightened that he was driven daily to work in an armored car, and his children had to go to school with a police escort. In search of any means of getting rid of the irrepressible D'Annunzio, he suddenly hit upon the brilliant idea of offering D'Annunzio Treasury support for an experimental air flight to Tokyo. So attractive did this exploit appear to D'Annunzio, that for a moment he almost forgot Fiume. Drunk with words, he issued a statement, "Let us go! Let us strike! We will soar alone into the unknown! We will dare the undared, we will attain the unattainable . . ." Nitti hoped, of course, that D'Annunzio would break his neck.

More extreme anti-government groups even planned, in August 1919, to set fire to the Palazzo Braschi, the Ministry of the Interior; and the poet Trilussa brought two tanks of petrol to D'Annunzio's hotel for the purpose. D'Annunzio had to persuade him that two tanks would not be enough. "Impractical as a poet!" he laughed. The editor of the *Popolo d'Italia*, Benito Mussolini, also joined the fray and even visited Fiume, to stir up public feeling. From Fiume he telegraphed to the poet, ". . . all the great family of the Italian people supports you with impetuous faith, unending admiration and undying sympathy"—to which D'Annunzio replied by telegram, "My thanks to you and your companions. I am ready. We are ready. All are ready. The greatest battle is about to begin. I tell you, we shall have the Fifteenth Victory." [1] The *Popolo d'Italia* now came out almost daily in favor of the Italian seizure of Fiume. When any inflammatory or libelous article was proscribed by the government, Mussolini would print his first page completely blank, with a small notice in the middle, "Censored and whitewashed by the orders of the pig Nitti, that vilest of Borbonic ministers. To him we shout in his ugly snout, *Viva Fiume Italiana . . .*" [2] In another place Mussolini wrote, "The capital of Italy is no longer on the Tiber. It is on the Carnaro."

To these men, the whole venture seemed simply a modern version of Garibaldi's expedition with his Thousand.[3] There were, in fact, many differences between the two. In 1860, Garibaldi and his men had the support of the Sardinian government and of Cavour, for their Sicilian expedition. In 1866, his 20,000 volunteers, marching on Rome, were looked upon as the IIIrd (if unofficial) Corps of an Italian Regular Army in the making. But D'Annunzio and Mussolini were now in open conflict with the government. D'Annunzio had described its Prime Minister as "*cagoia*," a crapulous fellow without a fatherland.

Of candidates for the role of an Italian Mirabeau there was no shortage, from D'Annunzio and various unemployed colonels (Mussolini was not yet senior enough), to the Duke of Aosta, the King's cousin, a tall and silly old man who happened to have

---

[1] There had, theoretically, been fourteen Italian victories in the Great War.
[2] Italian libel laws are less stringent than the British.
[3] *The Thousand.* It is interesting, incidentally, to note how people are easily moved by a clear, obvious symbol. A "Thousand" is a good round, masculine figure. If Garibaldi had had 752 men, his task would have been much more difficult.

been, during the war, at the head of "an invincible army." [1] It
seemed easy to stage a revolution in Rome, scene of past and future
glory, storm the hotel where Nitti lived near the Tritone fountain, expel or execute him, and wage war against Yugoslavia, and
the world—the real Italian war of expansion, after three years of
unsatisfactory alliances.

Nor was the Fiume project the first of its kind. As early as
1917, a General called Giardino had toyed with the idea of leading an armed insurrection, to form a republican constitution of
the Three Venetos with Dalmatia and Fiume. An unsuccessful
proposal had been made to Garibaldi's son, Riciotti, to lead another "Adriatic expedition." An attack on Spàlato had also been
planned, quite irregularly, for the month of June 1919. General
Caviglia, in his *Conflitto di Fiume* published in 1948, writes:
". . . the first assault division in full battle array and commanded
by General Zoppi was returning home from Libya at the time.
The officer intended to land at Spàlato and occupy it in the name
of Italy. But General Zoppi made the condition first that the
Commander in Chief, Badoglio, should be informed. Badoglio
did not oppose the idea openly, but he said the action should be
postponed, so as not to prejudice negotiations going on at Versailles. On account of these and other indecisions, the project was
never implemented. . . ."

A good eye-witness account of D'Annunzio speaking to the
crowd at this time is given in *The Waveless Plain*, by Walter
Starkie who heard him talking about Fiume in Venice:

"Suddenly I was roused from my meditations by a roar from
the crowd. Looking up, I saw a tiny, bald-headed man upon the
balcony. He stood motionless for a moment before beckoning the
crowd to be silent. He then began: '*Volete dunque che io parli?
Avevo rifiutato quando mi fu chiesto. Perchè mi forzate?*' (Do
you then want me to speak? I had refused when they asked me.
Why do you force me to do so?) As I gazed at the little man, all

[1] The Duke of Aosta had become such an admirer of D'Annunzio that he
even imitated the poet's handwriting.

my illusions fell in a heap like a house of cards. I had created my image of the poet from a world of towering supermen: instead I see before me a dwarf of a man, goggle-eyed and thick-lipped— truly sinister in his grotesqueness like a tragic gargoyle.

"Is this the man that Duse loved?

"Little by little, however, I began to sink under the fascination of the voice, which penetrated into my consciousness, syllable by syllable, like water from a clear fountain. It was a slow, precise voice accompanying the words right to the last vowel, as if he wished to savor to the utmost their echoing music. The tones rose and fell in an unending stream like the song of a minstrel, and they spread over the vast audience like olive oil on the surface of the sea. Never a hurried, jerky gesture: occasionally one arm raised slowly as though wielding an imaginary wand. He went on to tell how he had come among the Venetians as a Venetian, wishing to pay tribute to this sacred city. But it is no longer the time for words—'We have,' he cried, 'been too prodigal of words ever since we stood with arms at the ready. If words belong to women and deeds to men, then today every fighter silently takes his place in the ranks. Yesterday on the field of "La Serenissima" I spent two quiet hours adjusting my machine gun and packing bombs in my airplane.'

"The crowd in answer shout the words 'La Serenissima,' for they remember that this was the name of the poet's squadron of planes, so called in honor of Venice.

"The poet continues: 'The machine gun is silent until the practised hand presses the trigger; the banners are silent until the storm of battle descends upon them. This banner of Fiume does not speak—it commands. Out of the distant centuries it commands the future like the gesture of the returned *condottiero,* like the bronze of Alexander of the Horse.'

"Again the multitude burst in chorus with the shouts of *'Viva Fiume!'*

"The voice of the poet rose sharper in tone in continual crescendo. He played upon the emotions of the crowd as a supreme violinist does upon a Stradivarius. The eyes of the thousands were fixed upon him as though hypnotized by his power, and his voice like that of a *shanachie* bewitched their ears.

" 'The standard of the Dalmations today waving in the sunlight takes on again its original color of red. Today red overshines all our banners. What do we care about green in future? What do we care about hope?' "

It was not until September 1919, that a serious proposal was made to D'Annunzio, by discontented junior elements of the Army. Some months before, these young officers, fearing that the Allies might give Fiume to Yugoslavia, had formed a corps of volunteers to "defend it"; they had enrolled in three companies, which took their names from three Italian heroes killed in the war, Noferi, Baccich and Angheben. Their commander was Captain Host-Venturi, and he had about 1,000 men under him. Their oath was, "We swear to be faithful to the sacred cause of Fiume, and will never allow it to be taken from us. Fiume or Death!" Two of their officers, the Grenadier Major Rajna and Lieutenant Grand-Jasquet, came over from Ronchi, where their troops were quartered, and asked D'Annunzio, who was then in Venice, if he would lead these Grenadiers to take Fiume. They represented, they claimed, a majority of the younger officers, of the Italian Army. They warned him that if matters were delayed, the Jugoslavs might do the same thing. If the stroke were made now, they were sure the Italian Government would not dare to send troops against Italians, because a large part of public opinion was still on their side. More problematical was their contention that the statesmen at Versailles, representing the power of the entire western world, would remain inert. They even believed that Nitti might give tacit consent, because a *fait accompli* in Fiume would strengthen his hand in the Versailles bargaining.[1]

Not only did D'Annunzio agree to this plan, but he imme-

[1] This, in fact, was so. Vincenzo Nitti, son of the statesman, wrote in *L'Opera di Nitti* (Gobetti. 1924): "My father was by no means dismayed at D'Annunzio's action, because it gave him more strength in his international dealings." Nitti himself later implied the same thing in his memoirs *Rivelazioni* (Naples, 1948): ". . . I was aware of the fermenting spirit in the north, and I instructed General Diaz to make a close inspection of the occupation zone." This of course he could not admit at Versailles.

diately wrote the first part of *Italia o la Morte* in the *Gazzetta del Popolo,* the clearest announcement of the expedition. His writing was becoming more and more biblical, ". . . and when the day of Pentecost was come, all were together of the same mind. On the one side was the notorious whited sepulcher of the Pharisees—on the other, the spirit. On the one side was the notorious usurer's board covered with the false linen of Arimathea—on the other, the spirit. Let us celebrate today, in the glory of Fiume and in the glory of the young lion of Italy the feast of the spirit. . . ."

He could invoke not only the scriptures but Italian religious art to support the claim to Fiume. In the Vatican is a baptismal font made by Carlo Fontana in 1698. It represents in bas-relief, Italy between her two seas, with the outline of Dalmatia behind, beyond the Dinaric Alps. A figure of Christ is seated on the western part, covering with his hand all of Venetia Giulia—the part contested by the Slavs. It could be deduced from the way the artist has depicted this that God was hereby marking out the confines of Italy. D'Annunzio, at least, interpreted it so; he wrote a sonnet on the subject: "The love of Christ with his blazing hand vindicates forever our soil—from the fountains of the High Adige to Valona, the Divine Right occupies the Alps and all the shore of Istria poured out onto the great Dalmatian brink."

To Mussolini, the night before he left Venice for Ronchi near Fiume, he wrote, "Dear Comrade, The die is cast. I am about to leave. Tomorrow morning I shall take Fiume by arms. May the God of Italy be with us! I rise from a bed of fever, but I can no longer postpone. Once again, the spirit dominates the miserable flesh. . . ." More uncertainly to his friends in Venice, he said as he left, "When I return, it will be to await trial and execution."

At dawn on September 12, 1919, he set out at the head of 287 men. His face was paler, it is said, than his shirt; and he wore dark glasses to conceal his eyes, which were still painful. He traveled in a car filled with flowers from his admirers, so that he seemed, at first, to be in a hearse. The first goal was Ronchi, a small town not far from Trieste, where there were about four hundred Grenadiers. The plan was to transport them in trucks to Fiume; but for some reason these vehicles were not available when D'Annunzio arrived, and the small contingent had to set out on foot. This gave to the expedition its heroic name of, "The Ronchi March." Fortunately, at Palanova, they found a military supply depot, where there were about twenty trucks and more discontented soldiers who joined them.

D'Annunzio's own description of the Ronchi March is given in *L'Urna Inesausta,* ". . . I was able to overcome all the problems and form up my column towards five in the morning. The stars shone as they shone at Quarto dei Mille. They were all propitious. Dawn was colored with a Garibaldian streak in the heavens. On the road to Fiume, Government troops began to join me. Only a few words from me were sufficient to enrol complete companies, battalions, and squadrons as we met them. Some kilometers out of Fiume, I disposed my columns in combat order, five vehicles in front and two behind. I was in front with Major Nunziante and Captain Sbacchi. I had with me the glorious Grenadiers of Sardinia, my first companions from Ronchi commanded by Major Rajna, the Fiuman volunteers of Captain Venturi, the sailors of Major Castracane; to which were added two battalions from the Sestia brigade, a battalion from the Lombardy brigade; artillerymen, Lancers, Bersaglieri; representatives of the entire nation, in fact. I had forces which were sufficient not only to give battle—but to win it. . . ."

At eleven o'clock that morning, General Pittaluga, an Italian but the Military Governor of Fiume and representative of the victorious Allies, was woken from his sleep and informed that an armed band of 1,000 men, under the poet D'Annunzio, had arrived to occupy his city. He immediately hastened with his troops to the suburb of Cantrida, where a stormy meeting took place between the two men.

"Poet!" exclaimed the General. "You will be the ruin of Italy if you do this."

"General!" replied the poet. "It is you who will be the ruin of Italy. If you withstand fate, and become the accomplice to a policy of infamy. I, Gabriele D'Annunzio, declare this city Italian. *Viva Fiume Italiana!*" He added that the General, as an Italian, should appreciate this. The General replied that he was in Fiume not as an Italian, but as an Allied general. He had his orders, and he would carry them out.

"I know," said D'Annunzio. "In that case, you will have to open fire on my soldiers, who are the brothers of your soldiers. If you must do so," he opened his great-coat, revealing his medals, "fire first on *this!*"

The General remained stunned, it appears, for three minutes by this patriotic reply. Then his Italian blood rose, tears came into his eyes, he began talking as quickly as Figaro, swore classical oaths, and gripped the rebel's hand. "Great poet!" he cried. "I do not wish to be the cause of spilling Italian blood. I am honored to meet you for the first time. May your dream be fulfilled! May I, too, soon shout with you, *Viva Fiume Italiana!*"

"*Viva Fiume Italiana!*" cried the poet.

"*Viva Fiume Italiana!*" cried the soldiers.

The two men embraced and went into the town together. That evening, the inhabitants of Fiume witnessed the remarkable spectacle in the Governor's palace, of the simultaneous arrival of a General entrusted with the command of a strategic area, and a Lieutenant-Colonel who threatened that area, on the best of terms, responding in a series of glasses of Vermouth to the repeated toast, *Viva Fiume Italiana!* [1]

In this way began the "Fiume episode," one of those peculiar brands of Italian heroism, half tightrope walking, half Grand Opera, with the nations of Europe all silent and admiring in the audience. On the operatic stage of any country such a scene would, indeed, appear perfectly reasonable. Only in Italy could it be possible in real life.

One of the best descriptions of D'Annunzio's arrival and of the

[1] Reported in *Il Popolo*, September 13th, 1919.

embarrassment it immediately caused the Government troops, many of whom did not know whether to join him or remain loyal, is given again by Giovanni Comisso in *Le Mie Stagioni.* He was then a subaltern in one of the Engineer units in Fiume. The senior officers seemed undecided, he says, but the younger ones were all unhesitatingly for D'Annunzio. Comisso's own Major, seeing that Comisso was wearing a Fiume cockade on his lapel, asked him, "If I give you an order, or D'Annunzio gives you one, whom will you obey?" Comisso replied that as D'Annunzio, a Lieutenant-Colonel, was the senior officer, he would obey him. Whereupon, the Major in a fury tore the cockade off his chest. Comisso says he returned to his troops, told them he was joining D'Annunzio, and encouraged all who wished to come with him, bringing any supplies and material they could carry. On returning to the center of the city, he found the whole population drunk with excitement. Soldiers and civilians were fraternizing in the cafés and bars, or arm in arm in the streets, crying: "Italy or Death! Fiume or Death!" D'Annunzio's Legionaries were already on guard at the crossroads, in front of the banks and municipal offices.

D'Annunzio's forces quickly increased, as a result of his initial success. Grenadiers, infantry, bersaglieri, artists, discontented politicians, civilian enthusiasts and loafers of all kinds soon flocked to join him. The entire crews of the Italian ships in the port went over to him.

Of the Italian regular Navy there was an important squadron in Fiume; the cruiser *Dante Alighieri,* the destroyer *Mirabello,* and the torpedo boats *Abba* and *I.P.N.* For various technical reasons, they were not ready to leave Fiume (so their Captains claimed); in fact, their crews refused to leave. The crews of the *Bronzetti* and the *Espero* locked their officers in the mess room while they were lunching, in case they refused to join D'Annunzio. There were also the torpedo boats *Nullo,* the *Bertani,* the *66 P.N.* and the *68 P.N.* together with the transport ship *Cortellazzo,* and half a dozen small *mas.* This entire little fleet, which D'Annunzio now took over, was commanded by an officer with the charming name of Castruccio Castracane, who immediately sent in his papers to the Ministry of Marine in Rome, and joined D'Annunzio.

The Allied troops, French and English, under orders from Versailles not to cause "incidents," retired to barracks and shut themselves up. The city became a sea of Italian flags. Songs, tears, war cries, *alalas,* received the "Liberator" in the Piazza Dante. The crowd surged round him, trying to kiss his face and hands. It was nearly an hour before the Legionaries could tear him from the delirious mob that day, and he was carried half-fainting to the Hotel Europa, where he spent the night.

The next morning, September 14, he officially took possession of the city, marching with his troops to the Allied Military headquarters, which he declared non-existent; and occupying the building in the name of the State of the Carnaro. Without firing a shot, the French and English troops left the city, the French for Buccari, the English for Valosca. There were reports in the Italian press at the time that the English had sent a posse of 1,000 British policemen from Malta, to support the soldiers. And there were graphic descriptions of the "Bobbies" arriving in Fiume in their London uniforms, of their dismay at finding D'Annunzio in possession; and of their immediate retirement, discomfited.

The population of Fiume, on their knees in the piazza, now witnessed the act of occupation. Symbolically, the poet kissed the Italian Tricolor and declared Fiume Italian. In *Le Mie Stagioni,* Comisso says, ". . . D'Annunzio and Grossich, Head of the Town Council, came by car to Government House that morning. I opened the door for them, and D'Annunzio got out first. He looked extremely weak. He went up to the balcony and spoke. But it was a fighting speech. I remember in particular the phrase: 'In this mad and vile world today, Fiume is the symbol of Liberty.' He then read out the names of all the units who had come with him from Ronchi, and added that he had behind him, too, all the war dead of Italy. The crowd was beside itself, crying, shouting and cheering. A fat girl was continually clapping and crying *'Bravo!'* at every word. Another girl was dancing in the street with an Italian Tricolor round her shoulders, like a shawl. D'Annunzio then produced the Italian flag which I had seen a few weeks before in Rome, when he had vowed on the Capitol that he would hang it in Fiume. He seemed, indeed, a prophet of old come back to life. . . ."

To Mussolini that evening, D'Annunzio wrote: "My dear Friend, I have taken the supreme chance. Having given my all, I intend to take all. I am now master of Fiume, of a part of the armistice lines, of the ships in the harbor, of the troops in the city. They recognize only me as their head. No one shall dislodge me. I shall hold Fiume as long as I live. Although I am supported only by ill-armed soldiers, the inhabitants of Fiume have acclaimed me. If only half of Italy were like these people, we Italians would be masters of the world. For Fiume is only an isolated peak of heroism, where to die is sweet. I have not slept for six nights and am a prey to fever. But I am still upright on my feet. Ask those who have seen me. *Alala!*"

Meanwhile in Rome, the news had been given to Nitti who, at first, simply refused to believe his ears. The fat little Prime Minister was sitting in Parliament, at an ordinary session, when the Home Secretary came in and whispered to him. He made gestures of impatience and beat his hand upon the table. The news had to be given to the MP's and when he announced it, his incredulity got the better of him, and he said involuntarily,[1] "But such an expedition is inconceivable . . . this raid, this . . . adventure, this . . . something between romance and literature. . . . It is out of the question that such a thing should dominate the affairs of a country. [Loud applause from the Right; boos from the Left] . . ."

The Allies in Versailles, on the other hand, really believed that there were a number of leading government personalities behind the expedition (unknown, presumably, to Nitti, if he is to be believed), generals and high naval officers. The whole episode gave to the West the impression that Italy had been reduced to the level of a small Balcanic or South American state, still in formation.

[1] See *Da Giolitti a Mussolini* by Nino Valeri (Parenti, 1956).

17

The Lyric Dictator

Once the Allied troops, English and French, had left, D'Annunzio began to organize the city into what his secretary describes as "a state of patriotic disorder." He gave himself the title of *Comandante,* at the top of the pyramid; then came his chief of cabinet, Giovanni Giurati; then, the Foreign Minister, a Belgian Leon Koschnitzy, who sent telegrams and corresponded directly with Rome, Versailles and the Allies. A tribunal of Justice was set up under a former Cavalry officer. Federico Nardelli became Minister of Public Prosecution; and an attempt was made at instituting what we would call a Home Office. But as the police of Fiume were largely Hungarian, and many administrative employees were Austrian, it was found better to leave the preservation of law and order to the Legionaries, as D'Annunzio now dubbed his troops (to recall Roman greatness). After a few weeks, the Legionaries had designed a special uniform for themselves—black shirts with something Garibaldian about them, skulls and crossbones insignia. They all carried daggers. They also invented a new salute, the raised right arm, chosen from among the many gestures of Greco-Roman orators. It was clearly superior to the humble bow or bourgeois handshake; its limits seemed the sky. At the same time it seemed, symbolically, to thrust a dagger into the throat of an invisible enemy.

D'Annunzio wrote about his Legionaries in the first days to Albertini, of the *Corriere della Sera:* "I wonder if you fully realize what has happened. General Badoglio himself considers this is the finest exploit since Garibaldi's Thousand. I have succeeded. Everything is in my power. The soldiers obey only me.

Perfect order has been established. The city is quiet. I have organized the services. Even the local police collaborate—men commanded by a Captain with six medals for gallantry. There is nothing that can be done against us. The *fait accompli* will have to be accepted in Paris. If that rogue from Lucania [Nitti came from that province] were really wise, he would steer clear of things spiritual. No one will succeed in ejecting me from Fiume. I don't know what is *your* attitude, but as a good Italian be fair and inform all the people of this. One thing is sure; I shall hold the city at all costs. I shall hold the ships. I shall not hesitate before any decision. Four years of war are nothing to the energy I have spent in these last wonderful days. If you are able, and your conscience permits, to oppose the vile defamation and falsification of the Nitti gang, you will be rendering a service to the real Italy, *which is here on the Carnaro. . . .*"

Nitti had been unwise enough to describe D'Annunzio's Legionaries as "deserters." To this, D'Annunzio proudly replied, "The deserters are not *us*. The deserters are those who have abandoned Italian Fiume, who have refused to recognize it, who have repulsed it, calumniated it, thereby committing the most disgraceful sin against the Fatherland. Such men are no less ignoble than those who fled at Caporetto . . ."

New volunteers from all over Italy were now flooding in, and within a few weeks D'Annunzio had a force of nearly 3,000 men. He had calculated correctly. Neither the Italian Government, nor the Allies, were prepared to send troops against Italians. For fifteen months D'Annunzio, like some medieval *condottiere,* was to be undisputed master of a city-state. His arrogant claim, "to have pulled the beards of three old idiots" (Wilson, Clemenceau and Lloyd George), seemed true.

There is a poem by Carducci, in which he celebrates the virtues of a tiny Italian commune in the Middle Ages, where the General Assemblies of its Parliament were public and held out of doors. The Consul presided, promulgating laws, allotting fields and pastures, encouraging the shepherds to become soldiers in a just, defensive war, "whenever the Hun or the Slav is at the gate." "In the name of Christ and Mary," he would say, "I order you to take this action." Raising their right hands, the people would signify their approval of his decisions for the common benefit. A variant of this ancient state now came to life in twentieth-century Fiume.

The people and soldiers would gather daily in the *piazza* beneath the palace of the Government, D'Annunzio in his bemedaled uniform would appear on the balcony surrounded by his staff, to deliver a harangue, before asking for their approval. Raising their right arms, they would grant this with the cry, *"Eja! Eja! Eja! Alala!"*—the shout with which, D'Annunzio had taught them, Achilles used to spur his chariot horses.

D'Annunzio would then say, "To whom, Fiume?"

The unanimous cry would be, "To us, Fiume!"

He would then change from the belligerent note to a soft, tender, almost caressing tone, in Venetian dialect, *"Vu con mi! Mi con vu!"*

"You with us! We with you! *Eja! Eja! Eja! Alala!"* they would shriek.

From this balcony, D'Annunzio daily informed them of the international situation, of Italian politics and of his plans for Dalmatia. "Our brothers in Dalmatia!" he cried. "When I left Ronchi beneath the twinkling stars, to begin my march, a deep feeling of melancholy almost overpowered me. A thorn kept pricking my faithful heart. It was the thought of you all—the grief that I had not enough soldiers to carry the fire to Spàlato, to Cattaro, to Trau, to the whole Dalmatian coast. What will my Zara say and think of me, I asked myself, when she hears the news? What will my Sebenìco, my Curzola, my other sisters say? The anxious thought was ever with me, even in those hours when all my energy was needed here in Fiume. For ever amid the triumphal cries of Fiume, I could hear your tearful voices in the background. . . ."

The Great Powers in Versailles had done nothing against him; but D'Annunzio had always believed that attack is the best defense. The Allies, Great Britain in particular, came in for much abuse in his speeches, ". . . Britain, that voracious Empire, which has seized Persia, Mesopotamia, Arabia and most of Africa, and is still not replete. That gluttonous British Empire which is eyeing Constantinople, gradually swallowing up China, daily buying more islands in the Pacific . . ." With Fiume, he associated other countries "spiritually murdered by England," "struggling Ireland, black-jacked Egypt and downtrodden India." He ridiculed a British proposal that the League of Nations should take over Fiume, because the League, he claimed, was "nothing more than another instrument of Great Britain for oppression." Instead, against the British League of Nations, he now founded an *Anti*-League of Nations, a League of the Oppressed Nations, which would support all countries "dispossessed by England." He even wrote a letter on the subject to Sir Eric Drummond, the General Secretary of the League of Nations, informing him that henceforth Fiume would be the symbol of a sacred crusade against his country. (This letter received no reply, although both Lloyd George and Lord Curzon later referred to it in public speeches.) To a Japanese delegation which visited Fiume at this time, he said, "Let us liberate ourselves from the West, which neither loves nor wants us. Poor deluded Italy, betrayed Italy, impoverished Italy, turns her eyes again towards your Orient, on which has been fixed the regard of her proudest centuries. . . ."

This ambitious foreign policy was supported by an equally energetic internal program. He proclaimed "The Free State of Fiume," and began to elaborate the famous "Statute of the Carnaro," a constitution for Fiume, which now, in retrospect, seems an amazing mixture of Liberalism, Communism and Fascism, together with parts of Plato's Republic, and clauses about Equality for Women, Freedom of Religion, of Speech, and Inviolability of Domicile. There was to be compulsory physical training for the young, pensions for the old, education for all in special hygienic buildings, aesthetic instruction, and unemployment relief on a grandiose scale. Property was to be owned privately, but would be subject to state supervision, dependent on its "proper, continuous and efficient use." There were to be six categories of workers and producers, like those of the old Florentine guilds, all legally recognized by the State, and dealing with every aspect of commercial life. He also commissioned Pasquale la Rotella to compose an official anthem of Fiume, rewarding him with the new Order of the Gold Star of Fiume.

Everything D'Annunzio had ever dreamed of, or written about, seemed to come alive in the state of Fiume. He saw it all in terms of splendid uniforms, pennants, Apollonian youth, Poetry, Music, Liberty and Love. He was in the center of a stage larger than any dramatist had ever possessed, as both author and main character at once, able, as has seldom occurred in history, to give his poetic imagination full play in a political field. He believed, probably sincerely, that a new era for humanity was dawning, and he was confident that his example would be followed all over Italy. He gave orders that the words, *Italia o La Morte,* should be painted in monster characters on one of the large squares near the harbor; and the citizens were summoned to appear on parade at a certain hour, take their place within the letters, and thus form living words. A photograph of the inscription taken from the sky by an aviator was then to be forwarded to Paris, to convince the Allies of the "living Italianity" of Fiume.

The real problem in Fiume was administrative rather than military. The Legionaries were prepared to live "hard," on simple rations, but there was an entire civilian population of 50,000 to feed. Sooner or later, the blockade, which was at present only symbolic, would be imposed by the Italian Government. D'Annunzio, issuing his lyrical proclamations, presiding at patriotic gatherings, and founding new slogans, seemed unaware of this. As he became more firmly installed and letters from all over the world poured in congratulating him, or simply asking his advice, as in the past people used to come to some shrine or temple of miracles, he began to think he was infallible. "Every power, every obstacle, will fall before us!" he cried. "We must stay. *Hic manebimus optime!*" It was significant that he here used the phrase of the Roman soldiers when they occupied new territory. He had created in Fiume, in fact, the first dictatorship of modern times, a lyrical dictatorship, of great emotional appeal to the Italians, but lacking the practical qualities essential for government.

It took nearly a year for the famous Charter of the Carnaro, or the Constitution, with its liberal-humanitarian precepts, to be drawn up. Then, on September 8, 1920, on the balcony of the Government Palace, in an apocalyptic storm, D'Annunzio read it to the waiting Legionaries, to the people of Fiume, to Italy, to the world. Written on heavy, luxurious paper, with special inks and huge capital letters, it reads as if Ezra Pound had drawn up the *Code Napoléon*:

". . . a College of Ediles will be instituted in the Regency of Fiume. It will be elected with discernment from men of taste, ability and education. As with the Roman ediles, the Colleges will renew the officials charged with making the city beautiful— officials who, in the fifteenth century, would have constructed a road or a square with the same musical [*sic*] sense which directed them in the organization of a Republican display or a Carnival. The College will preside over the Beauty of the City, preventing ugliness in public thoroughfares and badly placed buildings. It will give to all Civic displays, whether on land or sea, a sober elegance, recalling our Fathers, for whom it was enough to accomplish miracles of joy under the sweet light of heaven. It will persuade the workers that the act of beautifying a humble dwelling with some element of popular art is an act of piety."

"There is a religious feeling of human misery, of deep nature," he went on, "in the most simple sign which is transmitted from generation to generation, symbols engraved or painted on a bread bin, on a cradle, on the loom or spindle, on a cupboard or yoke . . . the Ediles will attempt to give back to the people the love of beautiful lines and colors, in those things which belong to daily life, showing them what our race could do with a light geometrical

motif, a star, a flower, a snake, a dove, on a vase, a jar or a chest.
They will also show the people why and how the spirit of ancient
communal liberties displayed itself not only in the lines, but even
in the stamp, a man places on his utensils, which thereby come
alive. Lastly, the Ediles, realizing that a people can only have the
architecture which the strength of their bones and the nobility of
their brows deserve, will endeavor to make the contractors and
builders understand how they can profit from the new materials
of the century, iron, glass, cement. They will raise harmonious
lines in the new architecture . . ."

Articles XIV, XVI and XX are the same: "Life is beautiful. It
is worthy to be lived magnificently and severely, by man re-
established in all his integrity by Liberty. The complete man is he
who can daily recreate his own virtue so that, each day, he may
offer it as a fresh gift to his friends. . . . The act of work, even
the most humble, the most obscure, if well executed, tends towards
Beauty, and thus adorns the world. . . ." In article XVI he advo-
cates a return to the old civic corporations of Dante's day,
". . . whatever be the work furnished, manual or spiritual, of industry or art, it shall be inscribed in one of the Ten Corporations . . ." Article XX defines the most ingenious of these
corporations, which seems simply sub-lunar. ". . . it concerns all
the vocations but is without art, shadow or name. It will be reserved
to the mysterious and expanding forces of the people at work. It is
also a votive symbol dedicated to an unknown genius, the appearance of a new man, to the ideal transfiguration of works and days,
the victory of the spirit over unhappy anxieties and the sweat of
blood. . . . It is represented in the Civic Sanctuary by a burning
lamp which bears inscribed an ancient Tuscan word from the
epoch of the communal corporations, an allusion to a spiritualized
form of human labor, 'Effort without Effort.' " D'Annunzio did
not seem to realize that Beauty is not necessarily appreciated, or
even desired, by the masses.

There is one statute which deals entirely with Music in the
State of Fiume: "In the Italian Regency of the Carnaro, music

will be a religious and social institution. Every one or two thousand years, there surges up from the depths of the people a Hymn, which is eternal. A great people is not only one which creates God in its own likeness, but one which also creates its Hymn for its God. If every renaissance of a noble race is a lyrical effort, if every unanimous and creative feeling is a lyrical power, if every new order is a lyrical order in the vigorous and impetuous sense of the word, Music, considered as ritual language, is the exalter of the act of Life, of the work of art that is Life. Is it not true that great Music announces every time it is heard, to the attentive and anxious multitude, the reign of the Spirit? In all the communes of the Regency, male-voice choirs and public fanfares will be organized at state expense. At the College of the Ediles, a Rotunda building will be consecrated capable of holding a thousand listeners. It will be furnished with ample tiers and space for orchestra and choir. The choral and orchestral celebrations will be free. . . ." [1]

Plato's ideal state was said to have been written on the clouds. It is solid, earth-bound compared to this. The various statesmen of Europe are not accustomed to making such a show of aesthetics in their constitutions (their legislators remember probably that Plato expelled the poets from his Republic). But the poet-ruler of Fiume was clearly determined to initiate his people into the most refined of delights, of form, color and sound. Foreign aesthetes who visited Fiume at the time were naturally delighted. The English writer, Osbert Sitwell, contrasts Fiume most favorably with England, and says, "The constitution of Fiume offered an escape from the normal European misery and vulgarity"; and he acclaims the article on Music as, "the national religion of Fiume." "D'Annunzio, when I met him, did not," he says, "ask what new footballers there were in England—but who were our new *poets!*"—an incontrovertible proof of the quality of Fiume! He describes D'Annunzio elsewhere as "a far greater writer than Byron."

[1] D'Annunzio had a great feeling for music, contending that he had a particularly acute ear. "I once sat next to Toscanini when he was conducting a rehearsal," he told his secretary, "and to his amazement, I was able to inform him, that one of his instruments was slightly out of tune."

But there are two clauses in the Constitution about which most people will agree with Osbert Sitwell. The statute enjoins, for instance, that the Parliament of Fiume, or Council of the Best, as it was called, when debating shall speak little. Its sessions should be held with "notably concise brevity" (*con brevita spiccatamente concisa*). As for the second Chamber, the Council of Provisors, a kind of Fiuman House of Lords—the Statute demands from its debaters the most laconic language.

Comisso, in *Le Mie Stagioni,* tells of the various political and ideological groups which formed among the officers of Fiume, some of whose programs were even more fantastic than the Statute of the Carnaro itself. He says that some of his more fanatical friends formed a group "under the sign of Yogi," entitled, "Union of Free Spirits tending towards Perfection," with its center in the Palazzo del Fico. Here, they held evening sessions and discussed such things as, the Abolition of Money; the Ideal Fraternal Army; the Embellishment of Life; Free Love; the Abolition of Prison. Comisso, who was then only twenty-two, planned with his friend Keller to go to Russia, to encourage the Russian communists to visit Western Europe and destroy mechanical civilization, so that it could "be replaced by the spiritual civilization of Fiume." Their theory was that the nineteenth-century rule of the bourgeoisie in Europe was over, and that something new and better was about to take its place. The war had been won by the common people, not by the bourgeois, who had profiteered and falsified the traditional Italian spirit, importing from the mechanical Anglo-Saxons ideas that were foreign to the Latin genius. Comisso's group sympathized with all D'Annunzio's writings, and wanted to get away from the cities, "to the sea and the Italian countryside"; to enjoy the things of the spirit, "to believe in the magnitude of Italian individuality"; above all, to ensure that machine civilization did not increase. Every instant must, they contended, be deeply lived, while material needs are reduced to a minimum. They despised money and luxury, which they called "the creations of stupidity."

An article printed in the *Testa di Ferro* (Head of Iron), a weekly news sheet of the Legionaries, expressed their views on March 28, 1920:

"Fiumanism is no longer a name, it is a precise and palpitating fact. At last we have a great and clear mission in the world. We are the advance guard of all nations on the march to the future. We are the island of wonder, which in its journey across the ocean, will carry its own incandescent light to the continents stifled in the darkness of brutal commerce. We are a handful of illuminated beings and mystic creators, who will sow through the world the seed of our force, a force which is purely Italian, and will germinate into the highest and most violent irradiations.

"Is it to be a republic? Or is it to be a monarchy? Names are of no interest to us. Words do not affect us. These institutions are worm-eaten, and must have a radical renovation. That is the problem before us.

"If there were at the head of the Italian national not a small-minded King, but a vigorous brain, we should have no hesitation in following him. We should defend him unto death, with all the strength of untiring combatants, and we would not give a Jugo-slav krone for the republic. But today, faced with the alternative of preserving our fidelity to an old worm-eaten throne—which sends out no fecund energetic acts, but merely culpable deeds of solidarity with unclean ministers—or of supporting an honest and inspired man, who is ready to give to Italy the greatness it demands, our decision is an easy one.

"All the ancient faiths are renegade, all the ancient formulae are rent. Saving our duty to official Italy, we shall put our faith in and obey no man but our sole and marvelous leader, Gabriele D'Annunzio, who has given to Fiume that political constitution which will be best suited to the character of the city of Holocaust, until such time as a more zealous Government at Rome shall decide to accept that annexation, which has been so often proclaimed in vain."

All this was encouraged by the speeches of the *Comandante* himself. "Is there any man among you who doubts my faith?" he would cry to his Legionaries.

One sole cry from the Legionaries, "No! Never!"

"Is there any man among you who doubts my loyalty?"

"No! Never!"

"Is there any man who doubts that you are my brothers, whom I am worthy to lead?"

"No! Never!"

Then he would shout, "We no longer hope. We wish. Do you understand? We wish. Repeat that word!"

All the Legionaries would cry, "We wish."

What did they wish? It is doubtful if D'Annunzio knew himself. His language was becoming more and more high-flown and poetical. To someone who happened to say in conversation, "We have now been in Fiume two months," he replied indignantly, "That is not so! We have been in Fiume sixty days of passion, and sixty nights of anguish."

Caviglia, the General in charge of the blockading troops, told Nitti in April 1920, ". . . D'Annunzio makes the extraordinary claim to have formed a state in Fiume, *which can live on its own.* It is to be enlarged, to include Dalmatia, the islands and eastern Istria. He intends to rule it with the institutions of a medieval commune . . ."

But the state that was "to live on its own" found it increasingly harder to do so. Nitti at last began to impose a real, as distinct from a token, blockade. Bread was soon short, and the horses had neither hay nor straw. Meat was unobtainable, and to make matters worse, the influenza epidemic now ravaging Europe broke out. The need for drastic, practical measures to remedy his economy was naturally attributed by D'Annunzio to the blockade, and therefore to Nitti. While Nitti, for his part, in Rome, claimed that he had imposed the blockade because of the "remedies." It is difficult to assess which began first, but sometime in the spring of 1920, it had become clear that many of D'Annunzio's Legionaries had become simply pirates.

D'Annunzio had created what he called a "Minister of Supply," a remarkable old colonel, Vittorio Margonari, who had been one of the first senior officers to join. He had formed a special band of men, the *Uscocchi* (the old Adriatic name for a particular brand of pirate). The exploits of these men have since become legendary, and several books have been written about them. They captured ships, warehouses, cargoes; they raided local catering establishments; they stole coal, arms, meat, coffee, ammunition. A group of them, under the desperado, Melchiorre Melchiorri, laid an ambush for the government General who was visiting Italian troops in the neighborhood. They captured him and took him back to Fiume. They went as far afield as Genoa and Sicily; they captured a boat bound for South America, with a cargo worth ten million lire. They were pirates in the twentieth century.

18

Pirates

The exploits of these *Uscocchi* are important politically, because they reveal D'Annunzio's growing friendship with left-wing anarchical groups in Italy, a factor of great importance for the future of Italy. It was information received from the left-wing Federation of Mariners in Genoa which enabled his *Uscocchi* pirates to capture the *Cogne,* as well as the *Persia,* carrying arms for White Russia, and the *Taranto,* with a two-million-lire cargo for Albania.[1]

The *Cogne* episode is the most famous, because it gave rise to a number of learned books and treatises on International Law. Its legal repercussions compare with those of the *Alabama,* sixty years before. Was the capture made by the Armed Forces of a sovereign state, as the Regency of Fiume claimed to be? Or was it an act of piracy? Was D'Annunzio to have the protection offered to belligerent powers at war? Or was he to be hanged as a pirate? The matter was further complicated by the fact that he had sold back part of the cargo to its owners, for cash.[2]

His pirates operated by air and land as much as by sea; and on this occasion, when D'Annunzio heard that the *Cogne* lay in Genoa harbor with a valuable cargo, and that many of its crew were sympathetic to his cause, he gave his pirates permission to

[1] The Federation of Mariners. In December 1919 an attempt had been made at a compromise between the Italian Government and D'Annunzio in Fiume, by D'Annunzio's *capo di gabinetto,* Giovanni Giuriati. This failed and D'Annunzio replaced him by Alceste De Ambris, who negotiated instead with the important left-wing group, the Federation of Mariners.

[2] Most of these exploits are fully described in Tom Antongini's *Gli allegri filibustien di D'Annunzio.*

capture it. They intended to board the boat at night in Genoa, overpower its officers, and sail it round to Fiume. When they arrived at Genoa, they found that the *Cogne* had left for Sicily, to take on a fresh cargo on her way to South America. Undaunted, they took train for Catania harbor, where they found her being loaded. In the middle of the night, the six of them crept aboard, and the members of the crew who sympathized helped them to hide in the propeller shaft, the only place where there was no danger of discovery. Their plan was to wait until the ship was on the high sea, then emerge and overpower the officers and the rest of the crew. This was the most uncomfortable hiding place on the ship, particularly inconvenient because when the motors started, the *Uscocchi* had to stop sitting on the propeller shaft, which began to rotate, and crawl about on all fours.

After seven hours of a calm sea voyage, Cape Passaro came into view. The captain was on the bridge with the officers of the watch, and the other officers were sleeping in their bunks. The *Uscocchi* left their hiding places and made for the bridge, on the way cutting the radio cables, and throwing the aerial into the sea. When they reached the bridge, they produced revolvers and confronted the captain, who thought at first that they were stowaways. "Don't be silly!" he said. "Put down those guns! You're not the first stowaways I've had. I'll take you to America, if you behave."

The *Uscocchi* explained who they were, and told him they intended taking the ship east, not west, to hand it over to Gabriele D'Annunzio in the port of Fiume. The captain laughed and said that, in that case, they would only run into the blockade, which the Italian Government was now enforcing in the Adriatic. They left him under guard on the bridge, and set off to capture the other officers and the radio officer, who was now trying ineffectively to send out SOS messages. The remainder of the crew, sympathizers for the most part, agreed to help them take the ship up the Adriatic to Fiume. When the captain was informed of this by the boatswain, he agreed that he and his officers, while taking no part in the running of the ship, would accept the situation and remain in one of the state-rooms. This cooperative attitude of both officers and crew, was typical of the feeling of such people all over Italy towards D'Annunzio and Fiume.

The journey round Sicily and up the Adriatic was uneventful. It was not until they reached the entrance of the Carnaro itself that difficulties began. Night had fallen, as they had calculated (for they dared not enter Fiume harbor in the daytime), and the *Cogne* was suddenly caught in the searchlights of a government blockade vessel, which gave the signal for it to weigh anchor and be inspected. It was hopeless to try and run the blockade, so a device planned some time before, and often used later, was employed. The Yugoslav flag was run up, and the *Cogne* continued on a course towards the nearest Yugoslav harbor, Buccari. The Italian blockade ship was now faced with a difficult decision. She did not wish to enter Yugoslav territorial waters, nor did she wish to fire on the Yugoslav flag. She therefore followed the *Cogne* for some miles, until she saw her entering port, then turned about and steamed off westwards. The *Cogne* retreated out of Buccari and steamed north as fast as she could, in Yugoslav territorial waters all the way. It was a dangerous decision, for had the Yugoslavs known who was in charge of the boat, D'Annunzio's hated *Uscocchi,* they would have given them a warm reception. But they were not detected. In the small hours of the morning, the *Cogne* sailed into the port of Fiume.

The news that this argosy, the richest yet captured, was arriving, had already gone round Fiume. Long before dawn, crowds were collecting on the quays. When daylight came, and the boat was seen on the horizon, D'Annunzio himself came down to the harbor. To the strains of military music and the discharge of cannons, the *Cogne* entered port. D'Annunzio boarded her to congratulate his men, and address the crew. Such was the power of his oratory, that by the end of his speech, every one of the *Cogne's* crew was under the impression that he had come to Fiume entirely of his own free will, to put himself at the services of the *condottiere.* An exultant population flooded the streets, singing and shouting. They carried the *Uscocchi* off, covering them with flowers, flags and kisses.

When D'Annunzio returned to his headquarters, he found telegrams coming in from the offended parties, including the Italian Government. They condemned the theft as an act of piracy, and demanded an immediate return of the booty. This was found to consist largely of heavy engineering goods and some airplane parts. D'Annunzio summoned a conference at which various solutions were put forward for using these goods, which clearly had no immediate value to a population in need of food. D'Annunzio proposed that two of his representatives should go to Rome and bargain with the government for the sale of the merchandise.

This impertinent plan was actually put into practice, and three days later a Fiume delegation with full powers arrived in Rome. The Italian Government avoided the issue, declaring that the goods belonged to a private firm; D'Annunzio must deal with that firm direct. The incredible situation now arose, in which a government responsible for the maintenance of order in its own territorial waters had either to recognize these waters as not its own, or to recognize one of its own nationals as a pirate. The matter, when put to the Allies in Versailles, received no further clarification. D'Annunzio seemed the *de facto* ruler of a sovereign state at war with a private company. No international machinery existed for dealing with such a situation; so he told the firms concerned that if they did not buy their own goods back, he would sell them at an international auction. As a concession, he offered to let them have them for a percentage of their value. In these circumstances, he said, the *Cogne* would also be returned intact. Otherwise, it would join his Fiume fleet.

The shipowners and firms asked for ten days to consider this unusual proposition. They had no alternative but to accept, and their commission duly arrived in Fiume, to inspect the goods. Negotiations were protracted, while they attempted to play for time, still hoping International Law would somehow intervene.

But the twentieth century, with all its lawyers in The Hague and Geneva, was powerless against the sixteenth-century *condottiere*. D'Annunzio, in the face of these delaying tactics, ordered the ship to be unloaded immediately, and he proclaimed a public auction on the quay. The first goods were actually being unloaded and firms from Italy were arriving, prepared to take the risk and buy the bargains cheap, when the negotiators capitulated.

They signed an agreement by which, within five days, one of their banks would pay the required sum. As D'Annunzio had no use for draft and checks, he demanded the money in cash. To avoid being swindled, even here, he said it must be in 1,000 lire notes, none of them to be in a series of more than ten at a time. The representatives of the firms pointed out the unusual nature of this, apart from the inconvenience of transporting twenty million lire in small denominations to Fiume. But D'Annunzio insisted; and five days later, two huge leather trunks appeared in his headquarters in Fiume, where the notes were unpacked and meticulously counted. Two days later the *Cogne,* loaded with its cargo again, set out for South America. It had lost half its crew.

One other notable exploit of the *Uscocchi* is worth recounting, as it was this more than anything else the *Uscocchi* did which infuriated Caviglia, the General commanding the surrounding Italian troops. He took it as a personal insult and determined to expel D'Annunzio from Fiume as ignominiously as possible. It concerned the theft of forty army horses at Abbazia, across the bay from Fiume, stolen under the very noses of their officers. The reaction to this in Italian military circles was violent. As everyone knows, the greatest insult to a military man is to have his transport stolen; it is worse even than losing a battle.

A regiment of Italian heavy artillery had been stationed for some months at Abbazia. As the Legionaries' horses in Fiume had been reduced, by lack of fodder, to a pitiable condition, D'Annunzio decided to steal some new ones from the artillery. The lieutenant he put in charge of the enterprise found it easy to visit the artillery unit at Abbazia. The relations between the troops of the blockading forces and the Legionaries were always "correct"; officers visited one another, even dined in one another's messes. It was easy to discover where the stables were, and how they were guarded. The *Uscocchi* lieutenant pretended that he was the grandson of a well-known horse trainer, and his natural curiosity to see the stables was understandable. As he went round, he saw that the horses were in excellent condition.

When he returned to Fiume, he fastened a number of large army pontoons together, to be towed across the bay at night. Beds of straw were laid on them, to prevent any noise when the horses were rustled aboard. He then waited for a calm, moonless night. On the towing vessel and the pontoons, he set out with fifty Legionaries and a journalist, Mario Baffico, whom D'Annunzio used in Fiume as a kind of "public relations officer." The plan was to land some men who would make a diversion in the main camp, while the others stole the horses. The lieutenant, with some NCOs and Baffico, went forward to the sentry, whose exact position he had noted when visiting the camp before.

"Halt! Who goes there?" said the sentry.

"Inspecting officer," said the lieutenant. "Give me the password!" This unusual command temporarily unnerved the sentry. Strictly *he* should have asked for the password.

"Why don't you reply?" said the lieutenant severely. "Give me the password and call the sergeant of the Guard. And if, as I perceive," he indicated the journalist, Mario Baffico, who had come close, "you allow a civilian like this man to wander about the camp, you're doing your job pretty badly."

The sentry became confused. He stammered a few words of excuse and called the sergeant of the Guard. The sergeant, who was stretched out on the floor of the tent came sleepily to life and wandered out. There was an exchange of words, in which the lieutenant insisted on the inefficiency of his guard, which immediately placed the sergeant on the defensive. Then, while the sergeant was still attempting to excuse himself, the *Uscocchi* lieutenant took out a pistol and told him to put his hands up. As he did so, other Legionaries appeared and disarmed the sentry. Before any alarm could be given, they had occupied the tents and tied up the other sleepy members of the guard.

Meanwhile, the other *Uscocchi* had gone round to the stables, each man taking two horses out to the waiting pontoons. But the horses, with unfamiliar masters, began neighing and kicking. Some went loose in the dark and galloped about wildly with their heads down. To move them up the gangway and on to the pontoons seemed impossible, and several fell off the gangway onto the rocks. The confusion, the cries of the sentries, the pawing and neighing of the horses, the blows of the Legionaries trying to force them aboard, caused the alarm to be given at the other end of the camp. Sentries came running forward. Firing began.

Dawn was breaking, so the lieutenant decided that, having managed to embark a number of horses, he would abandon the rest. D'Annunzio's great principle had always been that Italians should not fire on Italians. Before jumping on board, he asked the unfortunate sergeant, who was lying bound hand and foot, if he would care to join their ranks. This always happened at each *Uscocchi* enterprise, and always new recruits were found. They threw down the gangway and were quickly on their way to Fiume, with forty-seven excellent horses.

Inevitably, General Caviglia took this as a far greater insult than any of the other exploits of the *Uscocchi*. The blockade of Fiume was made total; not even Red Cross supplies were allowed to enter. The War Department in Rome demanded immediate return of the horses. This time D'Annunzio, understanding military sensibilities, thought it better to comply, and he ordered the horses to be given back. But his *Uscocchi* were not to be cheated completely. They spent a week in the neighborhood looking for all the old broken-down jades and nags they could find. They painted them red, green and white, the colors of Italy; they then delivered them to the Italian Army Commission waiting at the barrier of Fiume.

The announcement in the press of this final insult caused such amusement throughout Italy, and sympathy for D'Annunzio, that the War Department decided they would make themselves look more ridiculous if they did not let the matter drop. The skeleton-like horses they accepted in exchange were dubbed by D'Annunzio: "My horses of the Apocalypse."

For six months, these acts of piracy continued, to replenish the exchequer, granaries and stables of the little state. As no government appeared able to unseat D'Annunzio, enthusiasts from all over the world still came to join up, although conditions were daily deteriorating. Old soldiers, lovers of uniforms, fire-brands, adventurers—D'Annunzio announced that he would die among them, and be buried in his uniform. With each new feat of his *Uscocchi,* D'Annunzio became more jubilant and self-confident. He seemed to live in the belief of those Carlovingian paladins, who inherited the individual vigor of each enemy they killed—as if a man worthy to live feels his strength increased with each new obstacle overcome.

But the mentalities of the enthusiasts who had joined in the hope of battle and loot, were less elevated and suitable for the task of government. They had come to fight, and found no fighting. Fiume was to them an occupied town, where they could pillage and rape in the military style. They treated the houses they were billeted in as their own, or as brothels. They carried daggers and stabbed one another in tavern brawls. They were like those famous loose squadrons of Turkoman cavalry, who served without pay and fought without discipline. Many of the Legionaries, like Giovanni Comisso, were sincere lovers of their country, anxious to obtain Fiume for Italy, men who felt that the cause they had fought for in 1915 had been betrayed by their government. Some were simple soldiers who had followed their officers to Fiume out of loyalty, as they would have followed them in time of war.

Osbert Sitwell relates that, owing to inactivity, amusements had to be arranged for these troops: "Weary of waiting for battle, they must fight one another, and in a sham contest it was no unusual thing for there to be many serious casualties from bombs and bullets." He says that once Toscanini was invited with his orchestra, and that, to divert the orchestra, one of these sham battles was arranged. Four thousand troops (says Sitwell) took part, among them two Garibaldian veterans, one aged 78, the other 84. "One hundred men were seriously injured by bombs. The orchestra, which had been playing in the quieter intervals, dropped their instruments. Fired by a sudden enthusiasm, they charged and captured the trenches. Five of them were badly hurt in the battle!"

General Ferrario, commanding the 45th Division encircling Fiume, reports that this diary was found on a Legionary, ". . . we get up at eight and play a bit, then some spaghetti and a walk in the town, where the women cost little . . . no one ever gives us a pep-talk, and we get paid 1.50 a day. Then in the evening, drinking in the *trattorie* and more women, even cheaper at night . . ."

Another report tells of some officers and men who deserted from the Italian army to join D'Annunzio, simply because, "they did not like having to get up early for parade in their own units." Comisso, in *Le Mie Stagioni*, says that the officers led a "completely free life in Fiume, spending their nights gambling . . . taking cocaine in the manner of the wartime aviators." During the day, he says, they strutted about the streets in their smartest uniforms, affecting the elegance of D'Annunzio. Monocles were in fashion, white gloves and scents. Keller, the wartime ace, boasted that he used "to eat sugared rose petals in Fiume." "Love in Fiume," says Comisso, "was truly without limits. If there had been any need of it, the city was completely Italianized, in blood at least. There was little jealousy among the men for the women, but much among the women for the Italians . . . in the general promiscuity, venereal disease was endemic . . ."

Osbert Sitwell endorses Comisso's words about the uniforms. "Every man," he says, "seemed to wear a uniform designed by himself; some wore beards and had shaven heads like the *Comandante;* others cultivated huge tufts of hair, half a foot long, waving out from their foreheads, and a black fez on the back of the head. Cloaks, feathers and flowing black ties were universal, and all carried 'Roman daggers'; and among this young and swaggering throng walked two veterans, in Garibaldian uniform, with red waistcoats and long white hair." He also says that there were criminals among the Legionaries. He writes of a man, "like a tiger, covered with medals instead of stripes—a Sardinian who had been imprisoned for murder but was released by the Italian government, so it was said, at the outbreak of the war, on condition that he promised to devote himself to slaying the enemy. He took thirty Austrian prisoners, and is reported to have strangled them with his own hands. This individual, however, was extremely shocked by the doings of the 'Black and Tans' in Ireland, and smashed an empty champagne bottle just behind our heads, in protest. . . ."

Antongini tells how one evening he and D'Annunzio, after a hard day's work, went out for a walk, to get some air. It was dark and they hoped they would not be recognized. But they were almost immediately accosted by a drunken Legionary who was singing lustily. Although they crossed the road, he recognized them, came right up and shrieked in their faces, "Viva il Comandante, Gabriele D'Annunzio!"

"What do you mean?" said D'Annunzio. "Don't you see that I am not myself!" and with an air of mystery, he added: "I am my son." (Gabriellino, his son, happened to be in Fiume at the time.)

Whereupon the drunk took off his hat, bowed ceremoniously and said: 'Allora, tanti saluti a tuo Papá!' And he continued on his way, singing at the top of his voice.

It was after incidents such as these, says Comisso, that D'Annunzio tried to tighten discipline. He describes how D'Annunzio called the more extravagant young officers before him: "the Comandante was waiting for us in his study, severely standing straight up behind the table. He shook us stiffly by the hand and then, putting up his monocle, began a tirade. 'It is strange,' he said, 'that it should be I who ask you to behave, I who have known only too well the excitements of youth. But I say to you here and now, that since I have been in Fiume, I have lived a life as chaste as that of a Franciscan monk. But you—your behavior—it is beyond all limits. . . . Your men must come under stricter control.' "

Comisso points out that this Dannunzian chastity was quite imaginary, for every evening when he was at the palazzo a young singer called Montresor used to be taken to his bedroom. She would leave the next morning, having been paid 500 lire.

Indeed, women in quantities flocked to Fiume in the first days when the situation had settled, some hoping for a place in the famous *Comandante's* bed, others spies or half agents in the pay of the various governments, Italian, Yugoslav, Allied. D'Annunzio was aware of this. But he was certainly no St. Francis (as he claimed) and he appears to have enjoyed these enthusiastic ladies in his usual way. He received them individually in private—and then played them a trick worthy of Boccaccio. To each lady whose favors he had enjoyed (and they granted them with immodest haste to the greatest poet of Italy and the *Comandante* of Fiume) he gave a large silk handkerchief, of unique design and color, of the kind which women tie around their heads.

His son, Mario, says in his book *Con mio padre sulla nave del ricordo*, that this habit continued for some time, and the higher circles of the Fiume Legionaries began to look on it with disapproval. They did not like to see their *Comandante,* of international fame, making an exhibition of himself with every kind of woman. In the words of Ovid—also an Abruzzese poet, who had written much about love—*non bene conveniunt nec in una sede morantur majestas et amor.* Letters of the following kind would be opened by D'Annunzio's chief of cabinet, "*Carissimo,* to remind you that we have fourteen guests to lunch today, and that we haven't enough food for all. So some must be content with drinks and biscuits. Love." Or: "*Mio Carissimo,* Tomorrow is the lunch for the Mayor. There will be about twelve, including five or six ladies and young girls. Good night, darling."

To extricate himself from a situation which was becoming embarrassing, D'Annunzio gave a reception at his headquarters where he invited all the women to whom he had given a silk handkerchief. Each apparently imagined she was its only recipient. The first lady entered the reception wearing, of course, the gift. All went well. But then a second arrived, then a third, then a fourth. Soon, there were nearly a dozen women wearing the same handkerchief. After glaring furiously at one another, they attempted individually to approach D'Annunzio. But he was inaccessible, surrounded by his staff and official guests. They left the room in a fury and, shortly after, Fiume. In the words of D'Annunzio's son, Mario: "Thus my father, with a few handkerchiefs and a lot of amusement, relieved Fiume of a number of potential intriguers."

This of course did not happen to all the ladies who came to Fiume. Important visitors, such as the Duchess of Aosta, visited him for more political reasons. In any case, D'Annunzio had a theory that women must be near him, for him to do good work. He considered them, he said, the *nemica necessaria.*

Costantini, the bishop of Fiume, also supports this view. In his memoirs, *Foglie Secche,* he says that if, in public, D'Annunzio behaved in an exemplary Christian way, the same could not be said of his private life. If he knelt regularly at the altar of the big church and kissed the holy relics of the Saints Vito, Modesto and Crescenzia, and always listened to the bishop with "that attentive deference and humility which was a part of his personal charm," he lived in private with a "woman who was not his wife." The bishop refused to visit him. With such an example from the *Comandante,* says the bishop, morals in Fiume were almost nonexistent, and people came from all over Italy for divorces. The city became "the Cocaigne of divorcees." Blood, music, poetry, voluptuousness and death—these had often been proclaimed by the poet in his work. Now they lived in his city.

Bishop Costantini says that although religion had a place in the Statute of Fiume which D'Annunzio had drawn up, he had instituted, in reality, his own cult, "with a civic sanctuary and a burning lamp—a purely pagan affair. Orpheus had replaced Christ in the Statute." The bishop continues by saying that the mistake of

D'Annunzio at Fiume was that he surrounded himself with inferior people, who listened to the poet and after being with him for a short time, thought of themselves, too, as divine geniuses, as infallible, "so many caricatures of the *Comandante.*" "The contagion of Greatness was the danger for whoever lived those days in Fiume," he says. "It was a comic and painful spectacle to see the transformation of these people when they approached D'Annunzio." The culmination came when some members of Parliament came to Fiume, to remonstrate with D'Annunzio for half a day. After two hours with him in anticamera, they came out infected with his enthusiasm, completely on his side.

The way in which D'Annunzio received these State visitors is described by Osbert Sitwell, in *Discursions:*

". . . we were shown into D'Annunzio's private apartment. The room was fairly large, with little furniture, the walls covered almost entirely with banners. On one side, supported by brackets, stood two gilded saints from Florence, whose calm eyes gazed out over the deepening color of the Fiume sea. On one of the tables near the fireplace stood a huge fifteenth-century bell—made by the great bell-maker of Arbe, and presented by that island to the Regent. On the central table were many papers, and a pomegranate (D'Annunzio's symbol). He was dressed in khaki, covered with ribbons, and on his left shoulder he wore the Italian Gold Medal for Valor, equivalent, or superior to, our Victoria Cross. Though he was completely bald, with one eye, nervous and tired, yet at the end of a few seconds, one felt the influence of that extraordinary charm which enabled him to change howling mobs into furious partisans. . . . First he talked of England, of his admiration for Shelley, of sport, and of English greyhounds, 'running wild over the moors of Devonshire' . . . We asked him to talk of Ireland but, with a true feeling of hospitality for his guests, he refused. Instead, he told us of Fiume, of his great loneliness there, of how he, who loved books, pictures and music, had remained there for fifteen months surrounded by peasants and soldiers—of how the Italian government, relying on his roving temperament, were trying to 'bore him out.' "

19

Fascists

We must now leave D'Annunzio in Fiume for a moment and visit Milan, where Benito Mussolini was beginning to make his presence felt. It was later to change the whole Fiuman situation. In one of D'Annunzio's early plays, *La Gloria,* written twenty-five years before, there is a remarkable portrait of a dictator, Ruggero Flamma. Even in the rubrics of this drama, D'Annunzio seems to have foreseen the man who was to rule Italy for the next twenty years. In the stage directions before the play opens, we have what might be a description of the Palazzo Venezia in Mussolini's heyday (yet written in 1898).

"A huge naked room with great solid stone columns. A heavy table occupies the center; it is piled with important-looking dossiers—as if belonging to a statesman who has been working late at night. There is an air of decision and authority, of unanimous consent [*sic*] to a controlled and individual energy. On the architraves of the doors, is sculptured the device of a flame burning in the wind, with the motto beneath, *"Vim ex vi."* Between the two doors on each of the opposite walls is a niche with traces of gilding. It contains a pedestal without a statue. At the back of the stage is a balcony which opens on to a city whose color is darkening as the evening fades. City lights begin to appear in the distance, like sparks alive beneath the cinders of a fire!"

Mussolini, it has been seen, had been violently against war until, with equal violence in 1915, he suddenly supported it.[1] For this, he was expelled from the Socialist Party, and accused of

---

[1] He only did his military service belatedly, in 1905-6, having been declared a draft-dodger.

being bribed by the French. Whether this was true or not, he had
strong reasons, perhaps even ideals, for the change. For a long
time, he had thought of socialism in terms of a patriotic idea
combined with social revolution; and the war had suddenly appeared to him to combine both these elements. He accordingly
cut adrift from the pacific side of the Socialist Party, which regarded action only in terms of the interior politics of the country,
and he became a war interventionist. Socialism, he considered,
had declined sadly in Italy. From being international, it had become national; from national, provincial; from provincial, local.
And now it appeared to be at some undefined, sub-parochial stage.

At the end of the war, his two pet themes, nationalism and
socialism, came closer together in his mind. Italy had been cheated
by the Allies—this was a nationalist theme. Italy was bedeviled
by communism, which was creating chaos in the country—this was
a socialist theme, or rather, a theme for *proper* socialism. Herein
lies his theory of a revolution, not of the masses, whom he now
began to despise for their lack of discipline, but of an élite. The
National Socialists! In short, something of the Dannunzian idea
now being given form in Fiume.

On March 3, 1919, six months before D'Annunzio took Fiume,
Mussolini's paper, the *Popolo d'Italia,* had called a meeting in
Milan of anyone likely to sympathize with his views. A most
heterogeneous group of men collected, with interests and politics
of every conceivable kind—socialists, nationalists, Mazzinian republicans, ex-prisoners of war, futurists, anarcho-syndicalists,
young men in search of adventure, together with one or two
straight conservatives of the old traditional kind. They took their
name, *Fascisti,* from *fascio,* or bundle, a well-known term in
Italian politics before the war (it originally belonged to a socialist
revolutionary group in Sicily). Mussolini adapted the word, and
founded the new movement under the name of *fasci di combattimento,* meaning literally, "bundles for combat." Its program
was as comprehensive as its membership. The fifty-odd founding
members who came together that day in Milan issued a manifesto

demanding an astonishing list of things—Nationalism, Socialism, Republicanism, Revolution, Order, International Peace, League of Nations, Dalmatia and Fiume. Mussolini's skill lay in fusing these elements. From the patriotic note to the social one, from the condemnation of imperial appetites to the exaltation of imperialism itself, from the solemn profession of democratic faith, to scorn for all parliamentary systems and the "sordid battle of the parliamentary vote," the gamut of politics was run. The "Bundles for Combat" then had, in fact, no concrete program, no prejudice for monarchy or republic; they were neither Catholic nor anti-Catholic, socialist nor anti-socialist. They described themselves not as a party but as a *movement,* aimed at "keeping united in a *super-party* Italians of all faiths and productive classes, to propel them towards the new inevitable battles that must be fought, to complete and give value to the great revolutionary war."

Two broad directions were given to the movement in foreign policy. One was a violent opposition to Russian communism which, their leader contended, could only bring disorder. The other was nationalism, on behalf of Fiume, Dalmatia and the Irridentist lands. On the domestic side, the program contained a host of attractive measures; an eight hour working day, old age pensions, universal suffrage, nationalization of armament production, together with one or two frankly Utopian things, such as the suppression of the Army and the confiscation of all religious property. Most of this was shop-window dressing. Mussolini was never a man for programs. At a meeting in Florence, he replied typically to Marinetti the Futurist's demand that the Pope should be expelled and "devaticanization of Italy" begin, "We Fascists have no preconceived doctrines. Our doctrine is acts. Acts and facts—these are our interests." [1]

New "Bundles for Combat" soon began to form in the north of the peninsula among the lower-middle classes, small shopkeepers, clerks, under-officers and petty bureaucrats. These people were all

[1] Marinetti wanted to swoop over the Vatican in an airplane, kidnap the Pope, and drop him in the Adriatic.

looking for something which would help them to resist, at the
same time, the communists, who were creating industrial chaos,
and the big industrialists, who had become enormously rich during
the war. These industrialists and *latifondisti* (land owners), who
disliked Fascism at first, soon approved of its anti-communism,
and were even prepared to finance it. Then, when the movement
showed financial power as well, a host of people from all classes
began to join, men with quick hands and elastic consciences,
anxious to obtain a position of power with as little effort as possible. That these middle class groups had little faith in the government's ability to deal with communism was revealed by the
titles of the various leagues or associations they had formed on
their own, before Mussolini appeared: the *Gruppi di azione
patriottica e di Difesa nazionale;* the *Unione Popolare Antibol-
scevstica;* the *Lega della gioventù latina;* the *Comitato di organiz-
zazione civile;* the *Lega nazionale;* etc., etc. None of these groups
had a proper leader, nor were they inter-related at the outset. The
nationalists tended to be upper-class and kept ostentatiously apart;
the Catholics often became strangely muddled up with the socialists in policy, although they were supposed to be mortal enemies.
The only properly organized groups were Mussolini's "Bundles
for Combat."

And at this point, something very fortunate happened for them.
The elections of November 1919 took place in Italy, and for the
first time, the socialists obtained a majority. This would appear,
at first sight, something of a setback for Mussolini and his "Bundles," who obtained a minute poll. It seemed that his public life
was over. But the socialists, unaccustomed to power, thought the
time was now ripe for a vast anti-capitalist gesture. They over-
played their hand. They began that series of great strikes and
invasions of private property for which the years 1919 and 1920
have never been forgotten in Italy. Their Peasant League, operating on the Ferrara-Bologna plain, instituted a sort of agrarian
terror. Workers' syndicates took possession of villages and mu-
nicipalities, ejecting the Mayor and his officials, and insulting

anyone who had fought in the war. If opposed, they used violence. They thought (as communists did everywhere) that it was only a matter of months before the whole of Europe had imitated the Russian Bolshevists; that the Soviets themselves would soon arrive. The future was theirs, because the Third International had been formed. Confident of this, they occupied all the big factories, using methods copied entirely from the Russian model.

But after some months, the expected Russian revolution did not arrive in Western Europe. Lenin was fully occupied at home. And the Italian workers, finding that the factories did not function efficiently under untrained direction, nor did they provide and sell goods, began to ask for a return to their old salaried positions, while still retaining co-operative control. This created the famous scission in the Italian Communist Party, leading later to the formation of distinct Socialist and Communist Parties in Italy, as elsewhere in Europe.

The impression that these forcible land seizures had made in Italy was immense. Everyone who had been doubtful about the "Bundles" now began to join them. They seemed the only party who could maintain law and order. The government's inability to deal with the situation in Fiume was bad enough. But faced with communist excesses, it seemed even more feeble. Nitti had a plan, a typical plan. He believed that the communist methods would fail of their own accord. His solution was therefore to do as little as possible, the famous "wait and see" of all good bourgeois statesmen. He contended that the socialist occupation of the factories, grave as it was, could only be a passing phase. But while he and the government were waiting, Mussolini was acting. Ever fertile in ideas, he decided to attack politics from a completely new angle, simply destroying the socialists physically, with squads and armed desperadoes. The popularity of his party increased enormously as a result of this. In a matter of months, it had leaped from a few thousands to over 300,000, with two thousand groups or nucleii all over the country. Intoxicated with success the "Bundles" now decided to push on to the complete extermination of their rivals. It was now that the notorious *spedizioni punitive* against the *Camere del Lavoro* began. Instead of socialist violence, Italy had Fascist violence. The destruction and burning of socialist buildings and HQs became a Fascist prerogative, combined with bastinadoes, castor oil and the shanghaiing of local syndicates. The young Fascists had learned from D'Annunzio that *la fiamma è bella*. So, hurling torches of burning oil, they set light to *Case del Popolo, Camere del Lavoro* and all the socialist newspaper offices. They had also learned from Fiume the novelty of castor oil, a beverage occasionally mixed with petrol or iodine which was administered to obdurate opponents, to purge them of wrong ideas. A column of Fascist vehicles would form up by night not far from the village or town to be "punished." On arriving, they would pillage and fire the buildings of the local socialist movement, and carry off the directors into the country, to be manhandled, and frequently shot.

The Labor Exchange buildings in Trieste had been dealt with in this way, as early as July 1920. In October, they burned down the buildings of the socialist paper *Il Lavoratore,* directed by Ignazio Silone; then the Socialist HQ in Fiume; then, in January, 1921, their HQ in Digniano. The buildings of the *Avanti* paper in Milan were sacked and the stocks of paper burned. The Labor Exchange in Trieste then caught it again, this time being reduced to cinders. Any town or village that had elected a socialist municipality was their target. In the province of Ferrara there were, for example, in November 1920, twenty-one socialist councils. By the end of April 1921, all but four had disappeared, "liquidated" by the "Bundles'" *squadristi* under Italo Balbo, one of Mussolini's most active lieutenants. In Rovigo, Matteoti, the socialist deputy, told the peasants not to reply to these provocations, but to keep calm, even, if necessary, to give the impression of cowardice. This availed them nothing. Not one syndicate or cooperative was left standing in that constituency; there were dozens of dead, 5,000 wounded, 300 private houses destroyed. During the first weeks of 1921, all Emilia, the Veneto and Lombardy passed under Fascist control. Only the Trentino and Tyrol held out in the North; and the far South, where there was nothing to destroy. Real civil war developed in Istria, with barbed wire fences and machine guns at the ends of the roads, villages burned and populations transferred. About 100 Slovene "circles of Culture" in the neighborhood of Trieste were also burned down for good measure.

Nitti seemed no more worried by all this than he had been by earlier socialist excesses. He believed that the Fascists, given their head, would also end by destroying themselves. At the beginning, he had even put public forces at their disposal; many demobilized army officers had been encouraged by his War Minister, Bonomi, to join the "Bundles."

Mussolini was meanwhile behaving in Parliament in an extremely astute way. In his speeches, articles and general attitude, he was full of humanity, asking for an end to the acts of violence on both sides. He demanded a reconciliation between socialists and Fascists, and he stressed the danger of state interference. "Dictatorship," he said to critics who mentioned the word in connection with himself, "is a very big card to play, involving for whoever plays it, terrible risks." As the communists would still not come to terms, he turned his "movement" into a "party," because it could be more easily disciplined.

All this, the socialist strikes, the strong feeling in Italy against them, and the development of the Fascist Party in its early stages, coincided exactly with D'Annunzio's first months in Fiume.

20

Italia o la Morte!

In Fiume, Mussolini had, we have seen, originally supported
D'Annunzio whole heartedly. On a visit to the city, just after
D'Annunzio's arrival, he had even offered to take all the babies
away, in case fighting might break out, a humane project which
proved easier to conceive than execute. He had been the first man
to open a pro-Fiume subscription, in his paper *Popolo d'Italia*, on
behalf of D'Annunzio's Legionaries, who were still in summer
clothes; they required boots, blankets, great-coats. After Mussolini's fall (in 1943), documents were published showing his part
in the Fiume affair. The *Civiltà Fascista* of June 1944, and
L'Europeo of June 6, 1948, reveals that as late as September, he
was still encouraging D'Annunzio to a military adventure in Italy.
One of his messages runs, "March on Trieste—declare the Monarchy invalid—nominate a government Directory composed of
Giardino, Caviglia, Rizzo, with you as President—prepare elections—declare, naturally, the annexation of Fiume—send reliable
troops to disembark at Ravenna and Ancona and in the Abruzzi to
help republican uprising."

In theory, everything about the Fiuman seizure should have
appealed to Mussolini; the *coup de main,* the uniforms, the
chauvinism, the mob oratory, the mysticism. But D'Annunzio was
now revealing that he had ambitions beyond Fiume. It was only
later, twelve yers after Mussolini's death, that documents revealing the differences then existing between the two men had
been made public.[1] The Fascists, when they were in power, nat-

[1] These documents have been analyzed by Nino Valeri in *D a Giolitti a Mus-*
solini (Parenti, 1956). Further information on the last days in Fiume has since
been made available in Foscanelli's *D'Annunzio e l'ora sociale.* Foscanelli, who
was in Fiume with D'Annunzio, had to keep silent during the Fascist period.

urally refused to allow them to be published, for they wished to capitalize on the supposed D'Annunzio-Mussolini friendship. Almost until he died in 1938, D'Annunzio was the most famous and popular man in Italy.

Nino Valeri, in his recent book, says that not long after D'Annunzio's arrival in Fiume, a document was drawn up by some of the Legionaries indicating the far wider scope the adventure was to have. ". . . at dawn on September 26," it reads, "the Legionaries in Trieste will arrest the military commandant and other local authorities, in the name of Gabriele D'Annunzio. All other government troops will submit and accept whatever orders the new régime lays down. At the same time, an ultimatum will be sent to Nitti announcing the annexation of Fiume and Dalmatia, under the threat that Istria and all Dalmatia will otherwise be absorbed by Yugoslavia. With the fall of the Nitti government, we shall hereby name an extra-parliamentary government with D'Annunzio at its head . . ." This is followed by an "account," from a certain Captain Ercole Miani, of how he intends to take Trieste on the night of the 25/26 September, and there declare "the provisionary government of the new Italy."

There can be little doubt that a march on Rome was in D'Annunzio's mind. He saw what was happening in Asia Minor under the leadership of Mustapha Kemal, against the Sultanate of Constantinople and the Western powers. In his poetic imagination, he was half a Moslem prophet himself, helping to dispose of the Balkan states and bring the Western powers to their knees. He felt at the same time, Dante in exile, Garibaldi the Liberator, Cesare Borgia building a state out of nothing, and Julius Caesar crossing the Rubicon.

Another letter quoted by Valeri is to "a dear friend in Fiume," written by a certain Francesco Giunta, on November 12, 1919 (two months after D'Annunzio's arrival in Fiume); it is about the preparations for an imminent march on Rome: ". . . Rome, situation favorable, both for garrison and the Republicans, the nationalists and Legionaries. The Republican Party is ready for mobilization. At Florence, bearing in mind the general skepticism and slackness of these Tuscans, things are as well as can be expected. But I can answer personally for the city. In the rest of Tuscany, we have our nuclei in all the big, principal cities. I have personally attended to principal cities, and local details. Only Pistoia, which is bilious and factious as usual, and Lucca (in the power of the priests) are uncertain. Elsewhere, we are in control. The Piombino-Livorno littoral is notoriously Bolshevist. We must bear this in mind and watch it carefully. At Livorno, I am in touch with a number of the garrison officers. I have also been in the Romagna, where I have learned something. Two trustworthy comrades showed me a letter from Carlo Bozzi, in which he asks all the cities and villages of the Romagna to send to Milan for the day a squadron of ten armed men, because in these days events may require our holding the city for 24 to 28 hours, *to give D'Annunzio time to come with the main forces*. The squadrons are now at Milan. Benelli is becoming reconciled with Fiume. More than this, he has decided to work and occupy, if necessary, Central Italy . . ." There is also a curious letter from the aviator ace, Keller, October 13, 1919, "To *Comandante*. Required only message of proclamation. Five days of silence and then—Action! Men divorced from the feel of steel now living in a bright light are ready . . ."

Caviglia, the General who blockaded Fiume, says in his book *The Conflict of Fiume* (which also could not be published until recently), ". . . D'Annunzio's aim was less to liberate Fiume from the Yugoslav danger, than to place himself at the head of a revolutionary movement based politically on Fiume, and militarily on the armed force in Venetia Giulia, with whom he hoped to make a march on Rome. The morale of our troops at the time rendered this perfectly feasible. Nor, at that moment, would there have been much resistance from troops in the rest of the peninsula. . . ."

This is confirmed again by the Bishop of Fiume. One evening, he relates, a friend of his, Count Tullio, saw notices inviting all officers and men to come to the Fenice Theatre for a meeting presided over by D'Annunzio. The Count went, and found D'Annunzio speaking most violently to his men. "I read on your faces, in your eyes," D'Annunzio was crying, "your indomitable desire. Comrades, whither now?"

"To Zara! To Zara!" they cried.

"To Zara only! Reflect a little," said the poet softly.

"To Spàlato! To Spàlato!"

"To Spàlato only! Look into your hearts, and read again."

"To Rome! To Rome!"

This was the reply he wanted. Then they all sang the song of the Legionaries:

> "With the bomb and the dagger,
> We will enter the Quirinale . . ."

D'Annunzio sang it with them.

Even Mario, D'Annunzio's son, says, "When on September 8, 1920, my father proclaimed the Regency of the Carnaro, plans were studied for a march from Fiume which, along the Ancona coast, could lead the Legionaries to Rome and the conquest of power. My father had even given the idea a motto: 'From Italy let us navigate to Italy!' "

Strong measures were also to be taken against any Yugoslavs who happened to be in the city. An unfortunate Croatian journalist, Krazmardic, a talented man capable of publicizing these plans widely, was jailed. Not long after, while taking exercise in the prison yard, he was hit by a revolver shot. The Legionaries declared: "hit accidentally by a soldier, who was cleaning his revolver." But an observer who knew the Legionaries better said waggishly: "shot deliberately by a soldier, who was accidentally cleaning his revolver."

It was the idea of a march on Rome by a man better known, and certainly more popular, than himself which incurred Mussolini's jealousy; and his attitude towards Fiume began to change. But another, almost as important, factor influenced him. With the publication of the Statute of the Carnaro and its articles about "workers' rights," and the association with the Mariners at Genoa, D'Annunzio had revealed himself less as a nationalist than as a socialist. Some people even said that the statutes about equality were "Bolshevist." Mussolini, originally an extreme left-wing socialist, was moving slowly Right, until Fascism became identified with the reaction of the monied classes—while D'Annunzio, a natural aristocrat and monarchist, was moving steadily Left, until he was seriously feared as a kind of Russian communist.

In April 1920, the secretary of the Hungarian Bolshevist, Bela Kun, was arrested by the Carabinieri in Fiume; and D'Annunzio unwisely ordered his immediate release, on the ground that the man was his guest. Every day more egalitarian ideas appeared in Fiume, clothed in D'Annunzio's ornate language, about medieval guilds and eternal brotherhood, all pointing to "communism." There are phrases in the constitution such as, "the power of productive labor," or "the state must amplify, sustain and elevate the rights of the producers," which were new in constitutional parlance in those days. After referring to the rights of Free Thought, Assembly and Press, it continues, "the state will not recognize ownership as the absolute dominion of the person over the thing, but it considers it the most useful of social functions"—a statement which can be interpreted in many ways. Then there is, "the sole lawful claim to dominion over any means of production and exchange is Labor. Labor alone is master of the product, which must be most advantageous and profitable to the general economy"; and "only constant producers of the common wealth, and constant creators of the common power, are the real citizens of our Republic." "Incorrigible parasites who are a burden to the country" would not be entitled to the enjoyment of political rights. No wonder people in Italy were tempted to ask if D'Annunzio was becoming a Marxist.

For the armed forces it was the same, ". . . the organization of the new liberating army. When the Council sits, the authority of the army ceases. In opinion and voting all councillors are equal. At the council table (in time of war) sit with the same rights, questioning and voting, a general, a major, a sergeant, and a corporal." Moreover, as quotations from Comisso's *Le Mie Stagioni* have already shown, some of the Legionaries were planning to go to Russia and ask the Soviets to march west. On April 13, 1920, Nitti's representative in Trieste telegraphed to Rome this startling news, ". . . reliable source indicates D'Annunzio addressing Pasiglia [1] with view to proclaim Communst Soviet Republic Fiume, extending Venetia Giulia, assistance local socialist parties stating if latter refuses co-operation will join Malatesta's anarchical element." (Malatesta was a notorious anarchist.)

Passiglia refused this association, but the mere idea that it had been considered, was good enough to offend the feelings of many officers and officials who had come to Fiume to *escape* communism, which they hated as international and unpatriotic. Many of the senior officers were Royalists, who had joined because they saw in Fiume an addition to the kingdom. Two generals, Ceccherini and Tamario, both of whom had sworn allegiance to D'Annunzio and his cause in Fiume, now foreswore their oaths and returned to Italy.[2] A number of other officials with markedly right wing tendencies abandoned the city when the charter of the Carnaro was proclaimed. Major Rajna, the first man to support D'Annunzio in the Ronchi march, wrote this letter to D'Annunzio in the middle of 1920, ". . . if we start anti-constitutional measures, we shall find that not we, but Malatesta and the anarchists, will benefit. You reprove me—because you wanted to use the whole army for this—and I did not. You have favored the acts of Keller, Benaglia and company, for a military-anarchist move on Rome. That too is why you protected Vecchi, Marinetti and Giunta . . . you wished to go to Abbazia, Trieste, Spàlato (announced in your hymn to the Fiuman troops), to Rome itself. You wanted a

[1] Passiglia was an extreme left wing socialist.
[2] The first returned to Italy, in particularly unhappy circumstances. When, some months before, he had been in Zara, he had announced blandly to the multitude, "Rather than go back on my oath to the *Comandante* in Fiume, I would prefer to lose the affection of my son." A short time after his return to Italy from Fiume his son, a distinguished war time aviator, was killed in an airplane crash.

coup d'état to support the Duke of Aosta. . . . Fortunately, none
of these projects has been put into practice. This is due, in great
part, to those who for three months have tried to avoid excess.
Now perhaps, a clearer vision of reality may take possession of the
Fiume High Command. But this does not mean I shall remain on
your staff. I no longer have faith in it. . . ." He was accused by
D'Annunzio of taking part in a "Palace Revolt" and was put
under arrest. He was later expelled from Fiume. But he had
voiced a discontent which was becoming general.

In Rome, the Prime Minister Nitti, when confronted with this
news about D'Annunzio's "Bolshevism," was delighted. To his
Chief of Cabinet, he sent this directive on April 16, 1920,
". . . there is no need to give this out officially, but the information that D'Annunzio is becoming republican and showing Bolshevist tendencies should be widely diffused. We are clearly dealing
with a man who, having claimed that his movement has a patriotic
base, is now attempting to spread anarchy. This news must
be gradually given to all press correspondents, the cabinet instructed . . ." This, he knew, would cool the hot heads and draw
sympathy away from D'Annunzio throughout Italy.

Defection among his own officers and the increasing blockade
had meanwhile convinced D'Annunzio that he must obtain support from outside, in Italy itself. He naturally turned to the man
who had encouraged the venture in the *Popolo d'Italia,* and whose
growing Fascist Party seemed to have so much in common with
the cause of Fiume. He sent his Chief of Cabinet, De Ambris, to
Milan to see Mussolini.

Mussolini accepted this invitation, but only after a surprising
delay, and after raising all sorts of objections. His secretary,
Fasciolo, explained with some embarrassment that Mussolini was
engaged at the moment in conference with Count Sforza in Milan.
As Count Sforza, the Foreign Secretary, was doing all he could to
evict D'Annunzio from Fiume, this was not a good augury. But a
meeting between De Ambris and Mussolini did finally take place,
in Trieste. Foscanelli, who was acting at that time as D'Annunzio's secretary, went with them, and he has revealed what hap-

pened at the meeting in his recently published *D'Annunzio e l'ora Sociale*. De Ambris opened the proceedings by saying that D'Annunzio was convinced that, with the support of the Fascist Party, he could withstand any attack the government or the Allies might make on Fiume, and that he could probably persuade contingents of General Caviglia's troops to desert to them. He said that D'Annunzio now had important naval units at his disposal. He then suggested something much more dangerous. He said that, with proper support, these naval units could make a landing half way down the Adriatic coast, near Ancona. If Mussolini would guarantee the important Fascist support in Central Italy, a march on Rome would be possible. Already, *Bersaglieri* regiments near Ancona were showing willingness to join.

As De Ambris explained this, Mussolini's eyes (Foscanelli says), opened wider and wider. At a certain point, he interjected, "And what about Bologna? The communist city? And the socialists in Upper Italy?" De Ambris was not discouraged. "The workers of Parma are on our side," he said. "We must let the masses of the working classes know that we shall spread the Statute of the Carnaro throughout Italy. Its laws will protect the rights of the workers. Ours will be a revolution of the people."

Mussolini now began to enumerate difficulties. He spoke of the extreme difficulty of getting supplies at this time of year; of coal and transport problems; he referred to the Yugoslav troops still menacing the frontiers of the state of the Carnaro. But he did not refer to the one thing that meant most to him. As well as being relegated himself to the second figure in such a "March on Rome," the socialist side of D'Annunzio's program would alienate the big industrialists and landed proprietors who had, in the past few months, begun to help the Fascists financially. The discussion finished in such a state of irritation that the secretary, who had been taking notes, was instructed to tear them up.

The economic situation in Fiume was by now becoming serious, and D'Annunzio was driven to all manner of shifts to deal with it. He ordered the National Council to hand over to him the entire municipal revenue, and to raise a mortgage on all public buildings. An airplane was sent to Paris to negotiate the sale of a cargo of postage-stamps, valued at over a million lire; but the cargo was confiscated by the French police. At one point, D'Annunzio even attempted to sell for 1,000 lire, a tablecloth with a large ink-stain on it, which was said to have been made while he was composing one of his harangues in the command HQ.

Meanwhile, in Rome important changes had taken place, which were to settle the future of Fiume. The High Command of the government troops "besieging" Fiume had been changed. Badoglio had not been a success, and the government had got rid of him, by the usual military method of promotion. He was promoted full General and made Chief of Staff. General Caviglia replaced him. More important still, Nitti, the Prime Minister, had been replaced by D'Annunzio's old enemy, Giolitti. Nitti had maintained all the time that "the Fiume affair would solve itself," with the two elements, monarchical and republican, tending to a kind of civil war. Telegrams he sent to Caviglia, the General in charge of the surrounding troops, describe what he hoped for:

"3 May. No: 9570. Riporta no. 1656. To General Caviglia. (code) Believe irregular situation Fiume will quickly right itself now. As soon as possible after, desirable our troops enter, restore order."

But by June 9, the situation was still out of hand, and it would have been quite impossible for General Caviglia to force an entry pacifically, to "restore order," because the civil war had still not broken out. It was now that Nitti resigned, and handed over to Giolitti.

The old man, whose first battle with D'Annunzio had taken place in Parliament over twenty years before, took office as Prime Minister for the fifth time in his career. He immediately announced to the nation that Fiume, far from being a local affair, "was infecting the whole national life, planting its poisonous roots all over Italy." This was not an unreasonable statement, for D'Annunzio's *Uscocchi,* intoxicated with their piratical successes, had now started a series of raids on other towns and ports. After the success of the *Cogne* negotiations, they seem to have gone completely berserk. On November 13, 1920, they occupied the islands of Veglia and Arbe in the gulf of the Carnaro; the towns of Tobia, Sedoci and Blasici round the gulf; and of Mount Luban, Martinovo, Selo on Recina, Svatsic, Ivrini and Polevic; while D'Annunzio employed biblical language to congratulate them, ". . . Today bread has been multiplied as in the time of the purification of the loaves. Today, God has sent us bread . . ." He was referring here to the capture of a grain boat, the *Barone Fejerway.* ". . . nearly 6,000 tons of the best grain," he said, "are in our port today. We have enough bread for eight months. In other words, for eight months our companions will have white teeth. No one shall starve us out. Help us unload the sacks. Help us fill the granaries. Help us work the mills. Help us stoke the ovens . . ."

Giolitti believed (wrongly, as it turned out), that Mussolini was still behind D'Annunzio, and would welcome a march on Rome when these Dalmatian plans were fulfilled.[1] He accordingly began the negotiations for what was later to be the Treaty of Rapallo with Yugoslavia. By this treaty, a sort of judgment of Solomon which gave satisfaction to neither country, but which solved the Fiume problem temporarily, Italy agreed not to annex either Fiume or the Dalmatian isles. Fiume was to be an independent state, "of an Italian character," while Susak, its eastern suburb, would go to Yugoslavia. This treaty was later confirmed in Parliament with a clear majority (including the vote of Benito Mussolini!).

D'Annunzio was naturally furious that he had not been consulted about these negotiations which contained, he suspected, a number of secret clauses. He was encouraged by the more violent

---

[1] Pini Susmel in *Mussolini,* vol. III, says that Mussolini was planning a kind of Triumvirate with D'Annunzio at the time—but not to take place till the spring of 1921.

Legionaries, who were desperate at the thought of having to return to ordinary life, after having reached "the peak of heroism" where, as D'Annunzio wrote to Mussolini on September 16, 1920, "it would be sweet to die, swallowing the last draught of Fiume's waters." He decided to adopt a heroic attitude. He probably still hoped that Mussolini and his Fascists would help him.

On the afternoon of November 21, 1920, the Italian Chamber of Deputies and the Senate ratified the treaty of Rapallo, and D'Annunzio became in Fiume a pirate, in name as well as in fact. The Italian Government had now, if only for its own prestige, to eject him as soon as possible. The blockade was to be replaced if necessary by military action. Admiral Millo, in command of the Italian fleet in the Adriatic, was ordered to stand by, and General Caviglia at last received the order to use force. Admiral Millo was by no means hostile to D'Annunzio,[1] and he asked D'Annunzio to meet him on his ship to discuss a friendly solution. This meeting was abortive, for D'Annunzio on returning to his headquarters in Fiume, only ordered a general mobilizaion of all men between the ages of 18 and 50, and women strong enough to bear arms. He took for himself the style and title of "Head of the Liberating Army," significant, in that many have since thought this indicated that the "March on Rome" was still in his mind, and that he hoped the government troops would desert to him. His only hope was, in fact, that the soldiers and sailors of Italy would refuse to fire on their fellow countrymen, as they had refused on the morning of the Ronchi march. This brings us to what D'Annunzio characteristically called "The Christmas of Blood."

He delivered this curious address to the Italian Navy about to attack him—curious in that it has an unexpected reference to Lord Nelson, whom he should have disliked as a British imperialist:

"Comrades! The orders you have received from your leaders in the Adriatic are a mortal insult to the honor of our nation, to the

---

[1] Millo was the admiral who had very nearly joined D'Annunzio in 1919. Only a signed letter from the King, written at the government's insistence, reminding the C.-in.-C. of the Italian Adriatic fleet of his oath of allegiance, had dissuaded him.

honor of Italy. I recall the words used by the great Admiral who won the battle of Trafalgar. Were he to arise again today, born an Italian, and to take command of your fleet, in face of the traitors in Rome, I swear on my conscience as an old soldier, wounded in the war, I swear the message he would deliver to you would be, 'Italy expects every man this day *not* to do his duty . . .' "

But morale was no longer high in Fiume. The scarcity of provisions, the danger of famine and epidemics, the discontent and discouragements after fifteen months of slow blockade—all this had changed the patriotic ardor of the Fiumans. A crowd assembled in front of D'Annunzio's *palazzo* and asked him to save the city from bloodshed. But D'Annunzio still lived in a rarefied atmosphere and he swore to fight to the end. To the Italian Government who had accused him of not "thinking in an Italian way" over the Treaty of Rapallo, he addressed this diatribe:

"If to consider as malefactors, the men who have fought valiantly and covered themselves with wounds for Italy, is 'to think in an Italian way'—then we do not wish to be Italians.

"If to insult, to beat, to handcuff, to imprison, to torture the soldiers of the Piave, guilty of not being the deserters of Caporetto, but instead men of the Ronchi march is 'to think in an Italian way' —then we do not wish to be Italians.

"If to use daily against our troops in Fiume calumny and abuse is 'to think in an Italian way'—then we do not wish to be Italians.

"If to help with all available means, of physical and moral force, anti-national measures voted by the most putrid corruption that ever came out of our legislative sewers is 'to think in an Italian way'—then we do not wish to be Italians.

"If to use as a pretext, a small raid by a despairing band of patriots, to attempt to destroy a city already tortured is 'to think in an Italian way'—then we do not wish to be Italians.

"If to stop the food and corn supplies of a famished city, to deprive them of medicines, hospitals, milk for their undernourished children, is 'to think in an Italian way'—then we do not wish to be Italians. . . ."

Had this speech been directed against the Yugoslavs, perhaps the people of Fiume, who were mostly Italian, would have supported D'Annunzio. But the troops and ships now threatening them were Italian. Tender, passionate, mystical, D'Annunzio's words had lost their old power. Three times a day, he fell on his knees before the flags. "This is the flag of Italy!" he cried. "The only flag of Italy. We shall defend it till we die. Those who survive will raise it again, even if it flies above a pile of ruins. They will see the people of Italy coming towards them again, unified with them as one. To rise again is to be reborn . . ."

But the people of Fiume did not want a flag over a pile of ruins, nor to be reborn. A large proportion of the Legionaries remained true to their leader, declaring they too would fight; but some who had joined in the first flush of enthusiasm drifted away, taking with them what money and goods they could lay hands on. When it was clear that the attack was about to begin, by land and sea, D'Annunzio sent emissaries to all the Fascists he knew, to Mussolini and his lieutenants. But no word of support or encouragement came back. Not only the Legionaries, but many Fascists, spoke openly of a fresh piece of treachery by Mussolini, recalling his conduct in 1915 when he deserted the socialists. D'Annunzio, when he heard this, confined himself to a pessimistic speech, ". . . and so we are alone again, alone against all . . . alone, alone with our courage . . . alone against a vast conspiracy of hired assassins guided by schoolmasters . . ." (this another reference to Nitti).

Military operations against Fiume began at 5 A.M. on December 24, 1920, and the first phase finished on December 26. The warship *Andrea Doria* sailed to within striking range, and General Caviglia left Sapiane to march on Fiume with 20,000 troops, against D'Annunzio's 3,000. Even then hope of a general Fascist rising all over Italy still stiffened morale in Fiume. There were rumors that one of Mussolini's lieutenants had set out from Milan with 10,000 men to their relief. Had this happened, a civil war on the later Spanish lines might have developed. But Mussolini had taken a longer term view of the role he and his Fascists were to play in Italian history. He knew he must wait. Perhaps he already foresaw October 28, 1922.

After a few hours of land bombardment, casualties had not been great in Fiume, but a municipal commission approached the palace, to ask D'Annunzio to capitulate; while another force of die-hard Legionaries vowed they would fight on to the end. On the 25th the action by the land forces was broken off, because Caviglia was still hoping for surrender. When it was clear that this merely strengthened D'Annunzio's resolve, a heavier bombardment was ordered, for dawn on the 26th. At noon, the *Andrea Doria* began to shell D'Annunzio's palace. It was then that the *Comandante* himself was wounded in the head, and some of the Legionaries were killed. D'Annunzio has described this bombardment:

". . . at last the *Andrea Doria,* in the height of its heroism, decided to fire on me personally. The windows of my room were easily recognizable, and here the glorious cannonade was directed. They had often seen me at my window. I was discussing with my officers, when a shell burst above the cornice immediately outside. It could have killed me then and there, in one swoop, thus resolving the problem of D'Annunzio for the benefit of the King's good government. Alas, my 'head of iron' was only chipped! Oh Cowards of Italy, how energetic you were in your cowardliness! The day before this I had already come to terms with my conscience, and would have defended my life with every available means. Indeed, I have offered my life a hundred times in the war, with a smile. But now, in this moment, I knew it was not worth while to throw it away on behalf of a people incapable for a moment of separating their greed from their Christmas debauch—whose government with cold determination was assassinating a people of sublime virtue, who for sixteen months had suffered and fought. . . ."

The Mayor of Fiume, Signor Gigante, and Bishop Costantini, had meanwhile asked Admiral Millo if he considered a general evacuation of civilians would be necessary. The Admiral replied that he hoped to avoid useless slaughter and, at the same time, he offered asylum to women and children on board the *Dante Alighieri.* The same city dignitaries asked the commander of the Italian land forces, General Ferrario, if the city would suffer further land bombardments without warning. The General replied that he had orders to start a heavy bombardment at 9 A.M. on the 29th, but that he would not execute the order if, by 2 P.M. on the 28th, the city had accepted the terms of the Treaty of Rapallo. With this news, Gigante and Costantini again came to D'Annunzio and asked him to capitulate.

D'Annunzio now did a very Dannunzian thing. He committed the issue to the toss of a coin, a golden *genovese.* Perhaps it pleased him to risk everything in a second, in an aleatory action worthy of his own sibylline utterances. In *Italia per gli Italiani,* he relates that when three of his Legionaries had been buried beneath the debris of the balcony in his palace, he had been deeply moved, because all the balconies of the houses looking on to the sea suddenly opened, and women came forth holding their babies, whom they pulled from their breasts, crying, "This one, Italy! Take this one! But not *Him . . . !"* This was perhaps poetic license. More probably, D'Annunzio suddenly passed without warning from the mysterious firmament of dreams and ideals among which he lived in Fiume, to resignation and despair. For with the fall of the coin, he announced that it was not worth the trouble to throw away any more lives in the service of the Italian people, "incapable for a moment of separating their greed from their Christmas debauch . . ." (In these scornful words are curious echoes of events to come, twenty-five years ahead, in a bunker in Berlin.)

He and a lady called Louisa Baccara took refuge in the Mayor's palace, and he convened the Council, declaring that, to spare further destruction and massacre, he would resign and hand over the Civil powers conferred to him on September 13, 1919, retaining only the command of his Legionaries. The city representatives returned to General Ferrario, and obtained a truce by accepting the terms of the Treaty of Rapallo.

The best description of the last days in Fiume comes from

D'Annunzio's own pen, in the letter sent on December 29 to the Council of the Regency, submitting his resignation. Through the bombast and verbiage, something pathetic and noble can be perceived. The reader suddenly feels that D'Annunzio had not been wrong in making his gesture of defiance and vainglory, to the assembled governments of the world. He had experienced the peculiar satisfaction, given to few individuals in history, of holding up powerful governments at the pistol point, of rendering the "power men" temporarily powerless; or in the more fulsome admiration of Piero Bargellini, "His supreme poetic effort was accomplished in Fiume. Diplomats, politicians, statesmen and Captains of Industry bowed their heads before him. The vague respect man has for poetry, the timidity they feel before its mystery and immortality, the suspicion of the divine and eternal which comes from Art, made the *condottiere*-poet almost inviolable. Perhaps no one could have held Fiume by force . . . Gabriele D'Annunzio held it in the name of poetry."

The letter D'Annunzio sent to the Council, explains this, ". . . I came on September 12, 1919, from the cemetery of Ronchi with a small band of men faithful to the memory of our War dead, I came to the gates of Fiume, I was determined to face the forces of the Entente, to fight against the Treaty of Versailles.

"I broke down those gates, I entered without striking a blow. The flags of France, of England and the United States, were lowered; that of Italy was hoisted. By popular acclaim, the devotion of Fiume to the Fatherland was shown. The National Council of Fiume, the legitimate representative of the people, conferred full powers, civil and military, on me. For fifteen months, I exercised those powers, suffering and struggling, so that the Fatherland might accept this offering, this reward for our sufferings.

"For fifteen months, these people suffered and struggled with my Legionaries. They were proof against all threats; they overcame all perfidy; they withstood all misery. The three foreign nations who had been most offended by the Ronchi march stood apart in silence. Italy alone became the implacable executioner of her daughter. To the tenacious devotion of that daughter she replied with constant persecution. She could have given support; instead, she deceived. She could have saved; instead, she betrayed. At Rapallo, she was the first to take part in the plot. What should have been remorse became only rancor. At Rapallo, Italy paved the way for the national death of an Italian city. The mask of Liberty covered the face of slavery.

"There can be no doubt that only through our resistance and perpetual will to struggle has Italy obtained the frontier of Venetia Giulia.

"There can be no doubt that Fiume has given this frontier to the Fatherland.

"There can be no doubt that the Fatherland has given Fiume to the foreigner.

"We fought against all insults and betrayals.

"For fifteen months, the Government of Rome used the weapon of famine against us. Now, they have decided to reduce us by force. They have surrounded us with a circle of iron.

"They have set all the armed forces of Venetia Giulia against a few thousand Legionaries.

"To the insane arrogance of these assailants, I opposed far-sighted firmness. On more than one occasion, by my acts alone, I avoided the spilling of fraternal blood. When the territory of the Regency was invaded (by an act of violence contrary even to the Treaty of Rapallo, a cruel injustice to all established rights), I ordered my Legionaries not to oppose. I ordered them to withdraw to a line of observation.

"The attackers were informed that they must not pass this line, if they wished to avoid disaster. The warning was proclaimed on large panels erected on posts, for all to see.

"They attacked without warning. We withdrew to our last line of defense, still hoping to avoid a mortal struggle. At last, we could relinquish ground no more. Our line ran from the Case degli Emigranti, by the Viale d'Italia, the Diaz Barracks, the Cosala, the Cavalry Barracks, the Enco, to the Porto Sanso.

"We fought as soldiers of the Carso, of the Alps, of the Grappa, of the Piave know how to fight. Our young soldiers followed their example. Sometimes they surpassed it.

"And the citizens were equal to the Legionaries. The women were heroines—like those who fed the prisoners of Caporetto, defying death by giving to Italian soldiers the bread taken from the mouths of their own babes.

"For five days, the government troops were repulsed—days which are among the most glorious in human history.

"At present, we still hold the line intact. The line is unpassable. Those who send their troops against us, making them first drunk with wine, with money and lies, admit it. They admit they can never break the heroic resistance of the Legionaries, unless they destroy the city totally, unless they slaughter defenseless citizens.

"So they now declare they will destroy the city without allowing the people to leave. 'We will destroy your house,' they say. 'We will bury you in ruins if the Legionaries do not given in.' Never has there been such abject behavior in the whole history of military ignominy. Teutonic ferocity was at least intelligent; here, it is surpassed by a cruelty as obtuse as stupid. And all this ferocity is directed against this miracle of life called Fiume, against this city of the Holocaust!

"The Legionaries are still firm on the ground, but they will not have the victory of arms because they renounce it. They will have instead the victory of the spirit.

"I cannot impose on this heroic city its ruin and certain destruction, which the government of Rome and the High Command of Trieste now threaten. I therefore hand over my powers. I place in the hands of the Mayor and the people of Fiume the powers conferred on me on September 12, 1919, and those further ones conferred on September 9, 1920, by the College of Rectors.

"In full confidence and goodwill, I leave the people of Fiume the sole arbiters of their destiny.

"We are proud to have given our blood, to have shown our devotion to a people of such pure and elevated character.

"I am today, as in the night of the Ronchi march, the Chief of the Legionaries.

"Only my courage is left me.

"I wait now for the people of Fiume to ask me to leave the city to which I came only for its salvation. I leave to it only my dead, my sadness, and my victory.

"Fiume, December 29, 1920. Gabriele D'Annunzio."

So finished the autocratic, oratorical Regency of Fiume. Just as there had been no bloodshed at D'Annunzio's arrival fifteen months before, so his departure was accompanied by little violence. Once Giolitti had made up his mind, a few shells from a warship were sufficient to destroy the little state. And yet, as General Caviglia said when he entered Fiume and took over command, D'Annunzio could have held out for weeks if he had liked.[1] The General found enough arms and ammunition to load eighteen ships. Giolitti himself said in Parliament, "Does this house realize what an enormous quantity of arms have been discovered in Fiume? Besides railway trucks, we have already loaded thirteen steamers with arms of every description, and the loading is far from completed. It was the preparation of a new war we prevented." Much of the material had come through the Socialist Federation of the Mariners in Genoa, confirming how closely D'Annunzio was in touch with that left-wing body, a contact he was to maintain, with unfortunate personal results, until the end of his life.

[1] General Caviglia's informative book, *Il Conflitto di Fiume,* was written in 1921; he rewrote it in 1925 and gave it to the press, but publication was forbidden by the government. This book, together was Marshal Badoglio's on the same subject, was published after the Second World War, in, respectively, 1948 and 1946.

21

The Lost Leader

D'Annunzio left Fiume with the reputation of being the first revolutionary in Western Europe (a role which he was soon to dispute with Benito Mussolini).[1] There was a moment when it seemed that the government would carry out their threat to arrest and try him. Had he shown signs of further political activity, they might have done so. But he was a tired man, who had lived since 1915 a life of such energy, that with the collapse of all his hopes in Fiume, a period of mental and physical lethargy set in. Immediately after leaving Fiume, he retired to Venice, and thence to the Lake of Garda, where he bought a house and lived quietly during the momentous years which brought the Fascist Party to power. He did not disturb the government; and the government did not disturb him. His popularity was still such that a trial could only have been an embarrassment. But his influence on Fascism was still important.

It was clear that the Fascists and his Legionaries could no longer work together, after Mussolini's behavior over Fiume; although Fascism was for years to try and enrol the Legionaries under its banner. D'Annunzio had taken out a membership card for the Fascist Party during the Fiume episode. But after the "Christmas of Blood," he did not renew it. He ordered his Legionaries not to follow Mussolini, because of the "Fiume treason." "We must remain distinct and separate," he said, "even if the Fascists today seem the movement which is most alive in Italy. There is no sincere political faith inspired by a clear philosophy in it at present.

[1] Lenin, at a Congress of the Third International in Moscow, remarked that there was only one real revolutionary in Italy: D'Annunzio.

Legionaries who join it, instead of remaining in the Legions, betray our cause and their Leader. . . ."

In spite of this, many people have since tended to confuse Fascism and D'Annunzio's Legionaries, as if the Ronchi march was a kind of forerunner of Mussolini's March on Rome, and D'Annunzio a kind of John the Baptist to Mussolini. His librarian, Bruers, later wrote: "The Ronchi march decided not only the fate of Italy, but of the world—in that the fortunes of Fascism began on that day. The Ronchi march made the March on Rome inevitable." There were similarities, it is true; the uniforms, the desperadoes, the oratory, the chauvinism. But there the likeness stopped. D'Annunzio's state was an aesthetic creation, possible only in an exceptional state of international politics, and for a limited time; in the long run, quite impractical. All the ceremonies in Fiume had a mystical character. The opening and closing of every meeting had a symbolic quality, classical or heroic. The newly enrolled deserters from an Italian warship would find the *Comandante* on his knees, as if in prayer, to receive them. And these men, his Lieutenants and Legionaries, were to D'Annunzio himself, by turns, Homeric heroes and Christ's apostles. His state, like Plato's *Republic,* or Campanella's *Città del Sole*, if it was written on the clouds, had, at least in D'Annunzio's mind, ideal purity. Mussolini's Fascists, on the other hand, were flesh and blood creatures, calculating, ruthless, who came down into the *piazza* and took an active part in politics.

D'Annunzio carried on his rites after his retirement. In the *Vittoriale degli Italiani,* the house he retired to after Fiume, is a small round garden, which he called the *Arengo* (the Assembly, or place for harangues), with marble seats and statues, which D'Annunzio used to treat rather as, one imagines, the Druids treated Stonehenge. Here at night, he would take part in special ceremonies celebrated with patriotic rites. Surrounded by a select number of the Faithful, by the light of the moon, among the twisted and stunted trees, he would speak of the Italians, of their land, their race, their war, their dead, their seas and their glory.

Here, he claimed, he was as happy as he had been in the trenches, or at Fiume. Here, far from strife even when an old man, he was in accord with his Legionaries again.

Signor Foscanelli, in his *Gabriele D'Annunzio e l'ora sociale,* sees the Legionaries, when they dispersed far and wide after Fiume, as so many apostles, whom he likens to Christ's disciples after the Crucifixion: ". . . and so the apostles of the blond Nazarene left to preach love—and they found only hate. They went to preach peace—and they found only strife. Yet their derided, persecuted religion triumphed. One of them, Thomas, had to touch the bleeding side of his dead Master, to assure himself and stop doubting—but when he did so, he became the most inspired of them all [this, perhaps a discreet reference to Mussolini, who was at the height of his powers when Signor Foscanelli wrote these words]. And so the Legionaries, those of them who were touched with grace, the elect who believed . . . took to the roads of Italy with their apostolic mission. *Tu es Petrus . . .*"

This sub-lunar view of D'Annunzio and his followers was not shared by everyone. The ex-Prime Minister, Nitti, now in retirement and immersed in his calculations in Rome, saw his late enemy, the man who had dubbed him *Cagoia,* as nothing more than a profiteer. "D'Annunzio came to Fiume a poor man," he writes in his memoirs. "And he went away a rich one. Certainly not because he had exercised any form of productive activity there. His only desire afterwards was to own a fine house, to furnish and occupy the villa and grounds of Cargnacco. He was not the pathetic, wounded hero he claimed to be; he was a man who was always skilful in finding a secure and comfortable life, preferably that of a Prince. . . ."

The house Nitti referred to was taken by D'Annunzio very shortly after he was expelled from Fiume. It was by no means princely when he arrived, a humble, almost rustic building, no more originally than a series of small outhouses around a farmhouse above the Lake of Garda. It had been the property of a German relation of Richard Wagner, but sequestrated as enemy property during the war. D'Annunzio borrowed 380,000 lire from the Bank of Rome to buy it, a sum which needless to say, he did not repay. It included a part of the neighboring hill overlooking the lake, and one or two small buildings. D'Annunzio called the ensemble the *Vittoriale degli Italiani,* which can best be translated by "The Shrine of Italian Victories."

"Already the ineffective singer of great palaces and sumptuous houses," he said, "I come to place my sadness and silence in this old farmhouse, not so much to humiliate myself, as to test my ability to create and transfigure . . ." He gave the difficult task to an architect Maroni—of conferring a monumental character on a group of modest buildings, without demolishing any of them. The setting for this work is one of the finest in Italy. The thin coast road below runs form Salò through Gardone and Fasano to Maderno, Toscolano and Gargnano, a herbaceous riviera gay with oleander and bougainvillea. Cypresses line the heights, pink and white stones gleam like opals among the scanty vegetation on the hills.

The grandiose palace that was finally built here became a kind of Delphic temple, visited by admirers from all over the world. From here, D'Annunzio despatched envoys to foreign parts and issued encyclicals like a captive pope. The slopes and dales around the house, the rivulets and groves, were hallowed with the personal emblems of his poetic and martial past. A discarded battleship was somehow hoisted to a hilltop. The airplane in which D'Annunzio had flown over Vienna during the war, showering that city with pamphlets, hung in one of the larger rooms. Guns, swords and pistols jostled manuscripts of lyrical, sacred and profane poetry. Books of devotion on tables and lecterns were set beside lewd prints. A model of Michelangelo's David was given a small skirt. Often, the poet would conceal himself for days in his library, in poetic composition, and then suddenly emerge at dinner in full military attire, like Ibsen's Borkmann, in the formal clothes of better days. Towards the end, with the presentiment of death upon him, he spent one night a month in a coffin.

Such was the regal grandeur he assumed that, when the Mayor of Florence asked him to give a speech at a Dante ceremony in his city, D'Annunzio replied: "If I speak, the King must be there to hear." The Mayor was ingenuous enough to go to Giolitti, and ask if the King could be persuaded to come. To this, Giolitti replied tartly, "As long as I am here, the King will not come. But I think he will not come, even if I am not here." The Mayor set off with this news for the *Vittoriale,* where D'Annunzio made fresh conditions. "I will speak only if my 8,000 Legionaries are allowed to come." The Mayor said there would not be room to lodge them in Florence; so D'Annunzio said he would bring only 3,000 Legionaries. Again, said the Mayor, there was no question of free lodging for such a body of men in Florence. The idea of the speech was abandoned.

When D'Annunzio arrived at the *Vittoriale* in 1921, as astonishing number of theories appeared in the Italian press about his future. He was aged fifty-six and there still seemed a political career before him. The paper *Pasquino* said, "He will retire into private life to write his memoirs." Another said, "It is whispered that he will go to Avignon and become a monk. But for a still active man, this seems improbable. Some say he is flying to America, visiting all the cities by airplane." One weekly paper forecast, "He is going to become an English clergyman," supporting this unlikely theory by explaining that D'Annunzio at the *Vittoriale,* "received a mysterious visitor yesterday evening—an Anglican pastor. They remained all night in conversation, and at dawn the poet came out into the garden and cut on a tree the words, *'Ubi Gabriel, ibi ecclesia."* [1] There were further sensational reports, that he was becoming a fireman, a Moslem, a sandwich-man, a piano tuner. These were in journals which had been continuously anti-Fiuman, and had always tried to ridicule him.

D'Annunzio, for his part, certainly encouraged these stories by his own eccentricity, which now began to increase in an astonishing way. He was followed once in the grounds of the *Vittoriale*

---

[1] "Where Gabriel is, there is the Church."

by an American journalist who took down every word he said.
D'Annunzio told him that in the hot summer months he sat under
a fountain naked, reading a Dante edition which he had had
printed specially on rubber pages, for use in his bath. He could
thus enjoy poetry without putting his arm out of the water. "Hygiene and literature at once," he said. The American journalist
telegraphed this to his paper and, having returned to America,
telegraphed D'Annunzio, asking for the address of the editor of
these waterproof classics. To another curious American journalist,
he said that the day before, he had eaten roast baby, and found it
most tasty. The American journalist also immediately telegraphed
this to his paper. "An American journalist," said D'Annunzio,
when he heard about it, "what is he but a man seized with an
uncontrollable urge to obtain sensational and unpublished news,
and cable it to his paper? And that is what I have given him."

Nor was he any politer with American cinema grandees, one of
whom wanted to make a film of *Il Fuoco,* showing D'Annunzio
with the Duse. D'Annunzio at first refused to see the famous film
star who was to play the part of the Duse, describing the idea as,
"profanation and sacrilege." But he finally received her for a half
hour, and then afterwards wrote her this letter: "I—the gentlest
of gentlemen—received you with a courtesy which surprised even
your concealed bad manners. I write to you with indelible ink,
these words: Your design for a film (a barbaric and commercial
word, anyway) is a defamation of Eleonora Duse and Gabriele
D'Annunzio, an ignominious and stupid piece of vituperation.
Your vulgar design is a tissue of lies, calumny and sadistic obscenity. You are the Marchioness of Sade, become stupid and
impudent, disguised as Saint Elizabeth the Leper. Good-bye! Leave
without delay! The *Comandante* orders you to leave your hotel in
Garda! And he forbids you to reply."

One anecdote tells of the Soviet Minister Chicherin's visit to
D'Annunzio in his palace. Dinner was served in the Franciscan
refectory. At the end, two Legionaries came in bringing a beautifully damascened scimitar and withdrew, locking the door after
them. D'Annunzio took the sword in his hand and fondled the

blade, gazing fixedly at his amazed guest. Then he said: "My dear friend, for certain reasons which I did not wish to tell you before-hand, I have resolved to cut your head off." Then he stopped and waited for the effect his words would have upon his guest. Chicherin grew pale, saying to himself, "Who knows what may happen? With this mad poet, anything is possible. If he does cut my head off probably Europe will not care." After a few moments' silence and fondling the blade lovingly, D'Annunzio frowned and said in a peevish voice, "What a pity! I am not in form tonight. I am afraid I'll have to postpone the matter till another day."

D'Annunzio's intention in retiring to the *Vittoriale degli Italiani* seems to have been to return to his old pre-1915 manner of life and writing. There is a letter to the Director of a local paper, *Provincia di Brescia,* denying that he now intends to have any-thing to do with politics:

"My dear Director,
A zealous friend tells me that there are rumors about my con-tinued silence. They are petty and false. He tells me that even your discreet journal is chattering about a *Lega Italica,* which I am to join. I pray you announce that I am again the solitary proud artist I was in 1915. For that reason, I have not the least interest in what goes on outside the *Vittoriale.* To write to me is useless, as it would be to come and knock on my door. The plain news from the *Vittoriale* is in three parts, if you want it. I have given the second tome of *Faville* to my publisher, Treves. For the poetry-shop [*sic*], I have finished the *Figures of Wax,* second of the studies united under the title *Aspects of the Unknown.* I have started my new novel *Buonarotta* for Olivetana. All the petty politicians, hostile or friendly, must therefore despair of me. . . .
From the *Priory of the Vittoriale,* September 2, 1925."

It was now that he began using the word Priory to describe how far he was from worldly things. He now announced that he had been converted entirely to the cult of Goodness. A phrase which he began to employ increasingly was *vincere sine strage*—to conquer without fighting. It was not inert Goodness, indulgent and flabby, he wanted, he said, but *male* Goodness, inspired and forceful. He wrote at length of the socialist Utopia connected with this, in his *Per l'Italia degli Italiani,* and hoped to encourage Mussolini to use it. But Mussolini knew that this love of Goodness is often perilous for rulers. It was "Goodness" that helped lose France to Louis XVI; it later helped lose Russia to Czar Nicolas. Mussolini had no intention of becoming involved in any of D'Annunzio's Utopian schemes. Moreover, a man who made statements such as, "What does it matter if I am conquered in space, knowing that I am destined to live in time!" could hardly be considered as a serious political force.

In spite of this, the Fascists tried to use D'Annunzio when they forcibly occupied the Palazzo Marino in Milan. This was before they had seized power in Rome; and Facta's democratic government was still in office. They had planted their flags on the balcony beside the statue of Leonardo da Vinci, and they were preparing to burn down the offices of the socialist newspaper, *Avanti.* It happened that D'Annunzio was in Milan at the time, visiting his publisher *incognito;* and they decided to ask him to come and speak from the balcony of the building they had just occupied. Two of his old Legionaries, Aldo Finzi and Attilio Teruzzi, who had now become Fascists, visited him in his hotel, saying that the crowd outside the Palazzo Marino was calling for a speech. D'Annunzio refused even to receive these renegades,[1] and said that he was in Milan on a private visit. Meanwhile the crowd, who had been told that D'Annunzio would address them, had increased and were calling for him in person. "It is not *we* who want you," the young Fascists said. "It is the people of Milan."

It was then that D'Annunzio gave way to one of his famous bursts of indecision. Hearing the shouting beneath the window, he hesitated. Then he turned abruptly and said: "All right. I will

---

[1] Aldo Finzi later redeemed himself. He was killed as an anti-Fascist in the German slaughter in the Ardentine Caves in 1943.

speak." He was taken by car up the via Manzoni into the *piazza*, which was full of a cheering mob. Alongside their own flags, the Fascists had ingeniously hung the red ones of the Regency of the Carnaro, a symbol which clearly would affect D'Annunzio. He darted forward onto the balcony to touch them; and when he spoke, he was visibly moved.

"People of Milan! This is the first time that I speak in public since the glory of Fiume, since the long and cruel sacrifice which should have brought our country to the confines of Venetia Giulia. I look around tonight for the flag of Italy. I do not see it. No matter, it will hang invisibly as I speak. We will see it with the eyes of our faith. It will fly in the wind of Justice, blown by the breath of Liberty. You are all aware that here in our country today is a false Italy, which does not wish to live as we did in Fiume; a false Italy which lives, not with its spirit, but with its stomach; an Italy which has forgotten the victory of our war. But there is, praise be to God, another Italy which remembers, which affirms, awaits and suffers. From this Italy, from its suffering and its steadfastness, will arise ardor and courage to fulfill our destiny. This is the Italy of the plough, the hammer and the scythe. . . ."

There was not a word in his speech about the Fascists, who were anxiously awaiting support. What D'Annunzio pronounced, for all its banality, was a paean of praise to Goodness, Fraternity, Peace, with a side reference to communism. He exhorted all classes of Italy to come together and love one another. "It is necessary," he finished, "to group all the sincere forces and direct them towards the great goal which has been fixed for Italy by the eternal faiths. From masculine patience, not from restless impatience, salvation will come. We must walk ahead, not through a dubious labyrinth, but on the well consolidated Roman road. . . ." When the Fascist secretary, Michele Bianchi, sent a formal and congratulatory telegram to D'Annunzio after his speech, finishing, "Long Live Fascism!" D'Annunzio replied with the telegram, "Long Live Italy!"

In spite of this, the speech was interpreted by many people in

Italy as an approval of the Fascists, because he had spoken on the balcony of a building they had just seized by force. Many liberals, who had looked on D'Annunzio as a potential supporter, if not a potential leader, now lost confidence in him. One of their delegates came to the *Vittoriale* some weeks later, to ask him what he had really meant by his speech in Milan. He replied that he had been perfectly explicit; he condemned violence of any kind. The liberal said that this was not the general interpretation given to his speech, because he spoke beside the Fascist flags. After a few moments of embarrassed silence, D'Annunzio indicated that the interview was over; he got up abruptly and left the visitor to find his way out alone. Nor was this the end of the incident. A few days later, D'Annunzio was found lying on the ground, having fallen fifteen feet from the balcony of his house. No one knew whether it was an attempt at suicide—in his depression at the way events were moving—or, as some said, that Mussolini's hired ruffians had pushed him out of the window, in the Matteotti manner. He did not die, although he suffered a severe head and neck injury. D'Annunzio himself hardly clarified matters by stating darkly that it was "Italy" who had pushed him off "the Tarpeian rock." With other incidents such as these, he became really "the lost leader," the one man in Italy who might have opposed Mussolini, but whose mind was no longer fitted for the task.

During the *Vittoriale* period, when Mussolini's rule was daily becoming more absolute, many political delegations came to the *Vittoriale,* hoping for guidance and advice. In particular, as the years passed, members of the Italian Confederation of Labor, who were suffering most from Fascist persecution, visited him. His utterances on these occasions became more and more sibylline. Once, he referred them to his play, *La Gloria,* written several decades before, in which he had said, "The land belongs to those who cultivate it," a statement with which they were entirely in agreement. But he did not specify how to achieve this desirable end.

His connection with Mussolini's March on Rome in 1922, although entirely negative, reveals much of the early Fascist movement. It is only now, after the post-war publications of memoirs and diaries like those of Foscanelli, Valeri, and King Victor Emmanuel's own private diary, that we can understand something of the forces operating around the man who was still the most popular figure in Italy. We can understand, too, how Mussolini, realizing the potential danger, nursed him skilfully, until he finally silenced him altogether.

A member of the government, Aldo Rossini, the Minister for Pensions, had foreseen the Fascist March on Rome of October 1922. He suggested that D'Annunzio should come to Rome and head the Old Comrades, a powerful non-Fascist body. Rossini was well aware of the anti-Fascist feeling among these old soldiers, for he had been present at a recent meeting in Zara, where a number of daring suggestions had been made, among them to appoint D'Annunzio as the leader against the Fascists. Rossini knew that the democratic government under the Prime Minister Facta was about to fall, because it had proved itself incapable of dealing with either Fascist or socialist excesses, and it was hopelessly divided into factions. The problem now was to let it die quietly and be replaced, without a *coup d'état,* particularly from the Fascists who were gathering their forces in Naples. During the first days of October 1922, Rossini was a frequent visitor to the *Vittoriale,* and he finally persuaded the poet to come to Rome for the Old Comrades rally; but simply, in D'Annunzio's words, as "a devoted Italian, an old comrade." The government knew that D'Annunzio's presence alone, if publicized, would act as a deterrent to the Fascists in Naples, who were already contemplating their March on Rome.

At first, D'Annunzio seemed delighted with the idea. In a letter to Rossini, he said that the thought of being with them all again on such an occasion made him touch "the pinnacle of joy," that a "mysterious force" would compel him to come to Rome. Moreover, he invited the leaders of the Old Comrades to visit him first at the *Vittoriale*. It seemed that he was at last about to take up a positive position over the Fascist question. But on October 13 (two weeks before the *coup d'état*), the director of the Old Comrades, who was coming to make the final arrangements, received this telegram from D'Annunzio, "Kindly defer Gardone visit. Unfortunately confined to bed. Will telegraph later."

Meanwhile the Old Comrades were arriving for the ceremony in Rome; and on October 20 they appealed to all their colleagues to support them with their flags, adding that D'Annunzio would be there. Just before this the politician, Orlando, had visited D'Annunzio urgently, to tell him that Fascist plans for a *coup d'état* were now well advanced. Only a powerful patriotic body led by someone with D'Annunzio's prestige could prevent their seizure of power. Orlando said that the Facta government had asked the King to form a new ministry, and that they needed D'Annunzio's help. D'Annunzio would not give a reply. But on October 25 a doctor's communiqué appeared in the local Gardone newspaper signed by Dr. Duse, D'Annunzio's personal physician, in which he asked, "the faithful comrades to leave the *Comandante* in peace," as he would make his way to Rome on his own, in a private capacity. That evening, the leader of the Old Comrades received another telegram, from D'Annunzio himself, in which he canceled the visit. Something had clearly happened behind the scenes. The publication in 1949 of Victor Emmanuel's diary reveals what may have happened. On October 11, there is this laconic entry by the King, "Mussolini visits D'Annunzio at Gardone." What happened at that meeting we can only surmise, for the King has told no more. It is possible that Mussolini came there to threaten D'Annunzio with arrest if he went to Rome, at the same time dangling before him the title of a Princedom if he stayed at Gardone.

The Old Comrades now decided to take matters into their own hands. Although they had been clearly told by D'Annunzio that they were no longer invited to Gardone, they decided to go there and demand an interview on their own. An imposing body of men arrived, to learn that the poet was furious that they were trying to use him for political purposes. From behind closed doors, he sent out messages of abuse. Foscanelli, who was with them, has related this visit in his *Ora Sociale*. In one message, D'Annunzio spoke of "disloyal maneuvers round my person," and of the earlier visits of Orlando. He also refused to re-open negotiations with Giolitti. "I will not go to Rome for any parade," he said. "In Rome I see not the Tarpeian Rock, but the *cloaca maxima*. My mind refuses to be contaminated with the sewer. It will remain absolutely pure. . . ."

The Old Comrades returned to Milan, and on October 27, 1922, the Fascist March on Rome took place, and the future of Italy was sealed for the next twenty years. Parliamentary government in Italy—which had lasted all D'Annunzio's life—was over. Mussolini was later able to make the sinister remark in Parliament, "I made my appearance in Montecitorio as a purely formal act of courtesy. . . . I could have made this hall dark and gray, a bivouac for my squads." D'Annunzio's threats about Parliament in the past, "the elected herd," the badly dressed members, his jokes that he "would bomb Montecitorio," were vicariously implemented.

What happened during that meeting fifteen days earlier between D'Annunzio and Mussolini has engrossed many historians. Antongini, D'Annunzio's secretary, says that Mussolini told D'Annunzio of his proposed *coup d'état*, but that D'Annunzio refused to believe it. We only know that after the March on Rome, the following letters were exchanged between the two men. Mussolini wrote:

"My dear *Comandante*,
The newspapers will have told you all. We were obliged to mobilize our forces, to put an end to an *intolerable* situation. We are now masters of a large part of Italy, and in other places we have occupied the nerve centers. I do not ask you to come and stand at our side—although this would give me infinite pleasure. But we

are convinced that you will not oppose our marvelous youth which fights for *your,* as well as our, Italy. Later, you will surely have much to say. I greet you with cordial devotion.

Your Mussolini."

D'Annunzio replied to this in his now familiar Delphic style:

"In the perfect purity of my heart, of which you are aware, I am ready to give my work, to put my robust and resolute shoulder to the wheel. Before withdrawing from the scene, I wish to achieve for the Fatherland the great and devout union of *all the workers.* The divine voice said to the Seraphim intent on gathering innumerable dispersed fragments (you remember?), 'From all these fragments make one sole host!' I cannot believe that you will hesitate to observe our first pact of fraternal pacification loyally— *incuratae foedus amicitate.* It is important that you free yourself of all unfavorable advisers, those who are impure. Then the pact, if faithfully observed and an amnesty granted, will be the foundation of our unified civil edifice. As for myself, I ask nothing. I want nothing. Do you understand? Absolutely nothing. If you cannot extract me from this sadness and spiritual uneasiness with fraternal care, I shall again go into exile, as I did in 1911. For I prefer exile to the daily torment. 'To see nothing, to hear nothing . . .' "

The letter was handed to Mussolini by Gabriellino, D'Annunzio's favorite son. The arcane language which revealed the cloudy thoughts of the poet was quite agreeable to Mussolini, who propagated anything likely to inspire apprehension about the poet's sanity among his followers. He not only gave large state contributions for *The Collected Works of Gabriele D'Annunzio,* a grandiose edition which D'Annunzio had set his heart on publishing, but he now began to pander to all D'Annunzio's whims in the strange furnishing of the *Vittoriale,* offering airplanes, cannons, speedboats and other expensive grown-up toys. Of the private seaplane which he gave D'Annunzio to keep on Lake Garda, D'Annunzio wrote, literally like a schoolboy: "My seaplane has arrived! I had with my *mas* acquired a third lung. Now I obtain two more. In all, seven powerful lungs!" (It is difficult to say what this symbol means—presumably, by moving more freely on water, and in the air, he could live, or *breathe,* more fully.) The *mas* was the boat he had used in the Buccari raid. This, too, Mussolini had presented on behalf of the nation to the *Vittoriale.* Shortly after, Mussolini arranged that D'Annunzio should be made a Prince.

The collected edition of D'Annunzio's works was published on June 21, 1926, by a special body Mussolini founded called "The National Institute for the Publication of the Works of Gabriele D'Annunzio." It was a limited liability company with a capital of six million lire, and it provided for 44 volumes, subdivided in four groups. The group titles are by D'Annunzio:

1st group *Verses of Love and Glory.*
2nd group *The novels.*
3rd group *Tragedies, Mysteries and Dreams.*
4th group *Prose of research, struggle, command, conquest: torment, divination, renewal, celebration, re-vindication, liberation: of fables, games and inspiration.*

In the list of books drawn up personally by the aging poet there are 80 titles (not 44), because the list also contains books to be published, which he had not yet written. One of these works is, for instance, *Violante,* a novel of which he had written to Mussolini himself, "I have finished a novel, *Violante.* A novel of flesh without flesh! Oh, what a scandal!" *Violante* was never published; nor is there any trace of it among his writings.[1]

D'Annunzio was also keen to possess an airfield near Gardone; and here too Mussolini was co-operative. But every time D'An-

[1] Shortly after the publication of the general edition, the Vatican came out with a decree placing all his works on the Index—*fidei et morum offensivum— omnes fabulae amatoriae, omnia opera dramatica.*

nunzio asked when the building would begin, Mussolini raised technical objections. Probably, Mussolini did not want D'Annunzio to have a *private* airfield, where persons who might be hostile to the regime, perhaps foreigners, could arrive and depart at short notice.

His control of D'Annunzio became firmer as the years passed. In 1924, classed as a kind of historical monument, D'Annunzio was given the title of "Principe di Montenevoso," the mountain that overlooks Fiume, endorsing the self-styled high-priest of Italian victory and heroism. He was also made an Honorary General of the Air Force, one of his dearest wishes. After this, Mussolini equipped him with a jailer, seizing the opportunity, when D'Annunzio deplored the numbers of people always coming to the house and importuning him, to send him this telegram, "Would you like energetic and intelligent official, your disposal, keep callers away? Affectionate and devoted wishes, Your comrade, Mussolini." D'Annunzio accepted this, and the "energetic and intelligent official" arrived, Commissar of Police, Giovanni Rizzo. He lived in the *Vittoriale,* and reported regularly to his master in Rome. This gave rise to the idea, in the foreign press, that D'Annunzio was now "the prisoner of the *Vittoriale.*"

Signs of the poet's lunacy now began to multiply. He had always avidly read the *Almanacco del Barbanera,* a kind of Italian Old Moore, and dozens of copies of this astrological work now lay about the *Vittoriale.* He wrote to his publisher that he was "in eruption, creating a new Helen to be in competition with the one who shines so brightly in the *Iliad.*" In this he claimed to be inspired by one, Elena Sangro; and he wrote verses about her of great banality:

> O Helen mine, how much I like you!
> More than every fruit and every flower,
> More than every fountain!

He gave the rooms of his house private names, often of a religious character. The hall where the guests took off their coats
was called the "Masking room" (because apparently here one put
on one's "mask of circumstance," before being introduced into the
presence of the *Comandante*). Then there was the "Monk's
Room," in which D'Annunzio claimed to reply to his correspondence. But he never replied to anyone, and this seems to have been
a subterfuge. "How can a monk possibly write letters?" he would
say. On the door of the guests' lavatory was the sign, "Little Dung
Library." Then there was the "Room of the Leper," also called by
the Franciscan *"Zambra del Misello";* and the "Cell of Pure
Dreams," its walls hung with gray chamois leather. D'Annunzio
wrote invitations like the following to his friends. "We will eat a
few red and yellow beans in the room of the Leper at 9 P.M.
Remember that you are entering a severe and silent hermitage. I
shall be in my hooded garb, of the old sailor condemned to fresh-
water—or perhaps in the tunic of an old Capucin. We shall be
alone. Avoid all magnificence. Your brother Ariel."

On the few occasions when D'Annunzio again tried tentatively
to touch politics—his support, for instance of his old friends, the
Socialist Federation of Mariners in Genoa, who had helped him
in Fiume—Mussolini gently but firmly told him that his place
was with, "the creation of immortal works of art." In spite of this,
the correspondence between Mussolini and D'Annunzio over the
Mariners' Federation reveals, in its elliptical tone, the suspicion in
which both men held one another. Mussolini telegraphed to D'Annunzio on January 7, 1923, ". . . as to the Mariner's pact, I have
been as good as my word, overcoming considerable difficulties on
behalf of it. If not all the minor objections have been satisfied, on
general lines the affair has been settled. . . ." He took the opportunity to add: ". . . because all the French newspapers which dislike
the New Italy have started a campaign quoting *you* as an adversary
of my government, would it not now be apposite for you to give
a sharp denial which, once and for all, will put an end to their

game? You must know that my ministers are not dealing with ordinary administrative affairs. But with vast problems, which previous governments did not dare to tackle. We all await fresh books from you, and remind you that what Italians expect from you is—Poetry. Cordial and respectful wishes, Mussolini."

These cordial and respectful wishes, containing a clear order to mind his own business, did not please D'Annunzio, who replied:

"Your telegram had that singular note which is perhaps fundamental to Fascism, but which is completely foreign to my spirit life. No one shall influence me—not the least of my opinions and resolutions. Since birth, I have always been the sole guide of my own life and actions. An heroic example of my invincible will bears the date: 'December 1919,' when I alone saved the Giulian frontier. One of your present ministers knows something of this, so it is redundant for me to repeat it. I only ask you to free yourself of the false politicians who are misleading you. Refuse to countenance, for example, those who in the *Marche* are carrying out the deepest and darkest 'Reaction' against the soldiers who fought in the trenches, and who oppose every form of dannunzian [*sic*] spirituality in Puglie with police methods. Fie on you! Has not the best of your so-called Fascist movement been generated from *my* spirit? How then can I be your adversary? And how can you be mine? And why do you ask me to stop a campaign against you in France, of which I know nothing? I offer you all my strength and patience in silence 'asking nothing, coveting nothing.' For myself, I will always help the workers to attain redemption, in the sense of certain spiritual pages which you will find in my 'messages to the men of suffering.' "

As long as he kept to these "spiritual" generalities, Mussolini was not disturbed. One of the shipowners, the Marquis de la Penne, who was naturally pro-Fascist and against the Mariners' Federation, also begged D'Annunzio not to waste energy on anything which took him away from his literary activities, tactfully pointing out that he could hardly expect to understand the technicalities of the mercantile marine. D'Annunzio replied that his mind was good enough to understand anything. To prove it, he reminded the Marquis sharply of his researches during the war on a new type of nautical propeller.

Nor did Mussolini approve of his preface to the book, *Contra uno et contra Tutti,* in which are the words, "As I was leader in the battle, so will I be leader in the *piazza,* and in other places. . . ." The publishers were not allowed to distribute this volume widely, nor to give it publicity.

It was not until the Abyssinian war that the two men came closer together again. Many years before, D'Annunzio had written his *Teneo te Africa,* and when Mussolini attacked Abyssinia, D'Annunzio wrote to him: "My dear Commander of Arms, of Arms, of Arms. . . . You can imagine with what fury we have learned of the presumptuous idiocy of the English [the sanctions over Abyssinia, presumably] . . . My comrade, I am almost ashamed to offer you this effigy in gold, offered to me by the exiled workers from Italy in the United States; and my seven military medals; and a small chest full of other medals and honors." Ugo Ojetti, an old friend of D'Annunzio, says that when he visited him in the *Vittoriale* he was "most cautious when speaking of the regime," and that on one wall was a photograph of Mussolini on a horse, carrying "the sword given him by the Arabs." It is only fair to add that when one day D'Annunzio was asked if he would like to write the biography of Mussolini, he laughed and said: "I have already written it. Have you not read my *Cola di Rienzo?*" referring to his only biographical work, his life of the thirteenth century upstart dictator who was later murdered by the populace on the Capitol.

About the Rome-Berlin Axis, which Mussolini founded after the successful Abyssinian war, D'Annunzio was less certain. When he met Mussolini at Verona after the Italian dictator's triumphal journey to Germany, he is reported by Rizzo to have said to Mussolini, who was leaning out of the carriage window, "I shall always admire you for this." But another version says that he went to Verona that day to warn Mussolini of the danger of

German commitments. Maroni, his architect at the *Vittoriale*, says he returned despondently that evening, exclaiming: "This is the final ruin!"

Speculation is difficult in the case of such a mind. He would presumably have warned Mussolini before, not after, the journey to Germany, had he been against it. Moreover, at this time Mussolini had not engaged himself formally with Germany. The signed agreement, the Pact of Steel, came later, after D'Annunzio's death. Also, when on December 13, 1937, D'Annunzio heard that Italy had withdrawn from the League of Nations, he wrote to Mussolini:

". . . you know how I have been waiting for the last five years for the courageous and incomparable gesture you have made. Many people are undoubtedly amazed and intoxicated by it. But no one has been as moved by it as I am, to my very depths—as by a kind of supernatural revelation. Not infrequently, I have understood you, and represented your myth with mystical purity. You have no more to fear! You have no more to fear! Never has there been such a complete victory! I remain proud at having foreseen it, at having announced it."

22

Il Vittoriale degli Italiani

The *Vittoriale,* on which D'Annunzio's interest at the end of his life centered, sums up in its architecture and layout much of the man and his work, ornamental, declamatory, bellicose and occasionally mystical. Here is incorporated every style, confused and jumbled together, in the familiar Dannunzian minner. Simple and complicated, proud and humble, sacred and profane, it is the dwelling of a man who had always been able to write a poem equally well about the death of a lily in a vase, or about machine gunners in Libya. It is also a monument to the decadent age of a *fin de siècle,* with the cushions, velvets, damasks, brocades and the scents of des Esseintes in the incense burners. It bristles with flags, daggers, medals, rifles, proclamations, machine guns and other implements of war; and yet a crucifix by Giotto will hang next to an airplane propeller. In the garden is a sizeable portion of the battleship *Puglie,* on which one of D'Annunzio's lieutenants, Tomaso Gulli, was killed in July 1920, in a raid on Split. Its radio masts stick up in the sky, in curious company with the cypresses and poplars above the Lake of Garda. In another part of the garden is the smal *mas,* the torpedo boat in which he accomplished the *beffa di Buccari* (*Eia! Eia! Eia! Alala!*). In the war-museum hangs the airplane in which he flew over Vienna, next to the car in which he made the Ronchi March. A statue of the *Vittoria del Piave* is chained, for symbolic reasons, to a pillar; and a bust is turned back to front. This is Vathek's magic castle.

Everything has "meaning and symbol." Among these bizarre relics of a heroic past, are also blocks of stone he had transported from the most mountainous and bloody sections of the war front, in the Carso. Maroni, his architect, learned to establish a kind of telepathic communication with him about all this. If D'Annunzio said: "Why did you do that? I didn't tell you to," concerning some new construction or arrangement, Maroni would reply: "But I heard your orders, *Comandante,* over the *zambracca.* There must have been a fault in the transmission." The *zambracca* was D'Annunzio's own name for telepathy. D'Annunzio would appear perfectly satisfied, as if with a logical explanation.

When he gave the *Vittoriale* to the nation in 1929, he said: "I give this as a testament of the spirit, immune from every illegal search or vulgar intrusion forever [a veiled illusion to Mussolini's guardian, Rizzo]. Not only every house I have ever owned, not only every room I have ever lived in, but every object I have ever chosen and collected in the various ages of my life, has been for me a perpetual means of expression, a form of spiritual revelation—as were my poems, my dramas, my political and military acts. Everything in this *Vittoriale* has been created and transfigured by me. Everything here displays the imprint of my style, in the sense that *I* wish to give to that style. My love of Italy, my cult of the past, my aspirations to heroism, my presentiment of the future of my country, all is here displayed in line and shape and color. . . . Do not the relics of our war bleed again here? Just as death will give my body to the beloved land of Italy, so I have been permitted to preserve the best part of my life in this offering to that same Italy. . . ."

All over the *Vittoriale* are verses or scraps of poetry, many written by D'Annunzio himself. In the bathroom, decorated with stucco and Greco-Roman engravings, is one of Pindar's epigrams, "Water is excellent." Elsewhere are such mottoes as: "If you take roses, beware of thorns"; "I have what I have given"; "To Dare, not to plot" (*Ardire non ordire*).

It seems that he could not see a blank space on a wall without putting an inscription on it. *Solitudo, Silentium, et Clausura* were placed above the doors and over his bed. On his bookplates was his personal motto, enclosed in a laurel wreath, *per non dormire.*

To add to the general confusion, he gave symbolic names to various parts of the garden; the Arengo, the Porziuncola, the Arches of the Heroes, the Christian Crosses, the Gonfaloni of the Carnaro, the Silver Lilies of Trieste, the Golden Leopards of Dalmatia.

The rooms often lead into one another, getting smaller and smaller, like those Chinese boxes which contain smaller boxes, which in turn contain still smaller boxes. In the Arengo, are a number of white marble columns, as many as there were Italian victories in the Great War. One of them has been blackened to symbolize Caporetto, which D'Annunzio considered a kind of moral victory which Italy had gained over herself. (We English have no business to smile at this, for we did the same thing at Dunkirk.) Another has the odd legend *Eireann abu!* which is Erse for "Long Live Ireland!" Yet another has "Come and see how people love one another!" Outside the Arengo is a small space dedicated, "To Slander, the poisonous plant which always tries to invade the domain of the loving ones, Good Faith and Good Will."

His treatment of his own beloved Legionaries of Fiume became very strange, at the end of his life. One of them arrived to see him, and D'Annunzio told his secretary, "I can't see him today, nor tomorrow, nor the day after, nor after that. But put him up at the Pesce d'Oro Hotel, and I'll see him later." A week passed, two weeks, a month, and the wretched Legionary was still there, having failed to see his *Comandante;* and D'Annunzio had failed to pay the bill. Every day, the Legionary would come up to the secretary, complaining that he had not seen his hero. At last, the Legionary came one day and explained to the secretary that he had just seen the doctor, who said he must go immediately into hospital for two months with chest trouble. The secretary told D'Annunzio this, shocked that the poor man should have waited so long in vain. "On the contrary," said D'Annunzio. "This is a piece of Providence, to prevent my having to see him. Put him in hospital immediately, at my expense. Tell them to cure him properly, and that there is no hurry. For two months at least, we shall have peace. I will pay the bill."

At the end the Legionary, after two months in hospital and being cured, returned to his native town, still having failed to see D'Annunzio. D'Annunzio was delighted. "It was well worth 3,000 lire," he said of the hospital expense.

He became more and more inaccessible at the *Vittoriale,* even to his own family. He had a notice placed over the entrance, *cave canem ac dominum.* This annoyed many Italians, particularly as the place was flamboyantly called *Vittoriale degli Italiani*—The Shrine of the Victories of the Italians—and the taxpayers now supported it. For by giving the place to the State he obtained, his son confirms, a large sum of money to spend on it (the first of the Italian landowners to recognize what we would call a National Trust). His motto, *"Io ho quel che ho donato"* could really be applied, the wags observed, to the *Vittoriale.* He also caused his birthplace, the house in Pescara, to be restored by the State to the point that it no longer bore any resemblance to the house where he was born. "My natal house," he said, "must harmonize with the *Vittoriale.*" This nearly caused a lawsuit with his sister, Elvira, who had been living peaceably on the second floor of the old Pescara house for thirty years. She refused to leave when he wanted the State to "restore" it, even though he offered her a new house. Bitter words were exchanged, and he spoke of the "obstinate profanation of my sister Elvira," and of, "my serpent relations."

He invited poor Elvira at last to the *Vittoriale,* to make amends, and she left Pescara looking forward at last to seeing her famous brother again. But unfortunately, he was in one of his *clausura et silentium* moods. Although a guest at the *Vittoriale,* beneath the same roof as her brother, she received only letters and gifts from him, and left finally without seeing him.

He also had long periods at the *Vittoriale,* when he refused to open letters and telegrams. He once sent a telegram to his son, Mario: "For two months I have not opened a letter or telegram, and I don't know what has happened to Marietta (the house-keeper); but today I have begun to suffer the martyrdom of opening the mail again."

It is fitting that one of the last facts to record is about a woman. Only a month before his death, he was writing to a young lady who had been staying with him at the *Vittoriale* letters full of "audacious eroticism," says his biographer Gatti, surpassing anything written in his youth. Unfortunately Gatti gives no examples of these but only refers to the "contrast between the daring suggestions made in the letters, and the trembling hand that penned them."

In the last year of his life, D'Annunzio still spent many hours a day at his desk, in theory in composition, although there is little to show for it. At night he would listen to music, often engaging musicians to come in and play for him. In particular, Beethoven pleased him. One evening, not long before he died, he exclaimed after listening to the slow movement of a Razoumovsky quartet, "This is it!" The musicians who came to play did not know that that night he was choosing the music for his funeral.

He seemed in good health throughout the winter of 1937, but in the following February he began to complain of loss of appetite. To the doctor who recommended stimulants, he said, "I shall eat three raw eggs at a gulp, and that will bring my appetite back." When the doctor disagreed about this as a cure, he said, "You know nothing. We in the Abruzzi cure ourselves like this, with raw eggs—and we live a hundred years. A shepherd on the Maiella knows more than you."

On the evening of March 1, 1938, he talked happily to friends about a dedication to Eleonora Duse which he wished to place in one of his books. It was suitable as a last dedication, in the true Dannunzian style: "To Eleonora Duse—the Veiled Witness—who suddenly knowing me kin to the splendor of her pre-age—wished through the vows of her forgiveness . . ." [1]

After this, dinner was announced, but he said he felt tired.

[1] Reported by Francis Winwar in *Wings of Fire.*

When his architect, Maroni, suggested that he should be brought some food, he laughed, "Yes please. A goblet of water, a goblet of pure water." He then walked forward towards the dining room, but as he did so he staggered and fell unconscious.

They carried him to a chair, and sent for a doctor. The breathing quickly became harsh and labored. Before the doctor arrived, D'Annunzio seemed almost dead, although the heart was beating faintly. The doctor gave him an injection to revive the heart, but it served no purpose, for he never regained consciousness. A sudden cerebral hemorrhage had killed him. A priest had also been called, and he gave extreme unction, although it is doubtful whether D'Annunzio was alive to receive it. The priest, who had known him well during this time at the *Vittoriale,* considered that D'Annunzio had lived as a Christian at the end of his life; and he recommended to his bishop at Brescia that the writer should be given a Christian burial. Although D'Annunzio's works were on the Index he had never been excommunicated.

Mussolini and Maria Gallese (who had been living quietly, chiefly in Paris, since D'Annunzio abandoned her fifty years before) were the chief mourners at the funeral, and behind them walked Generals, Admirals, Ambassadors, Legionaries, aviators, sailors and Fascists. Mussolini spoke at the grave-side. "You may be sure—you may be sure—you may be sure—Italy will arrive at the summit you dreamed of. I swear it. . . !"

That summit—was it to be 1940, when Italy attacked France? Or was it to be 1943, when Italy collapsed?

It is ironic that this last remark of the Dictator should sum up D'Annunzio's active life. For whatever judgment posterity may pass on his work—and it is certain to be less favorable than the judgment of his lifetime, when he and many of his contemporaries thought of him as a second Dante—in his life he was Mussolini's forerunner. Signor Aniente's title for his study of D'Annunzio, *John the Baptist of Fascism,* is not unjust. This hero of the First World War, in which he behaved so honorably, died on the eve of the Second World War, brought about by the dishonorable movement he did much to create. The Italy of Mazzini, of which we spoke in the preface, had been entirely destroyed, almost exactly within the span of his lifetime and for this he is heavily responsible. He had helped replace it by the Italy of Mussolini, which served in turn as model for the Germans. Yet his last writings show that he hoped for something better from posterity:

"If after having reawakened the world in every center of culture to the new Italy, re-animated daring spirits with the feeling of a new Renaissance, I am reviled by those who have failed, what do I care? My work is dedicated to Time and Hope . . ."

Bibliography

ANIENTE, D'Annunzio, Saint Jean du Fascisme

ANTONGINI, T., Vita segreta di Gabriele D'Annunzio

ANTONGINI, T., D'Annunzio aneddotico

ANTONGINI, T., Gli allegri filibustieri di D'Annunzio

BACCINI, D'Annunzio

BADOGLIO, Rivelazioni su Fiume

BALDINI, Gli Italiani del secolo XIX

BALDINI e TROMPEO, P. P., Roma senza Lupa

BARILLI, Al Vittoriale con D'Annunzio

BERTACCHI, G., dalle Odi Barbare Carduciane alle Laudi D'Annunziane

BERTOZZI, R. M., L'antirealisino di D'Annunzio

BIANCANI, L., D'Annunzio critico

BO, C., Otto studi

BORGESE, G. A., Goliath

BRUERS, A., Gabriele D'Annunzio e il moderno spirito italiano

BRUERS, A., Gabriele D'Annunzio—il pensiero e l'azione

BRUERS, A., Nuovi soggi D'Annunziane

BUCCO, G., Presepi Dannunziani

CAPPELLETTI, G., La Figlia di Jorio e l'amore d'Abruzzo

CARACCIO, A., D'Annunzio dramaturge

CASALEGNO, C., La regina Margherita

CASTELLI, A. (ed.), Pagine disperse di D'Annunzio

CAVIGLIA, Il conflitto di Fiume

CECCHI, R., Cloaca massima—cronaca scandalosa dei nostri tempi

CHIEPPA, V., Umanità di D'Annunzio

CIMORONI, O., L'altro D'Annunzio

COMISSO, G., Le mie Stagioni

CROCE, B., Storia (XIX Secolo)

CUCCHETTI, G., Il mio D'Annunzio

DAMERINI, G., D'Annunzio e Venezia

D'ANNUNZIO, M., Con mio padre sulla nave del ricordo

DEL GUZZO, G., D'Annunzio senza segreti

DENTONI, E., L'opera artistica di Gabriele D'Annunzio

DOLLOT, R., D'Annunzio e Valéry

DORNIS, J., Essai sur G. D'Annunzio

FALIGNI, E., Pietà per i vivi

FALIGNI, E., D'Annunzio e noi

FAURE, G., Au pays de Gabriele D'Annunzio

FLORA, F., Dal Romanticismo al Futurismo

FLORA, F., D'Annunzio

FOSCANELLI, U., D'Annunzio e il Fascimo

GALLETTI, A., Il novecento

GATTI, G., Vita di G. D'Annunzio

GATTI, G., Le donne nella vita e nell'arte di G. D'Annunzio

GERMAIN, A., La vie amoureuse de D'Annunzio

GIANERI, E., D'Annunzio nella caricatura mondiale

GIANNANTONI, M., D'Annunzio. Maestro di Vita

GRIFFIN, G., G. D'Annunzio. The Warrior Bard

HARDING, G., Age cannot wither (Eleonora Duse)

INCHIOSTRI, U., Ricordi Dannunziani

KOSCHINITZY, L., La quinta Stagione

LANCELLOTTI, A., D'Annunzio nella luce di domani

LUCINI, G. P., Antidannunziana

MACDONALD, J. N., A Political Escapade

MEOZZI, A., Significato della vita e dell' opera di Gabriele D'Annunzio

MONZINI, V., Commento al D'Annunzio romanziere

MOSCHINO, E., D'Annunzio nella vita e nella legenda

MURET, M., littérature italienne d'aujourd'hui

NARDELLI, F. V., L'Arcangelo

NARDELLI, F. V. and LIVINGSTONE, D'Annunzio

NARDI, Vita di Boito

NARDI, J., D'Annunzio e alcuni scrittori francesi

OJETTI, U., D'Annunzio

PALMERIO, B., Con D'Annunzio alla Capponcina

PANCRAZI, P., Studi del D'Annunzio

PAPINI, G., Stroncature

PERODI, E., Roma italiana, 1870-1895

PESCI, U., I primi anni di Roma capitale

PICCIOLA, G., G. D'Annunzio e le novelle della Pescara

PRARIO, L. N., Tre abiti bianchi per Alessandra

PRAZ, M., La carne, la morte e il diavolo nella letteratura romantica

PRAZ, M., La filosofia dell' arredamento

RHEINHARDT, E. C., Eleonora Duse

SARAZANI, F., D'Annunzio e l'arte di guardare Roma

SCARFOGLIO, E., Il libro di Don Chisciotte

SIGNORELLI, La Duse

SITWELL, O., Discursions

SITWELL, O., Noble Essences

SODINI, Ariel armato

SOLMI, A. ed.), Quaderni dannunziani

SQUARCIAPINO, G., Roma bizantina

SYMONS, A., Eleonora Duse

TONELLI, L., La tragedia di Gabriele D'Annunzio

TOSI, G., G. D'Annunzio et la France

TOSI, G., D'Annunzio en Grèce

TRAVERSI, C. A., Curiosità dannunziane

TRAVERSI, C. A., D'Annunzio nella vita e nelle opere

TRAVERSI, C. A., Vita di D'Annunzio

TROMPEO, P. P., Carducci e D'Annunzio

VALERI, N., Da Giolitti a Mussolini

VASILI, P., La société de Rome

WINWAR, F., Wings of Fire

Index

Labor, Italian Confederation of, 272
Lacerba, 164n.
la Rotella, Pasquale, 216
Lavoratore, Il, 242
League of Nations, 192, 215
Lenin, Nikolai, 241, 263n.
Leonardo, 65
Leoni, Barbara, 27
Lezzani, Marquis, 26
Lloyd George, David, 196, 213, 215
London, Treaty of, 165

Machiavelli, Niccolo, xv-xviii
Magnifico, Carlo, 69-70
Malatesta, 132, 249
Marconi, Guglielmo, 159, 177
Margherita, Queen of Italy, 23, 75-78, 169
Margonari, Vittorio, 223
Mariano Fortuny theatre, 156
Mariners, Federation of, Genoa, 224n., 248, 262, 279
Marinetti, 62, 66, 67, 70, 73, 201, 239
Maroni, 282, 284, 288
Matteoti, 242
Maurras, Charles, 156
Mazzini, Giuseppe, ix-xi, 192
Melchiorri, Melchiorre, 223
Miani, Captain Ercole, 245
Michetti, 27, 69, 117
Millo, Admiral, 254, 157
Mirabello, 209
Montanarella, Renata, 102, 123-24, 183
Morosini, Countess, 179, 184-86
Mussolini, Benito, 165, 193, 202, 206, 211, 238-41, 243, 244-46, 247, 248, 250-51, 253, 256, 263, 264, 265, 270, 272-82, 288, 289
Mussolini, Vittorio, xi
Mustapha Kemal, 245

Nardelli, Federico, 212
Nencioni, Enrico, 24-25
Nietzsche, Friedrich, 29-41, 193
Nitti, 41, 191-94, 196, 200, 201-3, 211, 222, 243, 249-50, 252, 265
Nullo, 209

Ojetti, Ugo, 58, 81
Orlando, Vittorio Emmanuele, 196, 274
Ortona, 76, 78, 87

Palli, Captain, 195
Palmerio, B., 121, 122
Papini, G., 164
Pasquino, 267
Passiglia, 249
Pélican, Zoé de, 152
Pelloux, General, 83, 86, 87, 95
Penne, Marquis de la, 280-81
Persia, 224
Pesce, Rocco, 133
Piave, battle of the, 173-75
Picciola, G., 70
Pichon, 195
Pittaluga, General, 207-8
Pius IX, Pope, 22
Poincaré, Raymond, 195
Pollio, General, 171
Popolo d'Italia, 182, 202, 238, 250

Raimondo, 166
Rajna, Major, 199, 205, 249
Randaccio, 183
Rapallo, Treaty of, 253, 254, 258, 260
Rattazzi, 78
Régnier, Henri de, 161
Regno, Il, 71
Reims, cathedral of, 159-60
Rivista d'Italia, 70
Rizzo, Giovanni, 278, 281, 284
Rome, Pact of, 191

About the Author

An Englishman, Anthony Rhodes is a graduate of Trinity College, Cambridge, and also holds a degree in Italian Literature from Geneva University. He was a Captain in the Army from 1936 to 1946. After the Second World War, he lectured in English Literature at Geneva University; since 1953 he has devoted all his time to writing.

During the last four years, Mr. Rhodes has spent much time as a Special Correspondent for the *London Daily Telegraph* in Eastern Europe. He was in Hungary during the Revolution and returned in 1957. He has also reported from Rumania, Czechoslovakia, Bulgaria, Poland and East Germany. His articles have also appeared in many English magazines, including *Spectator*, *Encounter*, and *The Listener*.

D'Annunzio: The Poet as Superman is Mr. Rhodes' eighth book. He has published three novels: (*The Uniform, A Ball in Venice* and *The General's Summer-House*), three travel books and *Sword of Bone*, the story of the Dunkirk campaign. He is now living in London and working on a novel.